The Ethics of Life Writing

■

Edited by

PAUL JOHN EAKIN

■

Cornell University Press

Ithaca and London

First published 2004 by Cornell University Press
First printing, Cornell Paperbacks, 2004

Printed in the United States of America

Library of Congress Cataloging-in-Publication Data

The ethics of life writing / edited by Paul John Eakin.
     p.   cm.
Includes bibliographical references and index.
   ISBN 0-8014-4128-5 (alk. paper)—ISBN 0-8014-8833-8 (pbk. : alk. paper)
   1. Autobiography—Moral and ethical aspects.   2. Ethics.   I. Eakin, Paul John.
II. Title.
   CT25.E88   2004
   174′.992—dc22   2003023062

Cornell University Press strives to use environmentally responsible
suppliers and materials to the fullest extent possible in the publishing
of its books. Such materials include vegetable-based, low-VOC inks
and acid-free papers that are recycled, totally chlorine-free, or partly
composed of nonwood fibers. For further information, visit our
website at www.cornellpress.cornell.edu.

Cloth printing   10 9 8 7 6 5 4 3 2 1

Paperback printing   10 9 8 7 6 5 4 3 2 1

The Ethics of Life Writing

Contents

Acknowledgments

This inquiry into the ethics of life writing began about ten years ago when David Parker and Richard Freadman invited me to contribute an essay on this subject to a volume they were preparing, *Renegotiating Ethics in Literature, Philosophy, and Theory* (Cambridge University Press, 1998). Intrigued by the subject, and believing that I had a lot more to learn about it, I persuaded my colleague David Smith to join me in mounting the collaborative, interdisciplinary investigation that led to this book. Drawing on funding from the Poynter Center for the Study of Ethics and American Institutions, which David directs, and from Indiana University's Department of English and my own research funds, we convened a colloquium in October 2002 at which preliminary versions of the essays collected here were presented. Craig Howes summarized the leading themes of the colloquium discussions during the concluding wrap-up session, which he chaired, and he presents his findings in the "Afterword" he has written to conclude this volume as well. As David Smith and I hoped, the colloquium generated some productive cross-fertilization, and readers will note that several of the essays refer to other essays in the collection and to things that were said in the October meeting or "seminar."

It remains for me to acknowledge David Smith's generosity and enthusiasm, without which the present book would never have emerged. My wife, Sybil S. Eakin, gave me the initial push—"Why don't you stop talking about this and do something about it?"—and

Mary Ellen Brown, director of Indiana University's Institute for Advanced Study, gave me a lot of encouragement along the way. Members of the faculty Life Writing Seminar that I convened at the institute were the target audience for the colloquium, and they sensitized me to the complexities of this subject. G. Thomas Couser was an early believer in the importance of my project, and I benefited enormously from his good coaching as it unfolded over the last three years. Sybil Eakin, Craig Howes, and John Schilb offered invaluable editorial advice about my introduction. I owe a special debt to Timothy Dow Adams, who read the entire manuscript with great care and insight. I thank Bernhard Kendler, my editor at Cornell University Press, for his unfailing acumen and speed. Thanks also to Amanda Heller, who gave the manuscript an expert grooming, and to Ange Romeo-Hall, who kept the production of the book running smoothly and on schedule.

The Ethics of Life Writing

Introduction: Mapping the Ethics of Life Writing

Paul John Eakin

utobiographies and biographies crowd the shelves of bookstores today, prompting columnists and reviewers to tell us that we live in an age of memoir, fostered by a pervasive culture of confession in the media. Life histories are also getting a lot of attention in many academic disciplines and professional practices, including medicine, history, anthropology, psychology, and journalism, as well as literary studies. Spurred by these developments, critics have coined an umbrella term, *life writing*, to cover the protean forms of contemporary personal narrative, including interviews, profiles, ethnographies, case studies, diaries, Web pages, and so on. At the same time, the revolution in Internet and Web-based communication has generated an unprecedented amount of personal exposure that challenges the very idea of privacy in the United States. Yet while our lives are increasingly on display in public, the ethics of presenting such revelations remains largely unexamined. What is the good of life writing, and how, exactly, can it do harm? The essays in this collection explore answers to these questions. They focus chiefly on autobiography and biography, but their findings apply to the entire class of literature in which people tell life stories.

Telling the Truth in Autobiography, Biography, and History

Did the Nobel Peace Prize winner Rigoberta Menchú tell the truth in 1983 when she presented her first-person *testimonio* concerning the

1

abuses she and her people had suffered at the hands of a repressive government and military regime in Guatemala? Was Binjamin Wilkomirski really the Holocaust survivor he claimed to be in *Fragments* (1995), his memoir of his childhood experience of the Nazi death camps? Both Menchú and Wilkomirski were accused of lying, and coverage of their controversial stories made not just literary but front-page news.[1] These high-profile cases caught the eye of the public because they challenge the meaning of hotly contested passages of twentieth-century history. In his essay for this collection, "Arguing with Life Stories: The Case of Rigoberta Menchú," Paul Lauritzen contends that Menchú's appeal to the truth of her own experience in support of her claims is vitiated by her recourse to fabrications concerning her purported eyewitness testimony. In order for the moral project of an experiential narrative to succeed, he maintains, the reader's trust in the narrator's credibility is crucial, the generic distinction between fact and fiction decisive. Doubts about factual accuracy generate "corrosive skepticism."

Like Lauritzen, the biographer Diane Middlebrook holds that when a writer addresses biographical and historical fact, telling the truth is essential. In "Misremembering Ted Hughes," she demonstrates that Emma Tennant, writer and sometime lover of Hughes, makes it impossible for readers to distinguish fact from fiction in both the novel and the memoir in which she recreates Hughes's story. Particularly striking is Middlebrook's claim that a writer's ethical responsibility to tell the truth about biographical fact extends every bit as much to the "nonfiction novel" as it does to memoir. Tennant's precursors in this documentary genre—writers such as Truman Capote and E. L. Doctorow—use it to make "imaginative interventions in order to fill gaps in documented events, and to create plausible inner lives for the protagonists in significant historical situations." Yet these "imaginative interventions" into the historical record are governed by the nonfiction novelist's ultimate obligation to the truth. As Middlebrook explains, "The nonfiction novel benefits artistically from being narrated by an ethically uncompromised literary persona." Tennant's *Sylvia and Ted* doesn't measure up to this standard, for the author's "personal ethical failure jams the signals by which a reader navigates the reality-effect of the nonfiction novel." The very idea that these personal narratives by Menchú, Wilkomirski, and Tennant can cloud our access to the historical record testifies to the potential power of life writing. When life writers fail to tell the truth, then, they do more than

1. For Menchú, e.g., see Rohter.

violate a literary convention governing nonfiction as a genre; they disobey a moral imperative.

You don't have to be a Nobel laureate or a Holocaust survivor, however, to get in trouble for telling less than the truth in a narrative that purports to be based in fact; you can be someone readers have never heard of before, so long as you have a good story to tell about your life. Judy Blunt found that out when she published a well-reviewed memoir of her hard years on a ranch in eastern Montana, *Breaking Clean* (2002). When her outraged father-in-law protested, she conceded to a *New York Times* reporter that she had invented the startling scene in the opening chapter "that has him smashing her typewriter with a sledgehammer" (Harden B1). But she does claim that "the old man pulled the plug on the typewriter and shouted and screamed" (Harden B3). Lying or fictional heightening? In any case, Knopf, her publisher, proposed to cut the scene from future editions.

Life writers are criticized not only for *not* telling the truth—personal and historical—but also for telling too much truth. As Paul Monette puts it in his hard-hitting account of a gay man's loss of his virginity, *"Is this more than you want to know?"* (144). In the explosion of autobiographical writing in the United States in the 1990s—Frank McCourt's *Angela's Ashes* (1996) and *The Liars' Club* by Mary Karr (1995) are only two of the best-known titles—victims of all sorts, shedding their inhibitions, claimed a prominent place.[2] The public airing of private hurt, however, was not universally welcomed; many of these narratives not only featured abuse as a primary content but also were perceived by some reviewers to *be* abusive in their candor. The heated reaction to Kathryn Harrison's taboo-breaking story *The Kiss* (1997), for example, a harrowing account of her incestuous relationship with her father which began when she was a junior in college, made clear that commentators were responding not just to this particular case but to the new frankness that seemed to be the hallmark of contemporary memoir. Thus "Women Behaving Badly," Michael Shnayerson's survey of autobiographies by women in an essay in *Vanity Fair* in 1997, interprets Harrison's book as part of a cultural trend, "a new wave of female memoirists, mostly young and attractive, . . . mining intimate details of their sex lives, alcoholism, mental illness, and even adult incest" (54). Maureen Dowd might scorn memoirists who wash their dirty laundry in public, William Gass might scold autobiography for its descent into an infantilized narcissism, but clearly life—and life writing—in the information age has meant the transmission of more

---

2. See Gilmore's case for "trauma's centrality to contemporary self-representation" (129).

and more personal information, often quite intimate, with less and less restraint. People may protest the loss of their privacy, but with an assist from computers and cell phones in these wired and wireless times, they are conducting much of their private lives in public places; as see-all, tell-all Web sites proliferate, a lot of people log on and look.

Life Writing as Moral Inquiry

Menchú, Wilkomirski, Harrison: the controversies surrounding these cases might suggest that an ethics of life writing is properly concerned with checking its potential for harm, displacing what has been recognized traditionally as its potential for good. We need only consider the Gospels and saints' lives, however, and the enormous literature of spiritual autobiography and conversion narrative in the West from Augustine's *Confessions* to Saint Teresa's *Life*, Wordsworth's *Prelude*, and Eliot's *Four Quartets*, to recognize just how often life writing features the examined and the exemplary life. In his essay on Edmund Gosse's *Father and Son*, David Parker invokes the work of the philosopher Charles Taylor to redirect our attention to these traditional goods of life writing. Building on Taylor's conception of the self as "something which can exist only in a space of moral issues" (49), Parker argues that Taylor's guiding question "What is it good to be?" is central to the project of living—and writing—any life. Following the logic of Taylor's vision of the self, life writing emerges as an extension and a further playing out of that capacity for narrative understanding which enables us to grasp what Taylor calls "life-plans" (25), our sense of the direction and meaning of our lives. If identity and morality are intimately and inextricably connected in this way, then ethics is not merely one possible perspective on life writing; it constitutes it as a practice. Thus Parker reads Gosse's story—and indeed all "self–life writing"—as a "progressive history of its narrator's current orientation in moral space."

Something like Taylor's view also informs John Barbour's "Judging and Not Judging Parents," in which he argues that the autobiographers he examines practice—and instruct us in the practice of—ethics. He analyzes three intergenerational memoirs in which adult children, now parents themselves, portray their parents. Investigating these lives by Paul Auster, Kim Chernin, and John Edgar Wideman, Barbour shows how each "offers not simply moral judgment but a self-critical assessment of the process of forming moral judgments." As these autobiographers grapple with the limits of moral agency, the nature of forgiveness, and the relevance of religion, they model the reading of

lives as a moral inquiry that offers "a paradigm of what moral deliberation ought to be in ordinary life." The upshot of such reading is self-
reflexive: "We encounter a perspective that makes us judge ourselves,
helps us to reevaluate our moral practice or ideals."

In addition to the explicitly moral concerns posed by Parker and
Barbour, life writing addresses other important goods, both psychological and social. When we tell or write about our own lives, our stories
establish our identities both as content—I am the person who did these
things—and as act—I am someone with a story to tell. And we do
something even more fundamental—we establish ourselves as persons:
I am someone, someone who has lived a valuable life, a value affirmed
precisely by any life story's implicit claim that it is worth telling and
hearing. In fashioning our identity narratives, relating our "life-
plans"—something we do piecemeal every day—we exercise that
"expressive freedom" which Taylor prizes as a defining mark of the
modern individual.[3] Members of oppressed and silenced groups instinc-
tively recognize this core attribute, making life writing a leading form
of expression in postcolonial and minority literature today. Closely
related to the function of life writing as a forum for the individual's
claims to freedom and dignity is its function as testimony, whether
addressing programmatic totalitarian assaults on those values—during
the periods of the Holocaust, for example, the Soviet gulags, the
Chinese Cultural Revolution—or more personal threats to the
integrity of the person, such as illness and disability. Essays in this
volume by Paul Lauritzen, Marianne Gullestad, G. Thomas Couser,
and Arthur Frank all treat this testimonial function of life writing.

If life writing as both act and content has the power to confirm our
status as persons, this social good also casts a shadow: Do you have to
have a story in order to be a person? The question isn't as odd as it
sounds, for in countries with aging populations, more than a few individuals, suffering from Alzheimer's disease and other forms of senile
dementia and memory loss, reach a point where they can no longer
tell their stories. We need to reckon with the fact that the self-
narrations in which we express our "life-plans" function as the mark

3. Similarly, the philosophers James Rachels and William Ruddick, making their
case for liberty as the basis of personhood, attribute to the free individual "a set of self-
referring attitudes" that "presuppose a sense of oneself as having an existence spread
over past and future time" (227). Unlike "victims of dire poverty, illness, and slavery,"
who "might retain the capacity for social responses and yet have none of the inten-
tions, plans, and other features of will and action that define a life," they argue, "only
persons have lives" (228)—and life stories, I would add, for life writing and telling are
primary manifestations of that capacity for making "life-plans" that Taylor, Rachels,
and Ruddick posit at the core of the free, modern individual.

not only of the free person but of the normal person as well. We inhabit systems of social intercourse in which the ability to articulate an identity narrative—whether written, related orally, or simply dropped piece by piece into the social discourse of daily life—confirms the possession of a working identity. Accordingly, when brain disorders of various kinds impair or prevent our saying to others who we are, our claims to recognition as persons may suffer irreparable harm. What are the responsibilities of the "normal" to those with apparently damaged identities? Meditating on the breakdown of narrative identity, the collapse, as it were, of "life writing" in any of its forms, has led me to think of ethics as the deep subject of autobiographical discourse, prompting the present inquiry.

Beyond Privacy: Life Writing and the Law

If there is new interest in the ethics of life writing today, however, it is not so much a function of its goods as a function of its perceived abuses and transgressions. Indeed, one might expect that a collection of essays on the ethics of life writing would be grounded in the law. When I first became interested in the ethics of life writing over ten years ago, I certainly thought so. I assumed that the primary transgression of such an ethics would be a violation of the individual's right to privacy and that the legal tradition of privacy rights in the United States would be an obvious point of entry to the subject. Now I've come to believe that there are two strikes against a privacy-based ethics of life writing, one legal, the other experiential. A right to privacy, at least in the United States, has proved to be not only legally ineffective as a bulwark against invasive life writing but also conceptually problematic, for it carries with it an assumption of autonomous individualism that is inadequate to model the experience of selfhood in our intensely interpersonal lives.

Following Karl Weintraub's *Value of the Individual: Self and Circumstance in Autobiography*, historians of the genre have linked the rise of autobiography in the West to the emergence of the individual as a primary cultural value. Reflecting on this linkage, Elizabeth Bruss observed that "autobiography could simply become obsolete if its defining features, such as individual identity, cease to be important for a particular culture" (15). The work of Weintraub and Bruss highlights the extent to which life writing and the values inhering in any ethics that would govern it as a practice are necessarily culture-specific. In the United States, for example, the legal history of the right to privacy dates from the publication in 1890 of a celebrated article by Samuel

D. Warren and Louis D. Brandeis titled, precisely, "The Right to Privacy." In defending the individual's "inviolate personality," Warren and Brandeis seemed to stake out a domain that life writing could not invade with impunity. In France, a right to privacy does afford legal protection to individuals resisting unwanted exposure in life writing, and books have been withdrawn from publication and reissued with blank spaces where privacy-offending passages have been deleted.[4]

In the United States, by contrast, the legal picture today is quite different, largely as the result of a strong tradition of First Amendment protection for freedom of expression, such that there is no case on record in which autobiographers and biographers have been sued successfully for violation of privacy. Commenting on the legal restraints in the United States that would restrict what an autobiographer or a biographer can publish about someone else, Roger Dworkin, of the Indiana University Law School, writes: "Basically, the likelihood of recovery by the subject of a biography is minuscule. Even apart from the Constitution, there has always been a newsworthiness defense to the embarrassing private facts branch of the privacy tort. Given the unlikelihood of writing a biography about a nobody, that provides pretty full protection. Add the constitutional protections when one writes about public figures (and, in this context probably even about private ones) and the chances of liability for publishing the truth become vanishingly small."[5] Moreover, the historian of constitutional law David J. Garrow, surveying the history of the right to privacy in the United States, concludes that the Supreme Court, once the champion of a constitutionally protected right to privacy in two landmark cases, *Griswold v. Connecticut* (1965) and *Roe v. Wade* (1973), has since abandoned it. The Court, he observes, is less open to privacy claims now than at any time in the last hundred years.[6]

4. See Lejeune for the legal picture as it applies to privacy rights vis-à-vis life writing in France.

5. Letter to the author, July 9, 2002. In the much-publicized case in which J. D. Salinger sued the biographer Ian Hamilton, infringement of copyright and not invasion of privacy was the ground on which Salinger sought to protect his seclusion. See Hamilton and Hoban.

6. Garrow made these observations in a public lecture on the history of the right to privacy in the United States at the conference on privacy at New School University, October 5–7, 2000. See Garrow for the published version of this lecture. See also Nelson for a fascinating study of the ways in which privacy as a value plays out in the intricate connections between literature and the law. Paying special attention to the *Griswold* and *Roe* cases, Nelson stresses the relativity of privacy as an ideal, tracing how conceptions of it have shifted radically in the United States over time, notably during the cold war years, which are the focus of her study. Especially interesting is her finding that concepts of privacy have been inflected by considerations of gender.

Is there any life remaining for the Warren and Brandeis ideal of privacy today? In *The Unwanted Gaze: The Destruction of Privacy in America*, Jeffrey Rosen seems to concur with Garrow's epitaph, conceding "the superiority of norms over law in protecting privacy" (219) in the United States today. Yet, recoiling from the "culture of transparency" (223) created by technologies of surveillance and cyberspace communication, Rosen invokes a "classically liberal vision of privacy" (218) along lines laid out by Warren and Brandeis: "A self-possessed private citizen has an inviolate personality, surrounded by boundaries of reserve that can't be penetrated casually by strangers" (201). Can one violate "an inviolate personality"? This apparent paradox stems from two competing versions of the self at the heart of the Warren and Brandeis model that Rosen embraces: the self as person, a "precious and incommensurable interior essence" (219), and the self as property, a storehouse of personal information. Grant that the self is truly private and interior, then its essence is indeed inviolable—in theory, at any rate. We may think that "the private citizen" is sacrosanct in a democratic state, where the brainwashing we associate with totalitarianism is unthinkable, yet coercive police interrogations remind us of concerted attempts to invade the space inside our heads.[7] A self conceived as social, however, has a reputation that can be damaged. To counter this danger, Rosen envisions an ideal culture of civility in which individuals would be "self-defining," deciding "how much of themselves to reveal or to conceal in different situations" (223). If the good of privacy is the right to control the disclosure of personal information, then it follows that the harm it guards against is public disclosure on someone else's terms, "the danger of being judged, fairly or unfairly, on the basis of isolated bits of personal information that are taken out of context" (200). It is the sense of this latent danger that leads Rosen to observe that "there are few acts more aggressive than describing someone else" (206). If Rosen is correct, life writing is headed for trouble.

Representing Others: Trust and Betrayal

The second strike against a privacy-based ethics of life writing is experiential. Because we live our lives in relation to others, our privacies are largely shared, making it hard to demarcate the boundary where one life leaves off and another begins. Resisting subjects of biographies

---

7. See Brooks, esp. 37–42, for an eye-opening account of custodial interrogation as practiced in U.S. police stations.

may claim that they own their life stories, but Janet Malcolm, meditating on the stormy history of biographies about Sylvia Plath and Ted Hughes, dismisses the notion as an untenable illusion: "As everyone knows who has ever heard a piece of gossip, we do not 'own' the facts of our lives at all. This ownership passes out of our hands at birth, at the moment we are first observed." For Malcolm, "the concept of privacy is a sort of screen to hide the fact that almost none is possible in a social universe." So much for Rosen's "self-defining" individual. Yet Malcolm is equally blunt about the privacy-busting nature of the biographer's art. The biographer is, she observes, a "professional burglar, breaking into a house, rifling through certain drawers that he has good reason to think contain the jewelry and money, and triumphantly bearing his loot away" (86). The ethical position of the biographer writing the life of a resisting subject, however, is deceptively simple in its adversarial posture; moreover, Malcolm's striking metaphor, with its notion of theft, plays right back into an idea of privacy she has already repudiated, that individuals could be thought to "own" the "facts" of their lives. Life and life writing are messier than a traditional model of ethics centered on privacy and property can handle.

Autobiographers, for example, aren't "burglars" in Malcolm's sense; often they've lived in the houses and sometimes even shared the beds of the other people they write about.[8] In fact, in recent years, reflecting the circumstance of our relational identities, autobiographies have become increasingly *biographical*, featuring those others in our lives— parents, siblings, lovers, friends, and mentors—who have shaped us decisively. Thus, in her essay, "Friendship, Fiction, and Memoir: Trust and Betrayal in Writing from One's Own Life," Claudia Mills poses quite a different ethical dilemma facing the life writer from the one Malcolm contemplates. Rather than the ruthless invader from without, Mills examines the case of the life writer working within the domestic circle. How can one "value one's loved ones appropriately," she asks, "while also drawing on their lives as material for one's work"? Measuring the benefits against the costs, including "the puzzle of posthumous interests," Mills submits a brief for the good of such stories, justifying "the public betrayal of trust" that life writing always

8. When Craig Howes and I discussed Malcolm's figure, he commented: "It's not just that an autobiographer is in a sense pulling an 'inside' job on the other people in his or her life. It's that unlike the biographer, who's rifling the house hoping to find some jewels, the autobiographer often knows what other people value most, and where they keep it. . . . In autobiography, the writer often takes and fences the one thing that the other person would not want taken and revealed" (letter to the author, February 24, 2003).

entails. Especially notable is her stress on "appropriate care and respect for the stories told," as opposed to the debasement of "talk show broadcasting"; to say that one is simply telling the truth, the usual all-purpose defense embraced by life writers whose motives have been impugned, is not enough to let one off the hook. In any case, though, Mills proceeds from the premise that the cost of telling someone else's story is inescapable: "The sharing of stories does require that stories be shared."[9]

There are many parallels between Mills's calculation of the costs and benefits of life writing and Richard Freadman's scrutiny of his own motives in "Decent and Indecent: Writing My Father's Life." "Writers have a right to write," Freadman observes, "but how far into the privacy of others does that right extend?" In particular, what rights do the dead retain that the living are bound to respect? Freadman subjects his motives to a rigorous analysis in an exercise of "imaginative modeling." Bringing his father back to life in order to hash out with him the propriety of writing the memoir, he interrogates the concept of trust which he hopes he has not betrayed. Weighing in the balance against the dead man with all his doubts and scruples is Freadman's evocation of himself as life writer seeking reassurance that his memoir has been loyal not only to his father's trust in him but also to his own trust in his "*best self.*" In this way, Freadman's representation of his father engages the fundamental question posed by Taylor and Parker, "What is it good to be?"

This question, in fact, haunts many of the essays in this collection, including Nancy K. Miller's essay "The Ethics of Betrayal: Diary of a Memoirist." Like Freadman, Miller is a critic of autobiography turned autobiographer who wrestles with her obligation to the other person in her memoir. Reconstructing her early life and marriage in Paris in the 1960s, she wants to use her ex-husband's letters to fill in the gaps in her memories of that time. Complicating the situation, and creating her ethical conundrum, is the fact that, as Miller reports, years ago she herself had been victimized by the unauthorized use of her letters in someone else's personal narrative. Will she now become complicit in a practice she condemns? Even if she steers clear of violating the legal constraints with regard to the letters by opting for paraphrase, how can she justify violating someone else's privacy? Is there such a thing as an "ethical betrayal"? Asking this question prompts another,

---

9. At the colloquium at which Mills's paper was delivered, Deborah Nelson observed in a similar vein that while life writing is always going to harm someone, the injuries have benefits. Ethically speaking, the life writer engages in a balancing act: "You do the harm," she said, "because you think the yield is great."

larger question, for telling the truth is not, she discovers, in and of itself enough to justify disclosure. Wondering whether her story is worth the telling, Miller sees in it a cautionary tale for women of her generation, who were "badly in need of a feminism that had yet to be invented." Of the young woman adrift who was her younger self, she writes ruefully, "If only she had had an idea of someone to become."

Acts of Resistance: Telling Counterstories

Whereas Freadman and Miller attempt to sort out their responsibilities to a single, featured other in their memoirs, Alice Wexler places this set of responsibilities in tension with those to a larger group in her essay, "Mapping Lives: 'Truth,' Life Writing, and DNA." Given that Huntington's disease, which afflicted Wexler's family, had functioned as a textbook stigma for proponents of the U.S. eugenics movement in the early twentieth century, Wexler's polemical purpose in her memoir *Mapping Fate* (1995) was "to show one such family, my own, from the inside, rather than as viewed through a clinical or eugenic lens." In so doing, she claims the right for those suffering from Huntington's disease and their families to "map" themselves, a right that many life writers feel empowered to take for granted. Thus, when Wexler confronts privacy issues surrounding genetic identity and other family secrets, she concludes that her solicitude for the welfare of the entire group of families with Huntington's disease should take precedence over her concern for the privacy of any member of her own family and its near relations. Yet an ethic of disclosure pursued to erase a legacy of stigma is not without its dilemmas: recognizing that life writing in an age of DNA carries risks, Wexler acknowledges that the revelation of genetic identity can trigger grave social and medical consequences, including the loss of jobs and insurance. Allegiances to privacy and to truth in many of these essays prove to be in tension; neither stands alone, reminding us that the goods and harms of life writing come inextricably intertwined. It is often this very tension between good and harm, moreover, that provokes life writers to reflect about the ethics of their practice.

The activist spirit that animates Wexler's approach to the identity-damaging stigma of Huntington's disease also informs the essays in this collection by Arthur Frank, G. Thomas Couser, and Marianne Gullestad, which champion the potential of life writing to resist and reform dehumanizing models of self and life story that society would impose on disempowered groups, whether the ill and disabled or racial minorities. Arthur Frank's essay, "Moral Non-fiction: Life Writing and

Children's Disability," makes clear the assumptions that underwrite the politics of life writing that these essays as a group project. Identities are narratively constructed, and because this work of construction takes place in a social context, "people are subject to stories others tell about them." The moral work of life writing becomes, accordingly, the writing of "counterstory," which Frank, drawing on the work of the bioethicist Hilde Lindemann Nelson, defines as "the narrative work of resistance that . . . 'damaged' people do to restore themselves to full moral respect." Frank illustrates counterstory by focusing on a subgenre of contemporary life writing that features "fully abled parents writing about their seriously disabled children." These stories demonstrate the crucial link between narrative and personhood. Commenting on one parent's determination to rescue his son from being "reduced to his disabilities," Frank sees the impulse behind the telling of this story as nothing less than the parent's justification of the child's right to exist. In a culture in which personhood and the respect that it entails are socially transacted through the exchange of identity narrative, the parent's justification requires making such a life "narratable," a special challenge, Frank suggests, when the child "is blind, . . . without speech, and is functionally quadriplegic."

The good of life stories, a constant theme in so many of these essays, acquires an existential urgency in the cases of grave disability examined by Arthur Frank and G. Thomas Couser: whether such lives should be valued and sustained may turn in fact on whether they can be told. Investigating "euthanography," "narratives in which euthanasia (in any form) is considered (but not necessarily committed)," G. Thomas Couser presents two narratives by parents of young men left catastrophically incapacitated in the wake of diving accidents. As these parents and their sons face daunting end-of-life decisions, the crucial issue becomes the ability to imagine a life with disability. Couser makes clear the more than literary nature of this narrative problem when he points to the "nonverbal prospective 'life writing'" that parents inevitably engage in as they conjure up "scenarios of children's futures" and seek to "script" them "to conform to an imagined life course." Had the young men fallen out of life (which is always the life of life stories) into an unthinkable because "unnarratable" limbo? Hence the importance of creating "scripts" for such damaged, apparently de-storied lives, "accounts that inscribe futures where no future seemed plausible." For Couser, as for Frank, telling counterstories enlists life writing in the service of social change, recasting the discourses of disability and euthanasia.

The work of writing counterstory may in fact be undone or at least compromised, however, by unconscious assimilation of the very story one is writing against, as Marianne Gullestad demonstrates in "Tales of Consent and Descent: Life Writing as a Fight against an Imposed Self-Image." Markets and democracies in postindustrial Western societies, she argues, "are kept together by meaning-making cultural production conceived metaphorically to be 'within' each moral individual." Specifically, it becomes the individual's task to create what Gullestad calls a "sustainable self-image," which "implies the possession of self-respect and dignity over time, in spite of challenges and attacks." This "focus on individuality, autonomy, and freedom ... conceals both institutional barriers to self-development and what one has received from others." Thus, a discourse of identity that speaks of young people "finding themselves" masks the extent to which identity formation is inflected by social, economic, and political forces. Individuals necessarily draw on the cultural resources available to them to fashion serviceable, "sustainable" identities—identities, moreover, that require confirmation by others to function successfully. Gullestad examines a set of brief autobiographical narratives by young persons of color in Norway for whom precisely such confirmation has been denied. In order to correct the racist stereotypes imposed on them by the dominant culture, these young men and women organize their identities around a model of roots, ancestry, and descent that seems to offer them a basis for pride and respect, the very model deployed in the dominant culture to provide a "natural" basis to establish the belonging of some and the exclusion of others. Ironically, their strategy for resisting stigma takes for granted the "hegemonic resources" for forming self-images which have victimized them: "caught in the dominant frame of interpretation," they have internalized the identity structures they seek to resist.

We do well to remember that it is not just special groups—persons of color, for example, or the disabled—who are shaped by dominant "frames of interpretation." We all risk being forced into reductive molds for identity and life story. Consider the case of the best-selling author Jonathan Franzen, whose blockbuster novel *The Corrections* (2001) was selected for inclusion in Oprah Winfrey's Book Club. In his *New Yorker* essay "Meet Me in St. Louis," Franzen relates a reluctant visit to his hometown with a film crew who want to shoot some footage of the author revisiting his birthplace for a brief biography to be aired on the *Oprah* show. "You're looking up at the tree," the producer coaches Franzen at one point. "You're thinking about your father" (73). The staged rendering of his life story, with the crew telling him not only what to do but also "what, approximately, I should be feeling" (70), comes across to Franzen as a denial of his identity: "This morning I have no subjectivity. . . . I'm a dumb but necessary object, a passive supplier of image" (71). In the media market, the self functions as a commodity. Juxtaposed against the falseness of the *Oprah* scripting of his story is Franzen's account of what he really felt: he opens up a cache of "painful memories" he hoped he'd left behind him when he left the St. Louis family home for the last time three months after his mother's death. This private material, withheld from exposure on *Oprah*, is revealed nevertheless—with accompanying epiphanies—in the *New Yorker*, so what's the difference? In the essay Franzen controls the script, yet this feeling of control may itself be partly an illusion, for he has in effect exchanged one conventional life story scene—the *Oprah* version of the author's nostalgic return—for another standard feature of autobiographical narrative, the author's definitive departure from his childhood home. Franzen resisting talking about himself, Franzen going all the way: the essay, for all its "counterstory" color, tells a familiar story after all. We are more involved in "dominant frames of interpretation" than we like to think.

All of the essays in this collection target texts and their authors, but to the extent that the kind of writing they discuss is an extension of the stories we tell about ourselves every day, we all engage in "life writing" constantly. When we read it, then, we are not merely disinterested witnesses of the ethical problems it entails; we are ourselves part of the game. In fact, I'd speculate that it is precisely the latent life writer in us that motivates our reading of others' lives. In this sense we are crypto-autobiographers, asking questions about our selves and our life stories indirectly by observing others as they struggle to find answers. What does it mean, though, to say that, ethically speaking, the reader is part of the game? In what ways does reading life writing entail moral responsibilities? Testimonial life writing, of course, as I've already suggested, makes direct and obvious claims on the reader as moral agent. As the Wexler, Frank, Couser, and Gullestad essays propose, when advocates of social change write counterstories, they assume that the values that oppress them—stigmatizing models of self and life story—are mutable, and they seek accordingly to alter them by changing readers' minds. Similarly forthright and insistent in its claims on the reader is the huge literature of spiritual autobiography and conversion narrative. Less obvious, but equally important to the moral work of life writing, is the kind of reflection about self and life course that is a constant theme in these essays as it is in so much life writing—indeed, all of it, if Charles Taylor and David Parker are correct when they urge that the self is "something which can exist only in a space of moral issues" (Taylor 49).

Reading these essays, I'm struck by the complexity of the issues and situations that an ethics of life writing must address. In the face of lived experience, these readers and the life writers they study steer clear of moral absolutes. Chastened, they embrace instead the good of stories. As Arthur Frank wisely puts it: "We do not act on principles that hold for all times. We act as best we can at a particular time, guided by certain stories that speak to that time, and other people's dialogical affirmation that we have chosen the right stories." As for our time, these essays affirm respect for the person, whether oneself or another, as a guiding value. Sometimes this value is posed in the case of specific individuals—Richard Freadman's father, for example, or Claudia Mills's children—and sometimes it is posed in terms of classes of persons—persons of color, the ill and the disabled. Frank's instinctive move to shift into the first-person plural—"we act as best we can at a particular time"—invokes a spirit of community in which, perhaps, the recurring tensions posed by life writing between a right to free expression and a right to privacy may find, if not resolution, at least what Henry James called "a *modus vivendi* workable for the time" (416).

WORKS CITED

Blunt, Judy. *Breaking Clean*. New York: Knopf, 2002.
Brooks, Peter. *Troubling Confessions: Speaking Guilt in Law and Literature*. Chicago: University of Chicago Press, 2000.
Bruss, Elizabeth. *Autobiographical Acts: The Changing Situation of a Literary Genre*. Baltimore: Johns Hopkins University Press, 1976.
Dowd, Maureen. "Banks for the Memories." *New York Times*, March 15, 1997, A19.
Franzen, Jonathan. "Meet Me in St. Louis." *New Yorker*, December 24 and 31, 2001, 70–75.
Garrow, David J. "Privacy and the American Constitution." *Social Research* 68 (2001): 55–82.
Gass, William. "The Art of Self: Autobiography in an Age of Narcissism." *Harper's*, May 1994, 43–52.
Gilmore, Leigh. "Limit-Cases: Trauma, Self-Representation, and the Jurisdictions of Identity." *Biography* 24 (winter 2001): 128–39.
Hamilton, Ian. "J. D. Salinger *versus* Random House, Inc." *Granta* 23 (spring 1988): 197–218.
Harden, Blaine. "Suffering and Creativity: Judy Blunt Took Bleakness and Ran with It." *New York Times*, May 28, 1982, B1, B3.
Harrison, Kathryn. *The Kiss*. New York: Random House, 1997.
Hoban, Phoebe. "The Salinger File." *New York*, June 15, 1987, 36–42.
James, Henry. *Autobiography*. Ed. Frederick W. Dupee. 1956. Princeton: Princeton University Press, 1983.
Karr, Mary. *The Liars' Club: A Memoir*. New York: Viking, 1995.
Lejeune, Philippe. "L'atteinte à la vie privée." In *Pour l'autobiographie: chroniques*. Paris: Seuil, 1998. 69–74.

Malcolm, Janet. "The Silent Woman." *New Yorker*, August 23 and 30, 1993, 84–159.

McCourt, Frank. *Angela's Ashes: A Memoir*. New York: Scribner, 1996.

Menchú, Rigoberta. *I, Rigoberta Menchú: An Indian Woman in Guatemala*. 1983. Ed. and intro. Elisabeth Burgos-Debray. Trans. Ann Wright. New York: Verso, 1984.

Monette, Paul. *Becoming a Man: Half a Life Story*. 1992. New York: Harper-Collins, 1993.

Nelson, Deborah. *Pursuing Privacy in Cold War America*. New York: Columbia University Press, 2002.

Rachels, James, and William Ruddick. "Lives and Liberty." In *The Inner Citadel: Essays on Individual Autonomy*. Ed. John Christman. New York: Oxford University Press, 1989. 221–33.

Rohter, Larry. "Nobel Winner Accused of Stretching Truth." *New York Times*, December 15, 1998, A1, A10.

Rosen, Jeffrey. *The Unwanted Gaze: The Destruction of Privacy in America*. 2000. New York: Vintage, 2001.

Shnayerson, Michael. "Women Behaving Badly." *Vanity Fair*, February 1997, 54–61.

Taylor, Charles. *Sources of the Self: The Making of the Modern Identity*. Cambridge: Harvard University Press, 1989.

Warren, Samuel D., and Louis D. Brandeis. "The Right to Privacy." 1890. In *Philosophical Dimensions of Privacy: An Anthology*. Ed. Ferdinand David Schoeman. Cambridge: Cambridge University Press, 1984. 75–103.

Weintraub, Karl J. *The Value of the Individual: Self and Circumstance in Autobiography*. Chicago: University of Chicago Press, 1978.

Wexler, Alice. *Mapping Fate: A Memoir of Family, Risk, and Genetic Research*. Berkeley: University of California Press, 1995

Wilkomirski, Binjamin. *Fragments: Memories of a Wartime Childhood*. 1995. Trans. Carol Brown Janeway. New York: Schocken, 1996.

Part I

TELLING THE TRUTH IN AUTOBIOGRAPHY, BIOGRAPHY, AND HISTORY

CHAPTER I

Arguing with Life Stories:
The Case of Rigoberta Menchú

Paul Lauritzen

I t seems fitting to begin a chapter on assessing life writing as a form of moral argument by relating a story. In fact, I begin with a bit of autobiography that is itself about appealing to personal experience as a kind of moral argument. Here, then, is my story.

In 1996 I published an article in which I drew on my experience of being infertile and of seeking to become a father to discuss a range of ethical issues raised by reproductive technology. Convinced by critics of traditional moral philosophy that ethical reflection is impoverished when we fail to attend to both fictional and experiential narratives, I discussed in detail the nature of my infertility, the tests and procedures my wife and I tried, and other generally private matters. I suggested that all serious moral reflection must involve a dialectical movement between general principles and concrete cases and that proper moral deliberation involves attending both to rules and to the affective responses of particular moral agents facing particular decisions. I thus appealed to my own experiences as part of a project to assess various objections to reproductive technology that had been raised in the literature of medical ethics. Although I did not develop a defense of my use of personal experience or seek to elaborate a critical apparatus for mobilizing experience in the debates about reproductive technology, my appeal to experience as a touchstone of moral analysis was not so different from what a growing number of writers were and are doing when addressing issues of applied ethics.

My article was well received, and one reason was surely that readers conceded to me a kind of authority that comes from firsthand experience. If I spoke of feeling a sense of coercion in the mere offer of various reproductive interventions, this feeling could be cited as corroborating feminist objections that reproductive technology is coercive to women, and apparently men as well. Who would know better than someone who had been through the ordeal of infertility treatment? Because of my experience in dealing with infertility, many readers found my analysis of reproductive technology both compelling and persuasive.

Then a curious thing happened. Colleagues who had read and commented favorably on my article were annoyed to discover that my wife and I had been successful in our efforts to conceive a child. Although my article indicated that we had about exhausted the range of medical interventions available to us, by the time the article actually made it into print, our first child had been born. Yet instead of eliciting expressions of congratulations or happiness at our good fortune, news of our son's birth was frequently met with anger and dismay by those who had read the article. What could account for this response?[1]

The answer to this question is instructive in helping us to see clearly the importance of providing a framework for assessing appeals to life writing as a form of moral argument. The most obvious answer is that news of my son's birth, following so quickly upon the publication of the article, could lead readers to believe that I had lied. Perhaps I had simply imagined what it might be like to undergo infertility treatment and then reported these imaginary feelings as actual ones. If so, my article relinquished any privileged access to truth. Worse still, if the events I narrated had not happened, then I had betrayed the reader's trust. Neither the narrative nor the conclusions, reached partly through appeal to the narrative, could be trusted.

Although this is a plausible explanation of why some readers responded to the news of our success as they did, it is important to point out that this explanation rests on a certain (questionable) understanding about both the nature of "experience" and the role an appeal to experience plays in moral deliberation. On this account, experience is understood to be largely unmediated, a sort of brute fact on which one can build an argument. So the appeal to experience functions as an effort to reach moral bedrock. This is why the possibility that the experience is not factual is so threatening. If the experience is fictional, there is no foundation on which the arguments finally rest.

---

1. I discuss the issues raised by this reaction at length in "Ethics and Experience: The Case of the Curious Response."

As plausible as this explanation is, we can see that appealing to experience is a much more complicated matter than this picture suggests by attending more carefully to why my article should be thought to be persuasive if the events I narrated "really happened" but not if they didn't. One reason has to do with the fact that we usually draw a very sharp distinction between fact and fiction, and we usually think about "experience" falling on the factual side of this divide. Notice, however, that the contrast between "really happened" and "imagined," or between "fact" and "fiction," will not be as easy to sustain as might initially be supposed. To be sure, either I was treated for infertility or I was not. But in describing my infertility treatment, I was not merely providing a chronicle of events at a clinic. Of what value would it be to the project of assessing the morality of assisted reproduction to give a catalog of procedures, along with the dates and times they were undertaken? No, I was recounting the lived reality of these events; I was relating the meaning these events had for me. Yet, seen in this light, the contrast "actually happened" versus "imagined" appears problematic. In what sense can the *meaning* of these events be said to have actually happened?[2]

The difficulty of answering this question highlights the general difficulty of thinking of experience as foundational. Experience is simply not transparent in the way required by the foundationalist account—at least not in a way that is useful for moral reasoning. To be useful to moral deliberation, the appeal to experience must be more than a mere cataloguing of events in the life of the agent; the events must be drawn together in a meaningful pattern. Yet to acknowledge this point is to acknowledge that an experiential report does not map reality in an uncomplicated way; indeed, it might be better to say that an appeal to experience provides an interpretation of reality. So whatever persuasive force an appeal to experience has cannot be accounted for by thinking of experience as an unimpeachable record of what actually happened.

At the same time, however, if an appeal to experience is to function as a kind of moral argument, the distinction between what actually happened and what was imagined or between fact and fiction must be maintained. To see why this must be the case, I turn to one of the best-known recent cases of life writing that functions as a kind of moral argument, namely, the work of Rigoberta Menchú.[3]

2. See White, *Content of the Form.*
3. Although I frame my reflections in relation to the contested story of Rigoberta Menchú—and controversial Holocaust narratives—I obviously do not mean to equate the significance of my narrative with these.

The story of Rigoberta Menchú is by now relatively familiar. In 1992 Menchú won the Nobel Peace Prize. As the Norwegian Nobel Committee put it, the award was given "in recognition of her work for social justice and ethno-cultural reconciliation based on respect for the rights of indigenous peoples" (Abrams 27). Her work on behalf of the rights of the Mayan Indians of Guatemala came to international attention after the publication of her *testimonio, I, Rigoberta Menchú*. This book, which is the transcribed and edited text of Menchú's interview with Elisabeth Burgos, describes in vivid detail Menchú's life in Guatemala during one of the most brutally repressive periods in the country's history. In the course of narrating her life story, Menchú details the horrific working conditions on the country's coffee plantations, which led to the death of two of her brothers. She describes the kidnapping, torture, and murder of her mother and another brother, and she recounts the death of her father when Guatemalan soldiers set fire to the Spanish embassy in Guatemala City, which her father and other activists had occupied to protest human rights abuses by the government. Thirty-nine people died in the blaze.

The power of the book can perhaps be conveyed through a brief but representative excerpt. In this passage, Menchú describes how army officers tortured and killed fellow villagers, including her brother Petrocinio, to make a point about cooperating with the guerrilla army. "In my brother's case," Menchú writes,

> He was cut in various places. His head was shaved and slashed. He had no nails. He had no soles to his feet. The earlier wounds were suppurating from infection. And the woman *compañera*, of course I recognized her; she was from a village near ours. They had shaved her private parts. The nipple of one of her breasts was missing and her other breast was cut off. She had the marks of bites on different parts of her body. She was bitten all over, that *compañera*. She had no ears. All of them were missing part of the tongue or had had their tongues split apart. I found it impossible to concentrate, seeing that this could be. (178)

As this passage suggests, Menchú's account of her experiences is deeply moving. Yet Menchú's work is not only a powerful example of life writing, or at least of life narration, but also an exemplar of an appeal to experience that functions as a kind of moral argument. For in whatever (other) ways *I, Rigoberta Menchú* has functioned, it has certainly functioned as an argument in support of the rights of indigenous peoples. In her Nobel acceptance speech, for example, Menchú described how dedicated her people were to developing "the most convincing and justified arguments for the elimination of racism, oppression, discrimination, and the exploitation of those who have been dragged into poverty and oblivion" (Abrams 44), and there can be little doubt that many have seen Menchú's *testimonio* as just such an effort.

Indeed, *I, Rigoberta Menchú* serves as a wonderful example of the sort of work that critics of traditional moral philosophy say ethicists and others ought to consider when deliberating morally. Martha Nussbaum, for example, has noted that "an ethics of impartial respect for human dignity will fail to engage real human beings unless they are made capable of entering imaginatively into the lives of distant others and to have emotions related to that participation" (xvi). Nussbaum cited this obstacle to respecting dignity in the context of arguing for greater attention to fictional literature in the process of formulating public policy, but her point is certainly applicable to experiential narratives that foster emotional engagement with distant others.

Thus, although Nussbaum had in mind the importance of fictional literature in these comments, they highlight why life writing can be a significant resource for moral reflection and why Menchú's work had the moral impact it did. Both the appeal to fictional literature and the appeal to personal experience in moral deliberation involve a narrative approach to moral understanding of the sort recommended in recent years by scholars such as Nussbaum. Drawing on Nussbaum and others, Richard Kearney has provided a nice summary of this narrative approach in his essay "Narrative and Ethics," and it is worth attending briefly to his account.

According to Kearney, it is useful to distinguish a narrative-based approach to moral understanding from one that relies primarily on rules and principles. As he puts it: "The narrative approach argues for an ethical understanding that involves affective as well as intellectual characteristics, affording primary consideration to specific experiential contexts rather than to generalizable norms. The narrative approach, in short, considers ethics in terms of human desire rather than exclusively in terms of rules" (31).

For this reason, Kearney agrees with Nussbaum that moral philosophers should attend more seriously to fictional narratives when deliberating practically. Citing Paul Ricoeur, Kearney points out that vividly imagining forms of moral and immoral behavior, a process facilitated by fictional literature, may shape a kind of practical understanding when we come to make moral decisions. Moreover, narratives have the ability to "implicate" readers because a narrative has the ability to draw a reader out of "the narcissistic enclosure of the ego" in a way that a more traditional philosophical argument does not. Not only may fictional narratives function in this way, but so too may experiential narratives. Indeed, Kearney cites the importance of

Holocaust narratives in this regard. The commitment to narrate the experiences of the Holocaust became, for many survivors, an ethical imperative. The responsibility to implicate others, "to make others participate," as Primo Levi put it, so that the horror of the Holocaust would be remembered and never repeated, became a moral responsibility that no standard philosophical argument could easily discharge.

Kearney sums up his account of the role of narrative in ethics this way: "Certain injustices appeal to narrative imagination to plead their case lest they slip irrevocably into oblivion. Ethical experiences of good and evil, as Nussbaum says, need to be felt upon the pulse of shared emotions. Or as Ricoeur says, commenting on narratives of the Holocaust, the horrible must strike the audience as horrible. It must provoke us to *identify* and empathize with the victims" (43).

If this is a reasonable summary of some of the ways that life writing may function in ethics, then we can note at least two ways in which an experientially based argument such as Menchú's can function. First, experiential narratives may provide access to detailed information about specific contexts in a way that other forms of moral argument or other sources informing moral deliberation do not. Here the point is not merely that an objective report filled with statistics may not have the same emotional impact as an experiential narrative—though that is true and, as we shall see momentarily, important. It is that an eyewitness account may actually capture important details of an event that might otherwise be overlooked or inaccessible. Thus, if we are going to deliberate with the fullest range of facts available to us, experiential narratives may prove to be indispensable.

Second, because an experiential narrative can facilitate an emotional identification between the narrator and the reader, it can lead readers to attend more carefully to the consequences of their actions. In the case of *I, Rigoberta Menchú*, the emotional identification with Menchú that her narrative elicits may lead American readers to examine U.S. foreign policy more carefully and with a different set of questions than previously. An emotional identification with Menchú may also motivate readers to act differently once they begin to see U.S. foreign policy with different eyes.

Attending to the narrativist account of moral understanding also helps us to see why *I, Rigoberta Menchú* had the moral impact it did. The passage quoted earlier about the death of Menchú's brother, and many others like it, certainly led North American readers to identify and empathize with the victims in Guatemala. *I, Rigoberta Menchú* thus facilitated an emotional identification with a distant other, which Nussbaum rightly notes may be necessary to taking human rights seriously. Certainly the immediacy of Menchú's eyewitness testimony has the ability to elicit a passionate, engaged response. Indeed, one reason it was so celebrated by critics of U.S. foreign policy in Central America was that it connected readers in a direct way to the concrete consequences of that policy. For that reason, many professors on American college campuses adopted it for use in the classroom.

I hope that at this point the relevance of the story with which I began is clear. If my appeal to personal experience in arguing about the ethics of reproductive technology generated anger and dismay when there was reason to suppose that I had fabricated my account, imagine the reaction if Menchú's account of her experiences were fabricated. Of course, we do not need to imagine the reaction because we know what the reaction in fact was when David Stoll raised the question: What if Menchú's story is not true? That was the question Stoll asked in his 1999 book *Rigoberta Menchú and the Story of All Poor Guatemalans*. According to Stoll, important parts of Menchú's story were fabricated. Although Stoll does not dispute the brutality of the Guatemalan government during the period Menchú discusses, and although he concedes that her mother, father, and brother were all killed at the hands of the Guatemalan army, Stoll does question key factual claims made by Menchú in her book, including her claim that she was an eyewitness to her brother's torture and murder.

The reaction to Stoll's accusations was a firestorm of criticism of Menchú, followed by a counteroffensive by Menchú's supporters defending both her integrity and the legitimacy of the political conclusions she reaches on the basis of her personal experiences. Stoll's work has occasioned an acrimonious debate, played out mostly in the literature in the field of Latin American studies, between supporters of Menchú and supporters of Stoll on the role of the guerrilla movement in Guatemala, on the one hand, and on the genre of *testimonio*, on the other.

Although I draw on some of this literature later on, I do not focus primarily on these two contentious issues. Instead, I wish to ask how, if Menchú's eyewitness account of the atrocities visited on the Mayan Indians by the Guatemalan government is a kind of argument against the human rights abuses of the government, we should assess the argument if it turns out that Menchú was not, for example, a witness to her brother's murder. If *I, Rigoberta Menchú* functions at least in part as an experientially based moral argument, do David Stoll's claims, if true, undermine that argument? To answer that question, it is useful to examine the arguments that have been offered in defense of Menchú. Specifically, there have been two lines of argument defending Rigoberta Menchú against Stoll's accusations: first, that Stoll misunderstands the nature of *I, Rigoberta Menchú*; and second, that Stoll fails to appreciate the larger truth embodied by *I, Rigoberta Menchú.* Let us consider each of these responses in turn.

The Genre Argument

The first line of defense offered by supporters of Rigoberta Menchú is that Stoll fundamentally misunderstands the nature of the genre into which *I, Rigoberta Menchú* falls. The reasoning here is that it is a mistake to read Menchú's book as oral history or even as autobiography. Instead we must read it as a distinctive form of "literature" through which subalterns have found a voice in Latin America since the 1970s. Although there are disagreements over the precise nature of the genre, and the form of *testimonio* has changed over time, many would accept John Beverley's definition as generally accurate. "By *testimonio*," Beverley writes,

> I mean a novel or novella-length narrative in book or pamphlet (that is, printed as opposed to acoustic) form, told in the first person by a narrator who is also a real protagonist or witness of the event he or she recounts, and whose unit of narration is usually a "life" or a significant life experience. *Testimonio* may include, but is not subsumed under, any of the following categories, some of which are conventionally considered literature, others not: autobiography, autobiographical novel, oral history, memoir, confession, diary, interview, eyewitness report, life history, *novella-testimonio*, nonfiction novel, or "factographic literature." . . .
>   The situation of narration in *testimonio* has to involve an urgency to communicate, a problem of repression, poverty, subalternity, imprisonment, struggle for survival, and so on. ("Margins" 24–25, 26)

Because *testimonio* is not equivalent to autobiography, because it is inevitably a political act that seeks to elicit solidarity with the struggles of the poor and disenfranchised, it should not be read with the same expectations that would inform a reading of autobiography.[4] Many scholars of testimonial narratives, for example, point out that the first-person narrator almost always is emblematic of the larger group. She typically seeks to give voice to collective experience through narrating personal experience. The opening lines of Domatila

---

4. The genre of *testimonio* was first given institutional recognition in 1970, when Cuba's Casa de las Americas began awarding an annual literary prize in this category. Thus, from early on, testimonial literature had a connection with revolutionary politics. See Kokotovic.

Barrios de Chungara's *testimonio* about life in the mines of Bolivia capture this point nicely. Barrios de Chungara says: "I don't want anyone at any moment to interpret the story I'm about to tell as something that is only personal. Because I think that my life is related to my people. What happened to me could have happened to hundreds of people in my country" (quoted in Kokotovic 37–38).

So the problem with Stoll's response to Menchú's book is that it is rooted in a literalist reading of the text which the genre of *testimonio* renders inappropriate. As Carol Smith puts it, given the nature of the genre, students should be encouraged to read *I, Rigoberta Menchú* "as if it were a general rather than a particular depiction of life in Guatemala" (25). Thus, for Smith, Stoll's compulsion to refute a literal reading of Menchú makes little sense because a literalist reading of the text makes little sense, given the genre. Kay Warren puts this point even more directly. Stoll refuses, writes Warren, to read *I, Rigoberta Menchú* "as an instance of testimonial literature in which, by design, there is room for maneuver between collective and individual verities" (204).

According to this line of argument, if Rigoberta Menchú did not witness her brother's murder, if she did not work as a child under oppressive conditions on a ladino coffee plantation, if she was not deprived of education, as she says she was, these details do not matter. For the story she tells in *I, Rigoberta Menchú* is not just her own story; it is, in Menchú's own words, "the story of all poor Guatemalans." If these things are not literally true about her own life, they are certainly true of many in Guatemala. Indeed, this line of argument can be neatly summarized by slightly altering the opening lines of Barrios de Chungara's *testimonio*: What happened to hundreds of Guatemalans could have happened to Rigoberta Menchú.

In addition to, and as a variation of, the argument that the story-telling conventions of non-Western and oral traditions inform *I, Rigoberta Menchú* and frustrate any literal reading of the text, defenders of Rigoberta Menchú also cite postmodernist reservations about the referentiality of texts. For example, John Beverley, who in his early work on *testimonio* highlighted the fact that the narrator of such a work "is also the actual protagonist or witness of the events she or he recounts," has in more recent writings shifted attention away from the significance of testimonial referentiality. It would be a mistake, he says, "to grant testimonial narrators like Rigoberta Menchú only the possibility of being witnesses, but not the power to create their own narrative authority and negotiate its conditions of truth and representativity" ("Real" 276). Because the only evidence that Stoll can offer to impugn Menchú's account are other texts, referentiality is of little import. "There is not, outside of discourse," Beverley writes, "a level of social facticity that can guarantee the truth of this or that representation" ("Real" 277).

Not only are the postmodernist reservations about texts in play at this point, but so too are the concerns about the constructed character of memory and the nature of the self that is supposed to have these memories. As Elzbieta Sklodowska puts it, the "chameleonic nature of memory," combined with postmodernist skepticism about a biographical self capable of reflecting on a biographical reality, should cause us to be wary of engaging the Menchú-Stoll controversy in the terms in which Stoll has framed the dispute (257). Given "the text's artifactual nature, including the inevitable embroidery of the facts for dramatic, political, or aesthetic effect," says Sklodowska, "where Stoll spots lies and fabrications, I see allegories and metaphors. In short, I see a text" (256).[5]

Whether the argument is framed in terms of misreading the genre of testimonial literature or in terms of the ceaseless interplay of texts or in terms of a collective and personal self, in every case Stoll is guilty of a kind of theoretical naïveté. A more sophisticated reading of the text renders any concerns about factual inaccuracies inconsequential and fundamentally misguided.

The "Big Picture" Argument

The second line of argument pursued by defenders of Rigoberta Menchú is quite different. Instead of contesting the philosophic basis of Stoll's critique by repudiating the distinction between fact and fiction, some supporters of Menchú openly acknowledge that many of the details of her account are not, strictly speaking, true. Nevertheless, according to this line of argument, Stoll's criticism of *I, Rigoberta Menchú* is misguided because it misses the larger picture. Rosa Montero, for example, has made this point with admirable clarity. "It would seem," she writes, "that those who denounce Menchú, obsessed by small details, have lost sight of the big picture. The end result is plain nonsense because they do not want to see the substantial truth about Rigoberta" (76).

The substantial truth is that the Guatemalan military did systematically kidnap, torture, and kill Mayan Indians; the truth is that land is concentrated in the hands of a few and that landowners force

---

5. It is passages like this one that lead Misha Kokotovic to write that "for many theorists the testimonial subject becomes a kind of subaltern poststructuralist" (40).

workers to labor in unsafe and oppressive conditions; the truth is that Mayan Indians were forcibly relocated by the government. These truths are not in doubt. The Historical Clarification Commission's report, "Guatemala, Memory of Silence," documents these truths, as does a study of land concentration by the U.S. Agency for International Development, as well as countless eyewitnesses, whether they are missionaries, anthropologists, journalists, refugees, or UN workers (Chinchilla 33). So whatever minor details Menchú got wrong, they pale in comparison to the larger truth to which *I, Rigoberta Menchú* calls our attention.

In one sense, of course, the argument that Montero and others make about keeping the big picture in mind is a variation on the argument that we must remember that *testimonio* is a genre that allows the individual to speak for the group. If we blend individual and group identity, then we cannot distinguish between individual and generic claims. What matters is not whether the specific and concrete details of a *testimonio* are true but whether the general claims are. In other words, there is a difference between generic and individual claims, and what matters are the generic claims. If Mayan workers have been forced to toil in subhuman working conditions, if the government systematically tortured and killed innocent civilians, then it does not matter whether Menchú's brother was killed in front of her or whether he was burned alive, as she claims. However he died, the government killed him, and even if the government did not kill him, it killed someone's brother. As the Rigoberta Menchú Tum Foundation put it in an essay defending her *testimonio*, Menchú "had a right to assume as her own personal story the atrocities that her people lived through. Their dead are still dead, and that is denied neither by the researcher, nor his sources. . . . It is not important whether they were burned alive or if they were already dead" (104).

Perhaps the most dramatic manifestation of this argument can be found in the work of Georg Gugelberger and John Beverley. Both compare Menchú's recollection to that of Holocaust survivors; indeed, both point to the same story told by Shoshana Felman and Dori Laub about the testimony of an Auschwitz survivor who narrated the story of seeing four chimneys explode—during the uprising in the camp—for the Video Archive of Holocaust Testimonies at Yale University. At a subsequent conference at which the video was shown, historians pointed out that only one chimney had in fact been destroyed during the uprising, and they therefore questioned the reliability of this survivor's entire testimony. By contrast, Laub, a psychoanalyst, argued that the number of chimneys did not matter. What mattered was the fact that there was an armed Jewish revolt in the camp, and that this particular survivor, having been an eyewitness to this event, could testify to that fact.

The point of comparing the case of Rigoberta Menchú to this Holocaust case, of course, is to suggest that, just as it does not matter whether there were four chimneys destroyed at Auschwitz or only one, neither does it matter whether Rigoberta Menchú gets some of her details wrong. Both this Holocaust survivor and Menchú testify to a larger truth, and it is mere caviling to ignore this fact. Indeed, that is precisely what Gugelberger says. "Stoll's emphasis on numbers and inaccuracies," Gugelberger writes, "his insistence that Rigoberta could not have seen everything she claims to have seen, and his questioning of how much Spanish she knew when she got to Paris are hairsplitting of the worst kind" (49).

If these are the two lines of argument that have been used by defenders of Menchú in the face of the criticism by David Stoll and others, how should we think about their application to the issue of assessing the moral authority of Menchú's account as an argument on behalf of the rights of indigenous peoples? If Stoll's accusations are true, do they erode the moral force of *I, Rigoberta Menchú?* To answer these questions, let us return to the narrativist account of moral deliberation sketched earlier. I think we can see right away that, if experiential narratives function in the way that Nussbaum, Kearney, and others have suggested, then there are going to be serious problems with the defenses of Menchú I have just examined. This is perhaps most obvious in relation to the postmodernist arguments, but it is true of the other arguments as well.

Consider again the passage from John Beverley that I cited earlier. When Beverley says that Rigoberta should not be treated merely as an eyewitness, that we must allow her to create her own narrative authenticity, he is essentially jettisoning any concern about referentiality. In effect, he is saying that it does not matter whether what Menchú narrated actually happened. And Alice Brittin makes what is tacit in this passage explicit: "The important point for readers of *Me Llamo Rigoberta Menchú* is not whether Petrocinio was burned alive or died by other means but that Rigoberta deemed it necessary to describe in such vivid detail what she claims to have seen with her own two eyes" (110). Yet, if *I, Rigoberta Menchú* is morally important at least in part because it may provide us with access to the lived experience of those whose rights have been systematically violated, thereby galvanizing support for human rights, if *I, Rigoberta Menchú* is important for American readers because it allows us to see in a vivid way the concrete consequences of particular U.S. policies for specific persons and groups, then the eclipse of concerns about referentiality embedded in the claims of Beverley and Brittin is disastrous as a defense of Menchú, for at least two reasons.

First, to reduce the importance of the details of Menchú's brother's death to what it tells critics about Menchú's state of mind is to trivialize utterly the pain and suffering of Petrocinio and others at the hands of the government. Laura Rice-Sayre has written that *testimonio* "brings back the body to the abstract field of human rights" (quoted in Marín 59), but this is true only if what happens to the body matters. The problem with the postmodernist defense of Menchú is that it renders the precise details of what happened to the body of Menchú's brother irrelevant. Yet in reducing the significance of the details of Menchú's account to an issue either of rhetorical strategy or of individual psychology, Beverley and others have relegated the reality of oppression and exploitation to the background. As Misha Kokotovic puts it, in attempting to preserve Menchú's iconic status by defending her in postmodernist terms, her supporters end up recovering their threatened intellectual authority by "delegitimating the lived experience of the marginalized" (32). Not only has lived experience been delegitimated, but also the whole notion of "experience" has been undermined. When Mary Louise Pratt says that in *testimonio* the category of experience is "ruled simultaneously by paradigms of individualism (uniqueness) and of collectivity (exemplarity)," the integrity of individual experience is effaced (42). To be sure, there are no unmediated experiences, and Menchú's personal experience was certainly shaped by her Mayan culture, but this does not render irrelevant the question of whether Menchú witnessed her brother's murder. If Menchú's experiential narrative is morally important because it provides us with access to important details about the concrete consequences of U.S. foreign policy, then it makes a difference whether Menchú gets the details right.

Thus the problem with any defense of Menchú that sacrifices the importance of referentiality is that it leads to a kind of corrosive skepticism. Menchú's defenders properly point out that we cannot know the whole truth or truth with a capital *T*. But it does not follow from this epistemic humility that there is no truth to be had, and to suggest otherwise is morally dangerous. When Beverley writes that there is "no level of social facticity that can guarantee the truth of this or that representation," he in effect acknowledges that, for him, there is no way to decide the truth ("Real Thing" 277). Yet if that is the case, then there is no reason to prefer Menchú's version of events in Guatemala to that of, say, the military, except perhaps for aesthetic reasons. There is merely Menchú's "representation" and that of the military.

This point is made even more dramatically when we explore the analogy Beverley himself draws between testimonial literature and Holocaust literature. Consider the case of the Holocaust memoir *Fragments: Memories of a Wartime Childhood*, published by the German publishing house Suhrkamp Verlag in 1995. The work, by Binjamin Wilkomirski, purports to be Wilkomirski's disjointed, fragmentary memories of his experiences as a young Jewish boy during the Second World War. Published to critical acclaim, it was quickly and widely translated. It won a number of awards, including the National Jewish Book Award in the United States, the Prix Mémoire de la Shoah in France, and the Jewish Quarterly Literary Prize in Britain. Based on this memoir, Wilkomirski was compared favorably to Elie Wiesel and Primo Levi. Narrated from the point of view of a child whose very identity is shattered by the Holocaust, the book tells the story of how Wilkomirski, a Latvian Jew, was separated from his parents during the massacre of Jews in Riga and survived the concentration camps at both Majdanek and Auschwitz, ultimately to be adopted by a Swiss family after the war. The book narrates in chilling detail the life of children in the camps. We read of rats crawling out of the corpses of the dead, children standing ankle-deep in excrement to keep their bare feet from freezing, guards breaking off sticks in boys' penises as a punishment for peeing where they were not allowed, and other horrors.

Like *I, Rigoberta Menchú*, *Fragments* is a powerful book, and for similar reasons. Like Menchú, Wilkomirski provides an eyewitness account of a series of morally repulsive events. The kinds of details that provide the narrative force to *I, Rigoberta Menchú* are present in *Fragments*, and their emotional and moral impact is heightened by the fact that we receive them through the eyes and the voice of a child. The book is indeed a powerful testament to the unspeakable evil of which humans are capable.

Unfortunately, there is substantial evidence that Wilkomirski did not live through the horrors he narrates; that he was not orphaned by the war; indeed, that he is not even Jewish.[6] Instead, the evidence suggests that he was the son of an impoverished Swiss house servant who gave him up for adoption to a wealthy Swiss family. Indeed, most of the evidence points to the conclusion that he spent the war years in relative comfort in Switzerland (Lappin, Peskin, and Suleiman).

Now, if there is any question about whether the truthfulness of parts of *I, Rigoberta Menchú* makes a difference to how we think about that book, there can be no question about the case of Binjamin Wilkomirski and *Fragments*. To say that it really makes no difference whether

6. See Mächler, *Wilkomirski Affair*, and Eskin, *Life in Pieces*.

Wilkomirski is Jewish or whether he endured the horrors he depicts is to trivialize the suffering of actual survivors. To say that it makes no difference would be a failure to repay what Paul Ricoeur calls our "debt to the dead" (143). Indeed, Ricoeur's observations on the relationship between history and fiction are particularly helpful at this point. Ricoeur point out, for example, that the fictional element in the work of historians is extremely valuable. "Fiction," he writes, "gives eyes to the horrified narrator. Eyes to see and to weep" (188). Thus, when Ricoeur says about Holocaust literature that "either one counts the cadavers or one tells the story of the victims" (188), he makes it clear that telling the stories is extremely valuable, notwithstanding the fact that the narrative may inescapably contain elements of the fictional.[7]

Nevertheless, Ricoeur insists that in telling the stories of the victims—granting the fictional elements and their power to move us— we must maintain the distinction between fact and fiction. Precisely because of our debt to the dead, we must seek to know the past "wie es eigentlich gewesen" (as it actually happened). Thus, to say that it makes no difference whether Wilkomirski actually lived through the experiences he narrated or whether Menchú actually witnessed her brother's murder is to abandon any concern about history "wie es eigentlich gewesen."[8]

To jettison the distinction between the real and the unreal, to be willing to collapse the distinction between fact and fiction, is thus both to dismiss actual survivors' suffering as unimportant and to play into the hands of the Holocaust deniers. If, as Robert Scholes has said, "there is no mimesis, only poesis. No recording. Only constructing" (quoted in Foley 11), then Primo Levi's or Elie Wiesel's account of Auschwitz is no more truthful than a Holocaust denier's, like Robert Faurrison's. The fact that postmodernist historians who otherwise condemn what Pratt calls the "metropolitan cult of the fact" (43) shrink from drawing this conclusion demonstrates the moral necessity of the idea that there is a truth and a reality accessible to a careful investigator.

7. For other discussions of the fact-fiction distinction that may be helpful here, see Eakin, *Fictions in Autobiography* and *Touching the World*, and Timothy Dow Adams, *Telling Lies in Modern American Autobiography*.

8. It is worth noting here that part of what we take into account in judging the power of a realist work of fiction is how well it captures what we know from other sources to be the reality depicted. Indeed, one reason why Wilkomirski's work was not origi-nally suspected of being fraudulent is that it generally accords so well both with what we know from other documentary sources about the camps and with other Holocaust memoirs. But it is accurate in this way only because Wilkomirski was apparently obsessed with Holocaust literature and read countless survivor memoirs and other documents that record that reality.

The second reason why abandoning any referential status for *I, Rigoberta Menchú* is deeply problematic is related to the larger issue of genre. Had Stoll claimed that a putative work of fiction was factually inaccurate, his work would not have been taken seriously; he would properly have been dismissed as confused. The reason why Stoll's charges were taken seriously is that, despite the claims of Menchú's defenders to the contrary, *testimonio* literature has not generally been received as fictional. The early critical work on *testimonio* certainly stressed its factual nature, and it has been treated that way when taught in American classrooms, at least before the publication of Stoll's book. Daphne Patai made this point succinctly, if polemically, when she wrote:

> Postmodernist obfuscations notwithstanding, however, it is a fact that commentator after commentator has praised the reliability of Rigoberta's plainspoken narrative, treating as axiomatic the truth of what she recounts. It is this supposed authenticity that has made the book a staple in the classroom, where scores of teachers have, by their own reports, taught it as real history and not as a version of "truth" to be read like poetry and the novel, from which students are to draw no precise historical conclusions. (273–74)

Even granting the claims of defenders of Rigoberta Menchú that *testimonio* should not be read as oral history or autobiography, it is surely true that one reason *I, Rigoberta Menchú* has moved people morally in the way that it has is that readers have assumed that the events narrated in the book happened in roughly the ways described. Patai's point about authenticity is significant because it highlights the fact that the emotional identification I discussed earlier depends largely on a relationship of trust between the narrator and the reader. For this reason, it makes a difference whether the narrative is fictional or not, and whether it is represented as fictional or not. And about this last point the narrative itself is unambiguous. Writing about the event that resulted in the death of her father, Menchú remarks, "As I said to someone who asked me for specific details of what happened in the Spanish embassy, I can't invent my own personal version from my imagination" (187).[9] The clear implication is that Menchú has confined herself to describing events of which she has direct experience. If this

---

9. At the same time, it is important to note that there is considerable internal evidence from the book that Menchú repeatedly uses her imagination to fill in gaps. For example, in describing the torture of her brother, Menchú lists a series of questions that his interrogators asked him (174). There is clearly no way that Menchú could have known that these were the questions posed to him.

is not the case, and the reader is led to believe otherwise, then the reader is likely to feel manipulated and betrayed.[10]

Assessing the "Big Picture" Argument

If the arguments about referentiality and genre are problematic because they undermine the moral force of Menchú's experiential argument, what about the argument that Stoll misses the big picture by focusing on minor factual inaccuracies? The first thing to notice in assessing this argument is that it does not discount the significance of the distinction between fact and fiction. Those who defend Menchú in this way acknowledge that there are factual mistakes in *I, Rigoberta Menchú*; they do not try to gloss over these mistakes. Instead, their point is that Menchú's experiences are nevertheless a reliable guide to a larger truth and a larger reality than the truth of any single factual claim that Menchú makes.

If we may draw a comparison to the Holocaust examples introduced earlier, supporters of the "big picture" argument would claim that the case of Rigoberta Menchú is closer to that of the survivor of Auschwitz who remembers four chimneys burning instead of one during the camp uprising than it is to the case of Binjamin Wilkomirski. No one questions the fact that this survivor was at Auschwitz at the time of the uprising, just as no one questions that Menchú was active in opposing human rights abuses in Guatemala. The question is whether the fact that both get some details wrong undermines their credibility as witnesses to a series of events. The answer, according to this line of argument, is that it does not.

To this answer I want to say "yes" and "no." The reason I agree is that I take very seriously Tim O'Brien's reflections about the liminal status of war. As O'Brien puts it: "In any war story, but especially a true one, it's difficult to separate what happened from what seemed to happen. What seems to happen becomes its own happening and has to be told that way" (78). O'Brien is surely right. In the context of war, what seems to happen may become the reality that is remembered. The fact that a survivor of the uprising at Auschwitz remembers four chimneys being destroyed and not one does not mean that the reality of the uprising is called into question. There is a larger reality to which

10. In saying that it makes a difference whether a narrative is fictional or factual, I am not denying Kearney's point that fictional narratives move people morally and may even help us reason more effectively when we are deliberating practically. Still, there is a difference between fact and fiction, and the difference makes a difference.

the survivor remains a reliable witness, namely, the improbable uprising itself.

At the same time, however, there is a difference between being mistaken about the precise details of a given event (or being selective or
"biased" in the presentation of an event) and being mistaken about
whether, say, an event took place. The problem, then, with applying
this line of argument to Rigoberta Menchú is that she does not just
misremember particular details; in important ways she misrepresents
the events. For example, she now admits that she did not witness her
brother's murder. In one sense, of course, even this fact pales in comparison to the larger truth to which *I, Rigoberta Menchú* bears witness.

Still, it is important to note that, unlike the postmodernist defense
of Menchú, the "big picture" argument recognizes the significance of
getting the general details right. In other words, it recognizes the fact
that the emotional and moral force of an experiential narrative like
Menchú's does not flow merely from the disturbing images with which
she confronts us. Although Menchú certainly provides us with some
haunting images, images that may in fact facilitate the emotional
identification of which I spoke, ultimately it is the story Menchú tells
that will sustain or fail to sustain emotional and moral solidarity with
her movement. The danger here is that the story will be constructed
simply to promote such solidarity. When this happens, identification
has been privileged over truth, and the upshot is a kind of sentimentalization. Michael Ignatieff captures the problem with the process of
sentimentalization very nicely. Sentimental art, he writes, "sacrifices
nuance, ambivalence, and complexity in favor of strong emotion"
(293).

Ultimately, then, the "big picture" argument acknowledges that the
issue of credibility is important. Those who defend Menchú along
these lines believe that her credibility is intact even though her
narrative is admittedly flawed. Even granting the inaccuracies, the
argument goes, she is a reliable witness and one who can be trusted,
because she gets the larger story right. Whether in the end you agree
with this assessment or not, the important point to recognize is that
the question of Menchú's credibility is an issue with which we must
inescapably wrestle. If the appeal to experience is to function in the
ways that I sketched earlier, then such an appeal cannot be self-
validating; an appeal to experience cannot serve as a trump. If we are
to invite others to engage in social action in part on the basis of appeals
to experience, if experiential narratives are to inform practical deliberation, then we need to raise serious questions about the reliability
and credibility of experiential narratives and their narrators. Did the

events really happen? Is the narrator reliable? Are there competing narratives to which we must listen? These are the kinds of questions that we must answer if we are to draw on experiential narratives when deliberating morally. If we dismiss such questions, as it seems to me many have done in the debate about *I, Rigoberta Menchú*, then we deprive ourselves of a valuable moral resource.

In the end, if life writing is to be a useful resource for moral deliberation, then we must be extremely careful—much more careful than many defenders of Menchú have been—about distinguishing between fact and fiction. In an effort to acknowledge and do justice to the constructed character of experience, we must not collapse the distinction between what happened and what was imagined. Although there will be cases in which the distinction gets blurred, and although it may at times be very difficult to verify the authenticity of an experiential appeal, the centrality of the distinction between factual accounts and fictional ones cannot be lost. The stark contrast between the cases of Binjamin Wilkomirski and Rigoberta Menchú comes from the fact that Wilkomirski's narrative is fraudulent from start to finish. By contrast, no one, including David Stoll, denies the fact that Menchú, her family, and Mayan Indians generally, experienced extraordinary suffering at the hands of the government.

I end by returning to the story with which I began. When my colleagues responded to news of my son's birth, I was puzzled. I had expected jubilation and was met instead with anger. In retrospect, I think that that anger was understandable. My readers had relied on my experience of infertility, and I had (apparently) betrayed that trust. In the reaction to that apparent betrayal, we find clues to why appeals to experience matter morally and how we can begin to assess life writing as a form of moral argument. The account of my experience dealing with infertility assumed a kind of moral weight because I would presumably be alive to issues raised by reproductive interventions in a way that someone who had not experienced infertility treatment might not be. When it appeared that I might have fabricated the experience, both the expectation that I might see what others miss and the ground for emotional identification with me as a person suffering from infertility were stripped away. Nevertheless, this is not to say that a fictional account of infertility would be morally useless. Just as we ought to be concerned with the reliability of a narrator in a work of fiction, so too we must be concerned about the trustworthiness of the narrator of an experiential narrative. Indeed, we need to be particularly concerned about the reliability of the narrator of a life story, at least when that story is being put to work morally.

WORKS CITED

Abrams, Irwin, ed. *Nobel Lectures Peace, 1991–1995*. River Edge, N.J.: World Scientific, 1999.

Adams, Timothy Dow. *Telling Lies in Modern American Autobiography*. Chapel Hill: University of North Carolina Press, 1990.

Arias, Arturo, ed. *The Rigoberta Menchú Controversy*. Minneapolis: University of Minnesota Press, 2001.

Beverley, John. "The Margins at the Center." In *The Real Thing: Testimonial Discourse and Latin America*. Ed. Georg M. Gugelberger. Durham: Duke University Press, 1996. 24–41.

——. "The Real Thing." In *The Real Thing: Testimonial Discourse and Latin America*. Ed. Georg M. Gugelberger. Durham: Duke University Press, 1996. 266–86.

Brittin, Alice. "Close Encounters of the Third World Kind." *Latin American Perspectives* 22, no. 4 (1995): 100–14.

Chinchilla, Nancy Stolz. "Of Straw Men and Stereotypes: Why Guatemalan Rocks Don't Talk." *Latin America Perspectives* 26, no. 6 (1999): 29–37.

Eakin, Paul John. *Fictions in Autobiography: Studies in the Art of Self-Invention*. Princeton: Princeton University Press, 1985.

——. *Touching the World: Reference in Autobiography*. Princeton: Princeton University Press, 1992.

Eskin, Blake. *A Life in Pieces: The Making and Unmaking of Binjamin Wilkomirski*. New York: W. W. Norton, 2002.

Foley, Barbara. *Telling the Truth: The Theory and Practice of Documentary Fiction*. Ithaca: Cornell University Press, 1986.

Frank, Arthur W. *The Wounded Storyteller: Body, Illness, and Ethics*. Chicago: University of Chicago Press, 1995.

Gugelberger, Georg M., ed. *The Real Thing: Testimonial Discourse and Latin America*. Durham: Duke University Press, 1996.

Ignatieff, Michael. "The Stories We Tell: Television and Humanitarian Aid." In *Hard Choices: Moral Dilemmas in Humanitarian Intervention*. Ed. Jonathan Moore. Lanham, Md.: Rowman and Littlefield, 1998. 287–302.

Kearney, Richard. "Narrative and Ethics." In *The Aristotelian Society*. Bristol: Longdunn Press, 1996. Supp. vol. 70. 29–46.

Kokotovic, Misha. "Theory at the Margins: Latin American 'Testimonio' and Intellectual Authority in the North American Academy." *Socialist Review* 27, nos. 3–4 (1999): 29–63.

Lappin, Elena. "The Man with Two Heads." *Granta* 66, no. 2 (1999): 9–65.

Lauritzen, Paul. "Ethics and Experience: The Case of the Curious Response." *Hastings Center Report* 26, no. 1 (1996): 6–15.

Mächler, Stefan. *The Wilkomirski Affair: A Study in Biographical Truth*. Trans. John E. Woods. New York: Schocken Books, 2001.

Marín, Lynda. "Speaking Out Together: Testimonials of Latin American Women." *Latin American Perspectives* 18, no. 3 (1991): 51–68.

Menchú, Rigoberta. *I, Rigoberta Menchú*. London: Verso, 1984.

Montero, Rose. "Her." In *The Rigoberta Menchú Controversy*. Ed. Arturo Arias. Minneapolis: University of Minnesota Press, 2001. 76–77.

Moore, Jonathan, ed. *Hard Choices: Moral Dilemmas in Humanitarian Intervention*. Lanham, Md.: Rowman and Littlefield, 1998.

Nussbaum, Martha C. *Poetic Justice: The Literary Imagination and Public Life.* Boston: Beacon Press, 1995.

O'Brien, Tim. *The Things They Carried.* New York: Penguin Books, 1990.

Patai, Daphne. "Whose Truth? Iconicity and Accuracy in the World of Testimonial Literature." In *The Rigoberta Menchú Controversy.* Ed. Arturo Arias. Minneapolis: University of Minnesota Press, 2001. 270–87.

Peskin, Harvey. "Holocaust Denial: A Sequel." *Nation* 268, no. 14 (1999): 34–38.

Pratt, Mary Louise. "*I, Rigoberta Menchú* and the 'Culture Wars.'" In *The Rigoberta Menchú Controversy.* Ed. Arturo Arias. Minneapolis: University of Minnesota Press, 2001. 29–48.

Ricoeur, Paul. *Time and Narrative.* Trans. Kathleen Blamey and David Pellauer. Vol. 3. Chicago: University of Chicago Press, 1988.

Rigoberta Menchú Tum Foundation, "Rigoberta Menchú: The Truth That Challenges the Future." In *The Rigoberta Menchú Controversy.* Ed. Arturo Arias. Minneapolis: University of Minnesota Press, 2001. 103–6.

Sklodowska, Elzbieta. "The Poetics of Remembering, the Politics of Forgetting: Rereading *I, Rigoberta Menchú.*" In *The Rigoberta Menchú Controversy.* Ed. Arturo Arias. Minneapolis: University of Minnesota Press, 2001. 251–69.

Smith, Carol. "Why Write an Exposé of Rigoberta Menchú?" *Latin American Perspectives* 26, no. 6 (1999): 15–28.

Stoll, David. *Rigoberta Menchú and the Story of All Poor Guatemalans.* Boulder: Westview Press, 1999.

Suleiman, Susan Rubin. "Problems of Memory and Factuality in Recent Holocaust Memoirs: Wilkomirski/Wiesel." *Poetics Today* 21, no. 3 (2000): 543–60.

Warren, Kay. "Telling Truths: Taking David Stoll and the Rigoberta Menchú Exposé Seriously." In *The Rigoberta Menchú Controversy.* Ed. Arturo Arias. Minneapolis: University of Minnesota Press, 2001: 198–218.

White, Hayden. *The Content of the Form: Narrative Discourse and Historical Representation.* Baltimore: Johns Hopkins University Press, 1987.

Wilkomirski, Binjamin. *Fragments: Memories of a Wartime Childhood.* Trans. Carol Brown Janeway. New York: Schocken, 1996.

CHAPTER 2

Misremembering Ted Hughes

Diane Middlebrook

D uring his lifetime, the English poet Ted Hughes was notoriously reticent about discussing his personal history. In 1984 he was appointed poet laureate of England, which made him a literary celebrity. But he had always disliked the limelight, and even after assuming this public office he resolutely avoided making himself available to journalists and photographers. He was by disposition protective of his privacy, and his life had been marked by scandalous tragedies: his first wife, the American poet Sylvia Plath, had committed suicide after discovering, shortly after the birth of their second child, that Hughes was having an affair with a married woman named Assia Wevill. Six years after Plath's death, Assia Wevill followed Plath's example, gassing not only herself but the four-year-old daughter she had borne Hughes. Although these facts were well known in the literary world, Hughes did not permit himself to be questioned about them in public.

Ten months before his death in 1998, however, Hughes released a book of poems titled *Birthday Letters* which provided an intimate portrait of his marriage to Sylvia Plath. The book became a runaway best-seller on both sides of the Atlantic, indicating that the public took a great interest in Hughes's private life. Immediately after his death, memoirs and fiction in which Hughes figured began to appear. Significant publications included a memoir by Lucas Myers, an American who became a close friend of Ted Hughes's while at Cambridge University during the 1950s, and disapproved of Hughes's marriage to Sylvia Plath

(*Crow Steered, Bergs Appeared*); an autobiography by Al Alvarez (*Where Did It All Go Right?*), with whom Hughes had quarreled after Alvarez published an account of the suicide of Sylvia Plath in a London newspaper (this was a first serialization of Alvarez's book about suicide, *The Savage God*); an article by Peter Porter, an English poet who was Hughes's contemporary, and often reviewed his books unfavorably ("Ted Hughes and Sylvia Plath: A Bystander's Recollections"); celebratory essays by a number of contributors to a Festschrift (*Epic Poise*) planned for presentation on Hughes's seventieth birthday, edited by Nick Gammage; and two works by the English writer Emma Tennant, who was involved with Hughes in an extramarital affair during the 1970s (a memoir, *Burnt Diaries*, and *Sylvia and Ted: A Novel*).

A range of ethical questions is raised in each of these highly self-conscious publications, which offer personal recollections, moral judgments, and in some cases avid speculation about the character of Ted Hughes. Because Hughes guarded his privacy so aggressively, each of the writers is keenly aware of the value of information about him. Each had kinds and degrees of personal relationships with Hughes that might lead a reader to expect bias in their accounts of the man and his work. Each commands a sophisticated rhetorical style, usually deploying a narrative structure in which to situate recollections of historical incidents. Any of these early contributions to the posthumous assessment of Ted Hughes would be interesting to analyze on any of these points, but possibly the most problematic is the work of Emma Tennant, in which ethical problems are bound up with issues related to literary genres, and to the privileged position Tennant occupies as Hughes's intimate contemporary and memoirist.

Burnt Diaries

Emma Tennant was born in 1937 the daughter of the second Baron Glenconner and Elizabeth Lady Glenconner, and grew up in a family of aristocrats. She was educated at St. Paul's Girls' School in London, spent her summers at the family's castle in Scotland, and was presented at court when she made her social début at age eighteen.

From an early age Emma Tennant knew that she wanted to become a writer. At twenty she married the son of the novelist Henry Green; she frankly admits that the novelist father interested her more than the son. This was in 1957. When the sixties overtook London, Emma Tennant abandoned what she calls her "girlitude," the feminine expectation of being looked after by a father-husband. She got a divorce and went to work at *Queen* and then *Vogue* magazines.

Tennant's first novel was published in 1963, a satirical roman à clef about the London circle of upper-class young marrieds to which she had temporarily belonged. She says she wrote it in ten days (*Girlitude* 153), as a contribution to "the new wave of disrespect" (157) that had activated a taste for satire among the younger generation of artists. She toyed with a plan to call the book *Hurting*, in homage to her former father-in-law, who often titled his novels with gerunds—*Living, Loving, Doting, Concluding, Party-Going.* "It is no more my goal to hurt people than that of most writers," she explained (99); the point was, she *needed* to write, and this was the only world she knew. The novel was published not as *Hurting* but with the blander title *The Colour of Rain*, and under the pseudonym Catherine Aydy—a title and pseudonym fetched from a session at a Ouija board (154). Her former friends were not deceived. Moreover, they were not amused to find themselves and their possessions caricatured in her book. Lawyers were brought in to put Tennant through a bout of ethical consciousness raising (160–62).

Tennant survived the lesson. Hardworking and prolific, she went on to write twenty or so novels over the years between 1963 and 1998, when, at age sixty, she began to bring out a multivolume memoir of her life and times. *Strangers: A Family Romance* (1998) dealt with her early years and her colorful family. *Girlitude: A Memoir of the '50s and '60s* (1999) covered her experiences from eighteen to thirty. *Burnt Diaries* (1999) took her story through the 1960s and 1970s and through a serious episode of breast cancer. The 2001 volume, *A House in Corfu*, described her parents' escape from English life in the 1960s by building an isolated home on the Greek island near the spot where Odysseus was said to have been rescued after his shipwreck by the young princess Nausicaa.

The connection to Odysseus is far more significant to Emma than to the elder Tennants: literary self-consciousness is a feature of her memoirs. In *Burnt Diaries*, onto the chronological sequence that recounts Tennant's active professional and personal ups and downs during the decade of the 1970s is grafted a fairy tale: the story of her affair with Ted Hughes, shaped by the plot of "Bluebeard."

The best-known version of "Bluebeard" is by Charles Perrault, the seventeenth-century French *littérateur* whose lasting fame is based on his collection *Contes de ma Mère l'Oye* (Tales of Mother Goose), eight folktales that Perrault converted into charming literary works. In "Bluebeard," a beautiful young woman is courted by an older man with a mysterious past: a succession of young noblewomen have died after marrying him. Moreover—as his name suggests—his appearance is fearsome, bestial. But he possesses great wealth, gained in military exploits, and the young woman in the story accepts his offer of marriage after visiting his fabulous castle. Shortly after their marriage, Bluebeard is called away on business. He encourages his new wife to entertain herself lavishly during his absence, and to invite her sister Anne to join her for company. He gives his wife the keys to all of the household stores, but forbids her entry to one room. Of course she is overcome by curiosity, and when she unlocks the forbidden door, she is greeted by the sight of bloody corpses: Bluebeard's previous wives. The key magically turns bloody, and when Bluebeard returns and demands the keys, she cannot conceal her trespass. He condemns her to death but permits her to withdraw to her room for prayer. Terrified, she appeals to her sister to keep watch for the arrival of their brothers, who are expected for a visit. The brothers arrive just in time to decapitate Bluebeard, and to secure for the young beauty a tremendous fortune—and also to deprive her of feminine curiosity once and for all.

For Tennant, Hughes resembles Bluebeard in being a man who possesses a secret that can ignite in women a foolish, overweening curiosity. The nature of the "secret" Emma Tennant associates with Hughes is signaled in the title of her memoir. *Burnt Diaries* refers to the journals of Hughes's first wife, Sylvia Plath: specifically to the journal covering the last months of Plath's life, which Ted Hughes claimed he had burned because he did not want his children to read it; but referring also, by implication, to journals for the years 1960–62 that Hughes said, ambiguously, had been "lost" and might turn up at some future date. Because of his involvement with his paramour Assia Wevill at the time of Plath's death, Hughes's loss or destruction of these journals has often been regarded as a self-serving effort to keep his own affairs off the record. Moreover, though Hughes did not marry Assia Wevill, they had a child together, and were a couple for about six years before Wevill's death—were all but married, that is. *Burnt Diaries* is directed toward readers who are familiar with this terrible succession of suicidal women, and who are curious, as Tennant is, to find out the secrets about them that Hughes might be hiding under lock and key.

Tennant entertains the fantasy of joining this queue of wives. She falls like a fairy-tale heroine into an erotic obsession immediately upon meeting Hughes: "Like Bluebeard's bride, it appears, I have to know" (159). Because the tale is "Bluebeard," her prose begins to resonate with unacknowledged allusions to the work of his dead wife as soon as she takes up with Hughes. For example, Tennant says of herself, as she enters a house where she expects to find him, "I am an arrow," echoing Plath's famous line, from the poem "Ariel," "I / Am the arrow, / The dew that flies / Suicidal" (*Collected Poems* 239–40). A couple of pages later, "the coming together of myself and Ted . . . now appears to be written in the stars" (70, 75), Tennant writes, evoking Plath's poem "Words," which ends with the phrase "fixed stars / Govern a life" (*Collected Poems* 270). Tennant again recalls this poem when she and Hughes first make love. And so forth.

Hughes cooperatively slips into the role Tennant has assigned him. Like Bluebeard, he is huge and shaggy (though unbearded), and possesses a fearsome virility of a sort that Tennant associates with wild animals. He courts her with gifts of books that propose to initiate her into esoteric knowledge; at their third meeting, in front of his "present" wife, he offers to make a worktable for Tennant, an offer that she recognizes would "tip me into thc shoes of the woman who was once his wife" (82). (Tennant remembers that he made Plath an elm plank table.) Eventually, Hughes asks her to run away with him to Scotland (156–63), to live in the wilds. (Hughes had "run away" with Assia Wevill, leaving Plath to manage their home and children.) The plan did not materialize, though Tennant does not seem to have refused outright. On the occasion when their romance is drawing to its end, she and Hughes see a fox in Regents Park; Hughes tells her he had thought of bringing her a fox cub and tells her about the day he almost brought home a fox cub to Sylvia Plath—an episode recounted in Hughes's poem "Epiphany" in *Birthday Letters* (113–15).

Hughes links his desire for Tennant to his desire to write: Tennant is supposed to serve as a muse, the role Plath played in his life. Tennant ascribes her initial interest in Hughes precisely to her own fascination with the story of his relationship to this dead wife, a powerful woman writer. The mystery that surrounds this diary is the equivalent to that bloody chamber in Bluebeard's castle. Tennant says she had read Plath's journals closely and was obsessed with mysteries about the marriage which she thought Hughes would eventually explain to her, given the sexual intimacy that had developed between them. But when she began to question, Hughes cut her off gruffly, saying, "Don't talk about Sylvia" (154).

The hidden implication is that Tennant wishes to share Plath's fate—not to die, but to acquire the fortune of writerly power that Hughes seems to possess. The aspiration to be the consort of this magical power drives Tennant into the ethically questionable behavior that her memoir freely acknowledges: willingness to inflict collateral damage on other women. One cause of her cruelty is jealousy, when, like Plath, Tennant discovers Hughes's willingness to deceive. She learns, accidentally, that throughout their affair, Hughes has been intimate with a woman named Jill Barber, who followed him to

London after meeting him at a book festival in Australia. Like Plath, Tennant takes revenge on Hughes's (other) paramour, Barber, by writing about her. Tennant gave Barber such an unflattering disguise in *Burnt Diaries* that Barber produced a rebuttal, "Ted Hughes, My Secret Lover," which was published as a two-part article in a London tabloid.

Tennant, with Hughes's complicity, worked a more complicated kind of damage on Hughes's wife during their affair. The occasion was a gala public performance of Hughes's work at the National Theatre in London, followed by a VIP dinner at a restaurant. Tennant became a last-minute addition to this party, when Hughes, "looking at me from the corner of his eye, restraining his smile, lowering his voice (but not quite enough to prevent his wife from hearing)," asked her to come along. "I should have then decided to extricate myself, and go home," Tennant acknowledges.

> I hear Ted's words, when he speaks of his own home existence, casual and dismissive: "I? Oh, I'm in hospital."—I know that in alluding in this way to his wife, a nurse, he betrays his domestic happiness, he deceives *her*. But what am I doing, conniving at this? . . . I decide—I have already decided, I think guiltily, that tonight I shall most certainly take the King. . . . Why, as I press my knee against Ted's, do I care not at all who sees or becomes aware of my improper actions . . . . There cannot be any reason for the folly—and cruelty—of what I do, other than a desire for a brazen announcement to be made. . . . I have a wager with myself. He will come back to my house tonight, when the meal is finished.. What on earth do I imagine will happen to his wife? (142–44).

Tennant admits enjoying this situation, exulting in her own social advantages as a literary insider from a wealthy family, playing the role of femme fatale in Hughes's life. But she did harm; and her account of the event opens the way into a compelling analysis of the feminine psychology operational in this situation, the aspect of the memoir that gives it some heft. The folktale "Bluebeard" is classified in the scholarly literature as the type in which brothers rescue women from ruthless husbands or abductors. Tennant focuses on the female psychology latent in the tale. "Like so many women who read Plath's famous last poems in the late '60's, I feel I've lived through a climate of feminism in which . . . Sylvia stands for the martyred female and Hughes for the murderous male" (48), Tennant comments; perversely—like many women she knows, including feminist women—she is attracted rather than repulsed by the aura of danger around Ted Hughes. She calls this affliction "the Bluebeard syndrome": a need "to become involved with a man known for his terrifying and unacceptable treatment" (49) of women.

Tennant's *Burnt Diaries* will no doubt be quarried for anecdotes when future histories of this period are written. Situated as Tennant was on the lively periphery of 1970s literary culture in London, she is able to provide an insider's view of some of the major players, and her willingness to anatomize her affair with Ted Hughes will be useful to biographers who seek to comprehend the complexity of Hughes's relations with women. Using the tale of "Bluebeard" as a pathway to disclosing motives of which she was conscious only in retrospect, Tennant illuminates not only a recognizable aspect of a certain kind of female subjectivity, but also a motif of the folktale that—before feminism, before women's liberation from "girlitude"—had escaped the scholars' inquiries and categories.

Sylvia and Ted: A Novel

As a novelist, Emma Tennant frequently writes sequels to, or fantasias on, or parodies of, literary classics. Tennant's *Pemberley* continues the story of *Pride and Prejudice; Adela* is about the ward for whom Mr. Rochester hires Jane Eyre as governess in Charlotte Brontë's novel; *Faustine* is a modern-day update of the Faust legend. In *Sylvia and Ted*, she draws a framing device from Ovid's *Metamorphoses*, which Hughes had translated selectively at the end of his life and published as *Tales from Ovid*. The arc of the plot in *Sylvia and Ted* is loosely structured by allusions to the tale of Tereus, Procne, and Philomela, while smaller sections are shaped by Ovid's tales of Ceres and Persephone, of Europa, of Echo and Narcissus, and of Atalanta. Other literary works supply metaphorical ornaments: *Electra, Hamlet*, and at the end of the novel an unacknowledged borrowing from Emily Dickinson's "After Great Pain."

But the bulk of *Sylvia and Ted* is drawn from *non*fiction sources: the published journals and letters of Sylvia Plath, biographies of Plath, and interviews with living acquaintances of the actual persons on whom the principal characters are based. Tennant acknowledges the historicity of the novel in an author's note placed at the front of the book: "Events described in the book are based on fact, and in the case of the story of Assia Wevill, Sylvia's rival, who also committed suicide, many of the facts were previously concealed or unknown. *Sylvia and Ted* is, nevertheless, a work of the imagination." Though a fiction writer is free to use whatever material comes to hand, and to do so without citing her sources, Tennant's little phrase "many of the facts were previously concealed or unknown" raises a disquieting ethical issue, given the use she makes of information that is already in circulation about the marriage of Sylvia Plath and Ted Hughes.

If the fictional elements work to illuminate the historical elements in Tennant's memoir, the reverse is true of her deployment of historical elements in her fiction *Sylvia and Ted*. Tennant's literary method is pastiche, and readers who know the writings on which Tennant has drawn will readily recognize them as frequent sources of the "facts" on which the novel is based. The section titled "Boston 1959" in *Sylvia and Ted* is an unacknowledged condensation of Anne Sexton's essay on her friendship with Plath, "The Bar-Fly Ought to Sing." Paraphrased poetry by Plath and Hughes is also absorbed, without acknowledgment, into the narrative of actions and motivations in *Sylvia and Ted*. For example, a turning point in the plot is a dream in which Plath is visited by the ghost of Ovid's Procne. In the dream, "Sylvia stands by the window of the room that is white in the moonlight. She hears her children breathe and turn in their cots, in the little rooms where the shade from the yew tree brings peace and darkness. She tenses herself for [Procne's] last words" (120). Tennant is alluding to Plath's poem "Event": "The child in the white crib revolves and sighs / . . . Where apple bloom ices the night / I walk in a ring" (*Collected Poems* 194).

But, as might be expected, by far the greatest amount of source material is drawn directly from Plath's journal. Snippets of Plath's entries are embedded without quotation marks or other acknowledgment to embellish the prose. Tennant writes, "The gods threaten play with blood, lust and death" (86, 96); Plath writes, "The great gods play the drama of blood, lust and death" (*Journals* 471); while the narrative about "The Meeting" in *Sylvia and Ted* (35–43) is a flat-out summary of Plath's long journal entry for February 25, 1956. Examples could be multiplied abundantly.

Tennant uses Plath's journal as a point of departure for *invented* incidents in *Sylvia and Ted* as well. For a section of *Sylvia and Ted* subtitled "Lolita, 1962" (97–104), Tennant has apparently drawn on a set of notes about Hughes's interest in a teenage neighbor in Devon which Plath made in 1962. In her journal, Plath notices Ted's attention to the teenager's "shape" (referring to "Lolita") and grows alert with hostility (*Journals* 635–41). The "Lolita" section of Tennant's novel invents a fifteen-year-old babysitter, Kate Hands, who minds the children while Plath works in the morning. (The actual Hugheses had no babysitter; each took a turn minding the children each day while the other worked—Plath in the morning hours.) In the novel, "Ted is obsessed with her. He feels the unknown, unfinished quality of Kate Hands in the same way a farmer knows a heifer or a sheep" (98).

In the reference to the farmer knowing a heifer, Tennant begins setting up Hughes's sexual conquest of the teenager in terms that call to mind Ovid's tale, in *Metamorphoses*, of the seduction of Europa, the rustic princess whom Jove deceives by disguising himself as a bull. Like Europa, rustic Kate "knows . . . the interest that is being taken in her . . . some part of her acknowledges the approaching theft of her virginity" (99). Kate permits herself to be decoyed into a meadow near the high school. In Kate, Tennant writes, Hughes "has found his tabula rasa. Like Jove, he can start from scratch, invent the world anew. A language is his to carve out of the granite nothingness that is this fifteen-year-old girl. But in order to build his fresh lexicon, Ted must first seduce, enter, and possess Kate Hands" (101). In a graphic scene, Hughes deflowers the girl. Getting up from the grass, she stumbles against a discarded scythe and cuts her hand badly. But a successful cover story is arranged, and the two "lovers" continue to meet throughout the summer.

All of these details, as far as anyone but Emma Tennant knows, are fictional. But situated as they are in the larger context of well-known events for which the sources are largely historical, the seduction of Kate Hands carries the impact of a breathtaking transgression. Had Hughes been alive, the novel could not have been published. Can this episode possibly be true—based on facts previously concealed or unknown? Possibly. But if it isn't true, is it fair? And if it isn't fair, to whom is it *un*fair?

The use of real people in fiction is an established practice brought to a high degree of literary mastery in such contemporary "nonfiction novels" as—to name only a few relevant examples—*In Cold Blood* by Truman Capote; *The Executioner's Song* by Norman Mailer; *The Book of Daniel*, by E. L. Doctorow, on the Rosenbergs; and Robert Coover's satire on the same subject, *The Public Burning*. The ethical difference of Tennant's book from these other works lies, I think, in the authors' relationship to the sensational and disturbing historical materials on which they draw. Tennant's precursors make imaginative interventions in order to fill gaps in documented events, and to create plausible inner lives for the protagonists in significant historical situations. Tennant does something else. Adopting the stance of the gossip, she positions at the novel's front door an author who invites readers to assume that the most shocking, disturbing, and discreditable actions she represents in the novel may be "based on facts . . . previously concealed or unknown"—facts available to this author through personal access to witnesses and participants in the ugly story she tells. Under the cover of fiction, surreptitiously, Tennant offers insider knowledge of these famous people and their celebrated catastrophes.

What inferences can be drawn from the particular sort of disquiet Tennant's authorial strategy evokes? Perhaps just one: that the non-fiction novel benefits artistically from being narrated by an ethically uncompromised literary persona. In the cases of Capote and Mailer, the narrating point of view—usually transparent and impersonal—is that of the investigative journalist upholding a professional standard of objectivity. In the case of Doctorow, it is that of the historian observing a professional code of reliance on evidence. In the case of Coover, the venerable stance is that of the satirist, wielding exaggerated unfairness as a weapon against folly and vice. In each case the conventional authorial position is that from which the reader receives the blend of information and imagination that constitutes the "non-" and the "fiction," the documented actuality and the explanatory invention.

As we have seen, Tennant has written successful creative nonfiction in the form of social satire, in her first novel, *The Colour of Rain*, where legal advice helped her to a deeper understanding of the genre's rules. She has written successful nonfiction in the genre of memoir, *Burnt Diaries*, whose narrating persona discovers her psychological prototype in a fairy tale. But in *Sylvia and Ted: A Novel*, a personal ethical failure jams the signals by which a reader navigates the reality-effect of the nonfiction novel. If we dig here, Tennant assures us, we get not a fiction but the real thing: dirt.

WORKS CITED

Alvarez, Alfred. *The Savage God: A Study of Suicide.* New York: Random House, 1972.
——. *Where Did It All Go Right?* London: Richard Cohen Books, 1999.
Barber, Jill. "Ted Hughes, My Secret Lover." *Mail on Sunday*, May 13, 2001, 49–52; May 20, 2001, 54–55.
Gammage, Nick, ed. *The Epic Poise: A Celebration of Ted Hughes.* London: Faber and Faber, 1999.
Hughes, Ted. *Birthday Letters.* New York: Farrar, Straus and Giroux, 1998.
——. Foreword to *Journals of Sylvia Plath.* Ed. Fran McCullough. New York: Dial, 1982.
Myers, Lucas. *Crow Steered, Bergs Appeared.* Sewanee, Tenn.: Proctor's Hall Press, 2001.
Plath, Sylvia. *The Collected Poems.* Ed. Ted Hughes. New York: Harper and Row, 1981.
——. *Unabridged Journals of Sylvia Plath.* Ed. Karen Kukil. London: Faber and Faber, 2000.
Porter, Peter. "Ted Hughes and Sylvia Plath: A Bystander's Recollections." *Australian Book Review*, August 2001, 21–28.
Sexton, Anne. "The Bar-Fly Ought to Sing." In *The Art of Sylvia Plath.* Ed. Charles Newman. Bloomington: Indiana University Press, 1971. 174–81.

Tennant, Emma. *Burnt Diaries*. Edinburgh: Canongate Books, 1999.
——. *Girlitude: A Memoir of the '50s and '60s*. London: Jonathan Cape, 1999.
——. *A House in Corfu*. London: Jonathan Cape, 2001.
——. *Strangers: A Family Romance*. London: Jonathan Cape, 1998.
——. *Sylvia and Ted: A Novel*. New York: Henry Holt, 2001.

Part II

LIFE WRITING AS MORAL INQUIRY

Life Writing as Narrative of the Good: *Father and Son* and the Ethics of Authenticity

David Parker

Much recent attention to the topic of ethics and life writing has centered on a series of issues such as privacy and misrepresentation. The focus has been on the ethics of authorial performance. This has been important work, articulating the tacit moral assumptions we bring to the reading of lives and thereby outlining a new possibility in the way we think about the writing of them—the possibility that, in the memorable formulation of John Eakin, "ethics is the deep subject of autobiographical discourse" (123).

The fundamental question in this new work is: *What is it right for the life writer to do?* On any philosophical account of ethics, *What is it right to do?* has to be a central question. On some accounts, however, such as the one I draw on here, this question occupies only part of the space of the broader ethical domain, which is defined by the question as it was posed by the ancient Greeks: *How should a human being live?* My claim is that this broader formulation contains another question that can be found at work at the heart of most, if not all, written lives: *What is it good to be?*

I move toward this claim inductively by exploring a single example, the classic auto/biography by Edmund Gosse, *Father and Son: A Study of Two Temperaments* (1907). At the end of the epilogue, having quoted a painfully remonstrating and reproving letter of his father's at length, Gosse advances to his conclusion:

All that I need further say is to point out that when such defiance
is offered to the intelligence of a thoughtful and honest young man
with the normal impulses of his twenty-one years, there are but two
alternatives. Either he must cease to think for himself; or his individualism must be instantly confirmed, and the necessity of religious
independence must be emphasized.

No compromise, it is seen, was offered; no proposal of a truce would
have been acceptable. It was a case of "Everything or Nothing"; and
thus desperately challenged, the young man's conscience threw off
once for all the yoke of his "dedication," and, as respectfully as he
could, without parade or remonstrance, he took a human being's privilege to fashion his inner life for himself. (251)

Given its placement at the climax of the narrative, this is clearly
meant to be a key moment in the moral experience of the autobiographical protagonist. Later I shall define more precisely what I mean
by terms such as "moral" and "ethical." For now I simply mean that
the narrator describes this as a moment in which he exercises his "conscience" in a choice between "two alternatives": he must either yield
to his father's point of view or have the courage to think and choose
for himself. It is a moment of deliberation, of practical reasoning,
though of course the discursive mode is not philosophical in any strict
sense. We can, however, catch the shadow of philosophy in the way in
which the individual Edmund Gosse gives way progressively to the
more universalised figures of "a thoughtful and honest young man"
and finally "a human being." The procedural shadow is, if anyone's,
Kant's, though the focus on the "human being's *privilege* to fashion
his inner life for himself" sounds more like Mill. Either way, the focus
is on moral *action*: the key verbs are of *throwing off* a yoke and of
taking a privilege, complementary assertions of moral autonomy.

What is implicit in this ending is that, through this culminating act
of choice, the young protagonist is "confirm[ing] his individualism"
and existentially *becoming* the self telling the whole story. This is
what the whole story has been leading to. I put it like that to under-
line one of the ways in which ethics may be central not simply to
authorial performance but to the complex interrelations between narrated and narrating selves: their ultimate identity may be one of moral
choice. But this is only one of the ways in which ethics may be central,
namely, in the protagonist's deliberations and choices about questions
such as whether to yield to the opinions of an authoritative other or
to summon the courage to think for himself.

These questions still bear a broad similarity to the ethics of authorial performance in that they are within the space defined by the question *What is it right to do?* Here I must invoke Charles Taylor, who

provides a much broader picture of the moral life than the dominant one in contemporary Anglo-American moral philosophy, which gives constitutive centrality to moments of deliberation and choice—and to the question *What is it right to do?* According to Taylor's *Sources of the Self*, we cannot understand these moments properly if we detach them from the whole background of what he calls the "qualitative discriminations" that are woven into our language and into the texture of our thought. "Prearticulately," he says, "they function as an orienting sense of what is important, valuable, or commanding, which emerges in our particulate intuitions about how we should act, feel, respond on different occasions, and on which we draw when we deliberate about ethical matters" (77–78). According to Taylor's (partly Aristotelian and partly Hegelian) picture, conscious moral deliberation and choice are shaped from below by our mostly "prearticulate" but identity-orienting systems of value, commitment, and belief, which turn out themselves to be partly formed by practical reasoning of another kind. In our moral experience the question *What is it right to do?* is the merest tip of a volcano of moral feeling and intuition.

Father and Son makes this point of Taylor's quite clear. We can understand Gosse's identity-defining choice at the end of the epilogue only against the background of values, commitments, and beliefs the young man progressively distills from his experience. Some of his key moral feelings and intuitions are those he has toward his father's religion:

> Let me speak plainly. After my long experience, after my patience and forbearance, I have surely the right to protest against the untruth (would that I could apply to it any other word!) that evangelical religion, or any religion in a violent form, is a wholesome or valuable or desirable adjunct to human life. It divides heart from heart. It sets up a vain, chimerical ideal, in the barren pursuit of which all the tender, indulgent affections, all the genial play of life, all the exquisite pleasures and soft resignations of the body, all that enlarges and calms the soul are exchanged for what is harsh and void and negative. It encourages a stern and ignorant spirit of condemnation. (248)

I've called these feelings and intuitions "moral," but the sense in which they are moral needs to be defined. This example is deliberately provocative because certain expressions here remind us that Gosse is often seen in very different terms from the ones I've just used: I mean expressions such as "the tender, indulgent affections," "the genial play of life," and "the exquisite pleasures and soft resignations of the body." These surely place Gosse where the editor of the Penguin edition, Peter Abbs, squarely places him, alongside figures such as Wilde and Gide, in the decadent fin de siècle, in which art for art's sake defined itself explicitly *against* morality. Abbs talks about Gosse as a hedonist and an aesthete and quotes with approval a critic who says of Gosse's criticism that its criterion of aesthetic pleasure left it without any basis for the "sizing up of moral values" and therefore powerless to deal with the shock of the First World War.

There is truth in this conventional historical positioning of Gosse, but what it ignores is that aestheticism itself has its own typical commitments to what is valuable and significant. Gosse clearly believes, for example, that "all that enlarges and calms the soul" is more worthy than "a stern and ignorant spirit of condemnation." I put it that way to invoke Taylor's notion of "strong evaluation," which involves not mercly preference for one thing over another (e.g., Coke over Pepsi) but the belief that one thing is in some sense of higher value, more worthy of respect.[1] For Gosse, the engagement with books, poems, and works of art is not merely something more pleasurable or desirable than the pursuit of evangelical religion; it is more admirable because it enlarges the soul. And so it is a strongly valued good, part of Gosse's sense of what makes a human life worthwhile. To put it another way, being large-souled in these terms is part of Gosse's answer to the question *What is it good to be?* For Taylor, the question *What is it good to be?* is integral to ethics, not least because our sense of what is worthy of respect or admiration—and the reverse—plays into our conscious deliberations on the question *What is it right to do?*

In Gosse's case, his final choice "to fashion his inner life for himself" draws on lessons he has learned in growing up about what it is good, and not good, to be. In the final stages of this process, at about the age of sixteen, he begins to read voraciously, especially Shakespeare and the Romantics, and begins to experience the "extension of [his] intellectual powers." At the same time, he begins to estimate his father in a new light: "I began to perceive, without animosity, the strange narrowness of my father's system, which seemed to take into consideration only a selected circle of persons, a group of disciples peculiarly illuminated, and to have no message whatever for the wider Christian community" (230). He also perceived this narrowness as a major moral flaw in his father:

---

1. This distinction is crucial for Taylor and really deserves fuller discussion. Strong evaluations "involve discriminations of right and wrong, better or worse, higher or lower, which are not rendered valid by our own desires, inclinations, or choices, but rather stand independent of these and offer standards by which they can be judged" (*Sources of the Self* 4).

He who was so tender-hearted that he could not bear to witness the pain or distress of any person, however disagreeable or undeserving, was quite acquiescent in believing that God would punish human beings, in millions, for ever, for a purely intellectual error of comprehension. My Father's inconsistencies of perception seem to me to have been the result of a curious irregularity of equipment. Taking for granted, as he did, the absolute integrity of the Scriptures, and applying to them his trained scientific spirit, he contrived to stifle, with a deplorable success, alike the function of the imagination, the sense of moral justice, and his own deep and instinctive tenderness of heart. (231–32)

It is clear here that, for Gosse, his father's religious "system" can have pernicious effects on the human spirit: to have "imagination," "the sense of moral justice," and the "instinctive tenderness of heart" all "stifled" is not a good way to be. By contrast, literature, among other things, has enlarged Gosse's own capacity for moral perception and reflection. "I began to perceive," says Gosse, in introducing his new way of seeing his father.

In the terms Taylor uses in *Sources of the Self*, the younger Gosse has "lived through" a "transition" in his moral experience, and on Taylor's account such transitions are at the heart of practical reasoning: "Practical reasoning . . . is a reasoning in transitions. It aims to establish, not that some position is correct absolutely, but rather that some position is superior to some other. It is concerned, covertly or openly, implicitly or explicitly, with comparative propositions. We show one of these comparative claims to be well founded when we can show that the *move* from A to B constitutes a gain epistemically" (72). The notion of "epistemic gain" is central to Taylor's account. It means not simply gain in knowledge but a move to a new way of seeing things that constitutes a gain over the previous one. Its application to Gosse's text and to auto/biography in general soon becomes clear: "This form of argument has its source in biographical narrative. We are convinced that a certain view is superior because we have lived a transition which we understand as error-reducing and hence as epistemic gain. I see that I was confused about the relation of resentment and love, or I see that there is a depth to love conferred by time, which I was quite insensitive to before" (72). Taylor is of course primarily addressing his philosophical interlocutors here and is arguing for a different way of looking at practical reasoning from the procedural models used by the proponents of Kantian and utilitarian ethical theories. Part of his argument, developed in earlier chapters, is that one constitutive aspect of us as moral beings is that we grasp our lives as narratives that have a certain

direction. We see ourselves as beings who are "growing or becoming"—
or the reverse, as backsliding or diminishing; we know ourselves
"through the history of [our] maturations and regressions" (50).

By "narrative" Taylor doesn't in the first instance mean written or
even spoken narrative, but rather the mostly implicit stories we have
of where we are "at" in our lives—in relation to our understandings of
what it is good to be. What he is saying in the cited passages is that
practical reasoning comes to focus in the moments wherein these
understandings themselves change and grow. Part of our narratives will
be the history of these crucial "transitions" when we came to see
things—in our own terms—more deeply or truly. My claim would be
that these implicit stories, about where we are "at" in our lives and of
how we came to "epistemic gain," will almost necessarily contribute
to the shaping of our written lives. That claim may seem strong, but
it seems to me to be borne out by most of the autobiographies to which
scholars and critics have given serious attention.[2] I follow it with an
even stronger claim. If, as Taylor argues, it is a condition of being a
functioning self that I speak from a moral orientation I take to be right,
I simply *cannot* narrate the story by which I came to ultimate epistemic loss. I can tell the story of my backslidings, and I may see some
of my earlier changes of perspective as epistemic loss, but the final
move to *that* perspective must be gain—though of course others may
see my history differently. All of this follows from Taylor's opening
chapters, in which he shows how we need to be rightly placed against
a horizon of significance that gives our lives meaning and value. In his
own formulation, to "know who you are is to be oriented in moral
space" (28)—a space of strong evaluations, of goods you live by. I shall
return to this starting point of Taylor's presently.

Father and Son certainly does not disconfirm either of my claims.
It is a narrative marked by its protagonist's practical reasonings from
the evidence of experience, which are transitions in the progressive
history of its narrator's current orientation in moral space. Some of
these transitions involve inductive scientific reasoning, such as the
child's experiment with idolatry (66–67). But the epistemic gains that
seem to me to be dominant in the story are those that involve the protagonist's initiations into distinctively post-Romantic insights about

2. I return to this issue in my discussion of an apparently disconfirming case, that
of Carolyn Steedman's *Landscape for a Good Woman*. It is interesting to speculate
whether my claim would apply to celebrity or popular memoirs such as *Bad as I Wanna
Be* by Dennis Rodman. Such cases raise the question of the extent to which an ethical
framework of some kind may be partly constitutive of those texts that have become
canonical in scholarly and critical discourse. The question of ethics and the canonic-
ity of autobiographies is too complex to canvas here, however.

the importance of qualities such as imagination and *"instinctive* tenderness of heart."* I have said Romantic "insights," but it is equally clear that the initiation is also into Romantic concepts and vocabulary. Epistemic gains, in other words, will take place only in an available language and may in fact depend on a shift from one vocabulary or language to another. This too is part of Taylor's account. It follows from the fact that for him a "self only exists within" what he calls communal "webs of interlocution" or conversation in the widest sense (36). These webs include not merely the people we know but the interlocutors we read and who crucially seem to be able to read us. From them we are initiated into our "languages of moral and spiritual discernment" (35). I have taken to using the notation "LMD" for this crucial term of Taylor's because the more familiar term "discourse" has become irrecoverably mired in a certain poststructuralist conception of power before which we are relatively helpless. Talking of our LMDs stresses the agential nature of the self and takes language as empowering us to make "discernments," to pick out qualitative realities of experience such as acts of "courage," and to make qualitative distinctions that constitute acts of understanding. Gosse simply cannot discern his father's stifled "imagination" and *"instinctive* tenderness of heart"* within the language of his childhood religion. To become aware of them he must move to a new language. The epistemic gain he makes when he starts his voracious reading as a young man is "enabled," in other words, by the acquisition of a Romantic LMD.

I mean to show not only that *Father and Son can* be read by means of these adoptions from Charles Taylor's philosophy, but also that it may be illuminating to do so. The objection I am trying to meet is that my enterprise may be simply reinscribing familiar patterns of reading. There is nothing especially new, for example, in simply noticing the clash of languages in *Father and Son*. In an article published in 1993, Cynthia Northcutt Malone offers a Bakhtinian reading of the text in which she sees it as the site of a "polemical debate between the contesting voices and belief systems of Philip and Edmund Gosse" (16). She points out correctly that the debate is by no means that open-ended polyphonic contestation that Bakhtin so admired in Dostoyevsky, but more of an "internal polemic" of the kind found in confessions such as Rousseau's. Right from the opening of the narrative the reader is maneuvered into siding with the son. Malone quotes the opening, in which Gosse says that of "the two human beings here described, one [the father] was born to fly backward, the other could not help being carried forward" (35). She astutely analyzes the "double-voiced" irony here of the son's echoing of his father's letter, quoted in the epilogue, in which he talks of the son's "rapid progress towards evil." She concludes, "The inscription of the epigraph over the narrative juxtaposes directional readings of the son's 'progress': as sinful backsliding, on the one hand, and as intellectual movement forward, on the other" (18).

Analyzing the subtle polemical rhetoric of the text in this way is certainly insightful, but it does not capture some things that are for me central. The first is that the "voices" of father and son are not simply those of the two distinct individuals, but rather they also correspond to inner languages, LMDs, within the overall narrative of the protagonist's *becoming* the narrator. As I have tried to suggest, the narrator's identity cannot but be invested in a progressive story of ultimate epistemic gain, which in Gosse's case includes initiations into scientific and above all Romantic LMDs—and the leaving behind of the language of the saints. This is why it is misleading to talk of *juxtaposed* "directional readings," "on the one hand" forward and "on the other" backward, as we might ideally hope for in the open thought experiment of a Dostoyevsky novel. This is not to deny that the self may be complex and fragmented, multiply constituted in various languages, but to suggest that complete decentered openness is the wrong expectation in an auto/biography, as is the word "polemical," which implies that it would be better otherwise. Authorial neutrality over the matter of an autobiography's ultimate language(s) is not an available option. For all Gosse's scientistic talk of this memoir as a "record" or a "document," he writes it, as any autobiographer does, with a particular orientation in moral space, which means with a whole background of strong evaluative beliefs and commitments that are woven into his language(s).

■

It should be helpful at this point to pick up a couple of threads left dangling earlier, which will return us to the heart of our subject. The first is Taylor's starting point: our need to be oriented in moral space. The title of chapter 1 of *Sources of the Self* is "Inescapable Frameworks," underlining from the start Taylor's claim that having *some* sort of framework of significance and value is not an "optional extra" that we can choose or not as we wish. Here he parts company with the dominant strains of what he calls "naturalism" in current Anglo-American and neo-Nietzschean philosophy, which tends to picture such frameworks as optional projections onto the flux of morally neutral experience. In contesting that picture Taylor argues that naturalism is *inherently* mistaken by showing that identity, our sense of who we are, is a kind of orientation in moral space. To be without any evaluative framework at all would involve a profound psychic disorientation: such a person would not simply be morally shallow or unpredictable; he or she would be frighteningly disturbed, perhaps pathological. For a person of relative normality, the naturalist picture *cannot* obtain, simply on the grounds that such a person must be oriented in terms of the multiple evaluative distinctions needed to answer for herself coherently in everyday life.

Approaching more closely to our subject, I want to claim first that self–life writing cannot but reflect the self's orientation, or pattern of orientations, in moral space. Second, I see the autobiographical act as continuous with our attempts to answer coherently for ourselves in the space of questions in which we moderns increasingly live. I mean questions posed by a range of interlocutors, both implicit and explicit, about what we think is significant and valuable, about where we stand and the overall direction and meaning of our lives, questions that are at once about the goods we really live by and who we really are. If this is right, then autobiography will be *necessarily* a narrative of the good, and perhaps also, in some fashion, necessarily a narrative of epistemic gain.

The most I can demonstrate here, however, is that autobiography *can* be these things and perhaps often is. That may be enough for the purposes of the present book—that is, to show that the question *What is it good to be?* is one that an ethics of life writing should not ignore. To go further, as I wish to, and to advance the stronger claims of necessity involves testing them against more resistant texts than *Father and Son*. By this I mean, on the one hand, texts that do not recognize, or that may seem to oppose, the picture of the good that I am putting forward here; and, on the other hand, texts that are not organized with the teleological linearity of *Father and Son*.

In a 2002 paper, "Authenticity and Recognition in Intergenerational Auto/biography," I look at Carolyn Steedman's *Landscape for a Good Woman* as a resistant case in both senses. For Steedman, locating her "good woman" in the landscape of sociopolitical space involves reducing the good into the terms of power relations. Among other things, to be "good" according to her understanding is to be the pliable victim of the strong. If we accept Taylor's premise, however, then in order to make sense of her life, Steedman cannot reduce the good to a mere technology of domination. Reading her text against the grain of her neo-Marxist theoretical commitments, I argue that even her historical analyses of the exploitation of "good" working-class women are narratives of the good. They are so in the broader Taylorian sense in that they have meaning only within the moral landscape of a certain rea-

sonably explicit picture of what it is good to be. Her account turns out
to be partly oriented by certain post-Romantic goods not unlike those
underpinning *Father and Son*—goods of self-valuing, self-worth, and
self-belief. At another point I argue that other parts of Steedman's narrative manifest a rather unexpected but clearly implicit commitment
to an ethics of care, which I describe as a suppressed good of her text.
In other words, it is important to note that texts can have an ethical
unconscious, and that seeing autobiographies as narratives of the good
does not involve the old bugbear of the unified humanist subject.[3]

Landscape for a Good Woman is also a more resistant case in the
structural sense than *Father and Son*. Certainly at first sight it does
not appear to answer to what I want to claim about the necessity of
narratives of epistemic gain. The slender and circuitous life narrative
thread of *Landscape* is embroidered with parsimonious care and
painstaking control on a broad meta-discursive cloth. The narrative is
there only as "case study," to illustrate the powerful theoretical argument that generates the whole text. It is not a text in which abundant
recollections of the life can easily bounce back against the narrator's
will-to-meaning in order to qualify or complicate it. Nor is Steedman's
life narrative at all linear. Even so, pulling the diffuse narrative
together, I find a clear direction in it that pictures the narrated self as
going through various stages of growing toward and becoming the self
who is telling the story. According to my reading, she moves from
being a repressed "good child" to a resentful adolescent to an adult
who will not let herself be put down by middle-class women. At each
stage, Steedman lives through certain transitions in her moral experience: the "good" child comes to feel her resentment and its implications, that it is unfair of her mother to call her unfeeling when she has
made her so. Each stage involves clear error-reducing moves. She
comes to see that she is not, for example, as the "good" child believes,
to blame for everything. But then to the reflective adult her mother
turns out to be more than the rejecting adolescent thought: the mother
comes to be seen in some ways as exemplary, a "good woman" in a
final unreduced sense. Steedman's is a narrative of epistemic gain, in
other words, and its orientation is intelligible within the landscape of
the post-Romantic goods I mentioned earlier, goods of self-belief and
self-worth, of taking herself seriously.

---

3. In another paper on autobiographies by Eric Liu and Andrew Riemer, "Locating
the Self in Moral Space: Globalisation and Autobiography," I argue similarly for the
notion of a fragmented ethical subject, which follows from Taylor's thesis that we
inevitably live by more goods or moral languages, and our identities are more complex,
than we can easily recognize.

But here we need to extend the discussion to confront what must seem like the most commonsense of all objections. What does all this talk of self-belief and self-worth have to do with *ethics?* Ethics is surely the discourse that deflects attention from such me-generation preoccupations to demands that we think about our obligations to *others.* This is both a commonsense objection that many educated users of the English language might feel and at the same time the objection of many mainstream Anglo-American moral philosophers. For example, Thomas Nagel, in his book *The View from Nowhere,* argues that neo-Aristotelian philosophers of Taylor's stripe are wrong "because moral requirements have their source in the claims of other persons, and the moral force of those claims cannot be strictly limited by their capacity to be accommodated within a good individual life" (195). What Nagel is getting at is that (eudaemonic) philosophies of the good such as Taylor's take the aim of the ethical life to be the human flourishing that comes from the realization of a range of goods. The claims of others on us, however, may well frustrate and defeat the project of realizing this range of goods in our lives. For this reason, such claims cannot be adequately accommodated within an ethics of the good. The key question is what ought to give way under circumstances of conflict between the claims of self and the claims of the other? For a Kantian there is no problem. The procedure of universalization allows the claims of both to be weighed rationally and impartially against each other. Specifically, it is a procedure designed to neutralize the irrational prejudices of egoism, inclination, and self-interest that ever predispose us to self-preference.

Thus (deontological) philosophies of the right as opposed to the good tend to place their priority as Nagel does on "moral requirements" that have their "source in the claims of other persons." But there are powerful objections against this emphasis. They begin with the question of why the claims of others should virtually constitute the moral domain instead of being simply one sort of claim among others. What of the claims of self? Many contemporaries who ultimately derive their thinking from the Greeks keep returning to this question. They range from Michel Foucault, with his hedonistic ethics of care for self, to neo-Thomists such as John Finnis (107), who argues that there is scope for reasonable self-preference not because my own flourishing is of more value than that of others but because it is *mine,* and it is only by taking its claims seriously that I can begin to realize any good in my own life. Otherwise, where the procedure of universalization dominates practical reason, it is not so easy to see how what Bernard Williams calls "the *I* of my desire" (67) ever gets much mass in the moral scale against the omnipresent and arguably more weighty obligations I have to others. The heuristic of impartiality does not simply insist on the moral equivalence of selves; it gives no weight to my *particularity* as a self. In a word, it can find no place in the equation for the moral significance of my *difference*.

This is where Taylor's work is especially pertinent. In his book *The Ethics of Authenticity*, Taylor outlines what he calls the "moral ideal of authenticity," in which he pictures the modern project of self-fulfillment (or self-realization) as embodying a serious moral claim, "that of being true to oneself" (15). His argument provocatively takes on not only Anglo-American moral philosophy but also some popular analyses of modern culture such as Christopher Lasch's *Culture of Narcissism* and Allan Bloom's *Closing of the American Mind*. These tend to picture the modern emphasis on self-fulfillment as relativistic and self-indulgent, and as narrowing the scope of cultural attention to the private and away from the larger concerns that transcend self such as religion, politics, and history. Where these popular analyses join with Kantian ethics is in their assumption that the project of self-fulfillment will merely license irrational self-preference, self-interest, narcissism, or egotism—not to mention self-absorption and insouciance toward the needs of others. And so, one would have to agree, in many cases it does. So whence self-fulfillment as a specifically "*moral* ideal"?

Taylor begins to answer this question by presenting self-fulfillment as a strongly valued good, a notion outlined earlier by which he contrasts forms of life or ways of being that I merely prefer with those that I hold to be in some sense incomparably higher than others. Thus we moderns, he argues, tend to see a fulfilled life as higher, as more worthy of admiration, than an unfulfilled life. What lies behind this observation of modern anthropology is the whole historical analysis he outlines in *Sources of Self*, and in particular his reading of the profound contribution of the Romantic movement to the shaping of Western modernity. Following Rousseau, we moderns tend to subscribe to the notion of "self-determining freedom. It is the idea that I am free when I decide for myself what concerns me, rather than being shaped by external influences" (*Ethics of Authenticity* 27). But this notion gets part of its authority for us, he argues, from a slightly later one, namely, Herder's notion that "each of us has an original way of being human." Taylor writes: "This idea has entered very deep into modern consciousness. It is also new. Before the late eighteenth century no one thought that the differences between human beings had this kind of moral significance. There is a certain way of being human that is *my* way. I am called upon to live my life in this way, and not in imitation of anyone else's. But this gives new importance to being true to myself.

If I am not, I miss the point of my life, I miss what being human is for *me*" (28–29).

It is implicit in this notion that there is a sense in which I have a responsibility to and for myself. It is a responsibility not to yield utterly to demands from beyond myself to conform to some universal human template, but to attend to the claims of my own inner nature and to realize my own *particular* way of being human. What Taylor calls the ethics of authenticity is in short an ethics of difference, and it is ever called into being against the perceived oppressiveness of universalizing moralities both ancient and modern, be they Stoic, Judeo-Christian, utilitarian, or Kantian. The dictum of Blake's Hell captures this perception with memorable force: "One Law for the lion & Ox is Oppression."

■

One reason for broadening the discussion as I have here has been to remind us that moralities centered on, and constituted by, "the claims of other persons" can become vehicles of oppression. Specifically, they can become such when they afford no *moral* weight to the claims of self, particularity, or difference. Such claims can only be regarded as immoral, amoral, or merely sub-moral, and so they are rhetorically disempowered before other-regarding considerations.

I take this conflict between the moral claims of self and "the claims of other persons" to be the ethical center of *Father and Son*. The "intolerable . . . burden of Atlas" (81) laid on the conscience of the child by his mother's dying wish is intelligible as such within the framework of the ultimate moral language (LMD) of the narration, which I have described provisionally as Romantic, but which we can now call the language of authenticity. What happens at the end of the narrative is that, faced with his father's potentially overwhelming reminders of his obligations to his parents and to God, the young man is empowered by discovering authenticity specifically as a *moral* language that can provide not only an adequate counterweight to the Puritan LMD of the father but also an armory of terms in which to mount a critique of it. In fact, the end is implicit in the famous beginning: "This book is the record of a struggle between two temperaments, two consciences and almost two epochs. It ended, as was inevitable, in disruption. Of the two human beings here described, one was born to fly backward, the other could not help being carried forward. There came a time when neither spoke the same language as the other" (35).

Setting aside for the moment the importance of evolutionary language ("one born to fly backward, the other . . . forward"), we can clearly see the whole trajectory of the narrative as contained in the significance and weight given here to the innate individual difference between the father and son ("two temperaments"). That formulation of difference indicates the presence from the start of the distinctive "language" of the narrating "I." It is a language the narrated "I" will only acquire at length, leaving behind the language he and his father once shared, when they also shared a commonly framed "conscience." The two terms are intimately related. The "consciences" of the two men come to differ radically precisely because they are constituted by different "languages"—which means, as we saw earlier, different vocabularies of moral choice embedded in very different background pictures of what is valuable and what it is good to be. For this reason it is justifiable to talk of Gosse's two languages as "languages of moral and spiritual discernment" (LMDs) in Taylor's sense.

But the force of talking this way will not be obvious because authenticity in Taylor's sense is not a familiar part of ethics, nor the son's exercise of "conscience" at the end a familiar part of what we might call the spiritual life. A more usual way to read these things in *Father and Son* is provided by Linda H. Peterson's excellent chapter on Gosse in *Victorian Autobiography: The Tradition of Self-interpretation*, in which the son's gradual throwing off of his father's religion is seen as parodic of traditions of spiritual autobiography. There is certainly rich insight in Peterson's account of Gosse's baptism as the dramatic climax of the autobiography, in which we see a "simulacrum of true change of heart" (176). What her account occludes, however, is that there is a "true change of heart" later on, but that it takes place in terms of a very different LMD. For Peterson there is nothing counterpoised systematically against the father's Puritan LMD: the loss of religious "authority is not re-invested in a single, alternative system" but is "dispersed to a variety of interpretive strategies, which are applied locally rather than comprehensively" (182). While I would agree that there is more than one language of interpretation other than the religious one—the presence of naturalistic evolutionary language is quite pervasive—there is certainly a predominant one, which is the one I am calling the Romantic language of authenticity. The extent to which it is "systematic" can be glimpsed in the fact that the climax of Gosse's account of the baptism is the revelation that during the service in the Room he has put out his tongue in mockery to the other little boys. What is underlined here is that he is after all still a child, and what shapes our way of seeing this is a familiar Romantic model of self as an organism that unfolds in its own way and at its own pace.

In fact, self as an organism following—or trying to follow—its own inner laws is one of the major organizing metaphors of the narrative.

The terms in which the baptism is presented are prefigured by the visit to his Clifton relatives, where Gosse discovers a "healthy" and "wholesome" warmth that allows him to sink back, after many months of strain, "into mere childhood again." Here he lives the life of an "ordinary little boy relapsing . . . into childish thoughts and childish language" (84). The Clifton family understand that the soul has its times and its seasons and that childhood is not the time for the spiritual intensities and compulsions that have controlled and distorted his life at home. His home in south London is figured as a prison "cell," the child with his cheek pressed against the window looking wistfully out at the gray world of the street. Two memorable passages make the organic metaphor underpinning all this quite explicit:

> This, then, was the scene in which the soul of a little child was planted, not as in an ordinary open flower-border or carefully tended social *parterre*, but as on a ledge, split in the granite of some mountain. The ledge was hung between night and the snows on one hand, and the dizzy depths of the world upon the other; was furnished with just soil enough for a gentian to struggle upwards and open its stiff azure stars; and offered no lodgement, no hope of salvation, to any rootlet which should stray beyond its inexorable limits. (44)

> At this time I was a mixture of childishness and priggishness, of curious knowledge and dense ignorance. Certain portions of my intellect were growing with unwholesome activity, while others were stunted, or had never stirred at all. I was like a plant on which a pot has been placed, with the effect that its centre is crushed and arrested, while shoots are straggling up to the light on all sides. My Father himself was aware of this, and in a spasmodic way he wished to regulate my thoughts. But all he did was to try to straighten the shoots without removing the pot which kept them resolutely down. (210–11)

The passages both portray self as distorted by the parental religious system, in the one case by being half starved and frozen in a place offering no generous tending to the soul and in the other being crushed by an alien weight. In both cases the self longs for free and vigorous growth—to put out a straying rootlet or a straggling shoot—but this is rigidly repressed. The organic metaphor provides what Peterson would call a pattern of self-interpretation, but its function clearly goes beyond interpretation. These passages also show patterns of evaluation, of "qualitative discrimination," which is why I think it is more meaningful to see the Romantic imagery as a "language of moral and spiritual discernment" (LMD). The imagery gives the narrating "I" a vocabulary in which to discern repression as well as its remedy: the metaphor of the pot implies an obligation to remove it. When the time comes, the image of the crushed plant will help to justify the decision and action of the narrated "I" precisely as *moral* decision and action.

In this Gosse illustrates, perhaps in extreme form, a key point I am adopting from Taylor. It is that self–life narrators (like the rest of us), in accounting for key identity-forming decisions and actions, feel a need to speak from a moral orientation they take to be right. Gosse's case is extreme in that he is overthrowing the beliefs of a beloved parent, beliefs that cannot but continue to make a powerful claim on him, especially when that parent uses all of his considerable rhetorical powers to try to keep him faithful to them. The whole narrative in fact is a complex act of "othering" these beliefs, together with the claims of the father's "conscience" on him and the "language" that informed it.

An incident around his sixth birthday illustrates this process of "othering." Gosse is naughty, and his father gives him several cuts with the cane, justifying this by reference to Scripture: "Spare the rod and spoil the child." Gosse flames with a rage he cannot fully account for: "My dear, excellent Father had beaten me, not very severely, without ill-temper, and with the most genuine desire to improve me. But he was not well advised especially so far as the 'dedication to the Lord's service' was concerned. This same 'dedication' had ministered to my vanity, and there are some natures which are not improved by being humiliated" (65). As is evident here, the narrating "I" is conscious of the "genuine" other-regarding love driving the father to keep the child faithful to his dedication, but this very conscientiousness and selfless care make an opposing *moral* language of his own all the more necessary. Whereas the father's scriptural justification is founded on a universalistic proverb, the narrator's account scrutinizes the punishment through the lens of individual difference. The impact of the rod on "some natures" makes the proverb's validity dubious, and the attempt to improve these "natures" by discipline a morally dubious enterprise. The biblical language is thus subtly othered by reference to its others, those individual "natures" oppressed by its all-inclusiveness.

The narrated "I" comes to take his stand in moral space on that which is "innate" in him, his own "nature," which opposes the attempts to make him yield to the Puritan template of individual "election" and "dedication." Gosse discovers and holds to a different sort of individuality altogether, one that is ultimately hard and resistant:

> Through thick and thin I clung to a hard nut of individuality, deep
> down in my childish nature. To the pressure from without I resigned

everything else, my thoughts, my words, my assurances, but there was something that I never resigned, my innate and persistent self. Meek as I seemed, and gently respondent, I was always conscious of that innermost quality which I had learned to recognize in my earlier days in Islington, that existence of two in the depths who could speak to one another in inviolable secrecy. (168)

The hard nut recapitulates the imagery of the plant, with its organic implications of innate individual possibilities incipient within it and ready to unfold and grow under its own impulsion and blueprint, manifesting its own unique way of being human. But authentic being cannot find realization without protection against religious "pressure" from "without" ever ready to force it into conformity. Hence the *moral* force of the nut's hardness, emblem of the self's need to be "persistent" in the face of the system that seeks to assimilate it.

What this passage also reminds us is that the older child self can cling to the hard nut of its individuality only because the younger child self had first "recognized" it at a particular moment back in his "days in Islington." The trajectory of the whole narrative, as I have been arguing, is to chart the key "transitions" in the narrated self's progress toward the self-defining existential decision in the last paragraph. For Taylor, such "transitions" are achieved when, under the stimulus of new experiences, practical reasoning breaks through to epistemically superior insight. The Islington experiences conform to this pattern. They crystallize around the inference Gosse draws from two otherwise trivial incidents that his father is not omniscient. This inference provokes a true epistemic shift, from the mistaken belief that his father, among other things, could peer like God into his innermost heart to the knowledge that his inner life is opaque to him. The "thoughts" open up an altogether new "secret" space that "belonged" entirely to him and to an inner other who was also himself: "There were two of us and we could talk with one another. It is difficult to define impressions so rudimentary, but it is certain that it was in this dual form the sense of my own individuality now suddenly descended upon me, and it is equally certain that it was a great solace to me to find a sympathizer in my own breast" (58). Here the narrated "I" discovers all at once the greatest possible boon to his individual self-realization, that is, an existing self-conscious subjectivity that will both focus his difference and become the site of all future independent feeling and thinking.

What the narrated "I" supposedly finds ready-made, in fact, is nothing else but the Romantic "autonomous self," of which scholars such as John Eakin and Nancy K. Miller have made us all so properly skeptical. I have written in "Authenticity and Recognition" of my own take on this, namely, that while the "autonomous self" is ontologically dubious, autonomy makes sense as the goal of an ethical narrative, which I am calling here, after Taylor, the ethics of authenticity. The ethical goal of autonomy in *Father and Son* is clearly stated in the final sentence of this text: it is taking "a human being's privilege [I would add responsibility] to fashion his inner life for himself" (251). We scholars of life writing now have relational or dialogic rejoinders to all this which tell us that such self-fashioning is ontologically impossible: the sympathizing other of self-conscious subjectivity gets its force from real others, real interlocutors, who come to inform self-consciousness in all-pervasive ways.

In fact, future transitions in the protagonist's realization of moral autonomy are indeed more interlocutive, to borrow a term that will remind us of Taylor's emphatically dialogic ontology of the subject, cited earlier: "A self exists *only* within what I call 'webs of interlocution'" (36; emphasis added). The "other" within Gosse's self-consciousness is of course powerfully shaped by Puritan voices and texts, while the resistant sympathizing "other" of his individuality is also informed by real others such as the Clifton relatives and his stepmother. But some of the most significant interlocutors for Gosse are those found in the authors and heroes of the books he can manage to get hold of. An important turning point is the reading of *Tom Cringle's Log*, which he says "tinged my outlook on life." He writes: "I must not define too clearly, nor endeavour too formally to insist on the blind movements of a childish mind. But of this I am quite sure, that the reading and re-reading of *Tom Cringle's Log* did more than anything else, in this critical eleventh year of my life, to give fortitude to my individuality, which was in great danger—as I now see—of succumbing to the pressure my Father brought to bear upon it from all sides" (171–72). It is evident here that individuality isn't simply a hard nut, banging in a Darwinian contest of power against the individuality of the father, though that too is implied throughout the narrative. Individuality is also the fulfilment of "fortitude," of a struggle within that needs nourishment from without.

■

My reading has stressed the ethical dimension of Gosse's struggle against powerful moral pressure, to bring into being that necessary element of self-flourishing we can call moral autonomy. To achieve this he has to throw off the oppressive weight of other-regarding claims

CHAPTER 4

Judging and Not Judging Parents

John D. Barbour

Oने of the most significant ethical dimensions of life
writing is the writer's evaluation of his or her parents.
This process of moral assessment is not as parochial
or private as it might at first appear, for in thinking about one's parents,
a person may consider how one agrees or differs with parents' beliefs
and values related to religion, gender roles, work, race, political
matters, the natural environment, and many other ethical issues.
One's relationship to parents may also involve an evaluation of moral
character as the writer reflects on what virtues of a parent he aspires
to or admires and what characteristics he criticizes or rejects. A central
theme in many autobiographies is judging one's parents, as the author
sorts out what parental virtues and values he affirms and which things
he denies, at least as normative for his own life.

There are several reasons why we should be careful about judging
others, which are often condensed into maxims about not judging. To
the degree that a writer focuses on her relationship to a parent, she
must explore the parent's life, explaining how the parent came to have
specific values and a certain moral character. It becomes harder to
judge when one realizes how various influences shaped a parent's life—
including the fact that that parent, too, was once a child reacting to
family pressures. If "tout comprendre, c'est tout pardonner" (to fully
understand another person is to forgive), the autobiographer may find
that the project of life writing makes it difficult to judge. He may
recognize that a parent's character was formed by causal influences

73

implicit in his "dedication" and to take on the right and obligation of
fashioning his inner life according to the self-responsible ethics of
authenticity. In case this emphasis, for all my advocacy, still seems
eccentric, it may be as well to end by reminding ourselves of some
of Gosse's own formulations regarding *Father and Son*. In the preface
Gosse says that the book offers a "study of the development of moral
and intellectual ideas during the progress of infancy" (33). It is, he says,
"the narrative of a spiritual struggle" (34). In a letter to Sydney Holland
he outlines what is at stake in the struggle: "To tell you the truth,
what I should like to think my book might be . . . is a call to people to
face the fact that the old faith is now impossible to sincere and intel-
ligent minds, and that we must consequently face the difficulty of
following entirely different ideals in moving towards the higher life.
But what ideals, or (what is more important) what discipline can we
substitute for the splendid metallic vigour of an earlier age?" (quoted
in Thwaite 432). The final question, I take it, is rhetorical. *Father and
Son* has answered it by advancing the new "ideal" of authenticity
which, while never "substituting" for the claims on us of other-
regarding morality, is a necessary complement to it.

WORKS CITED

Eakin, Paul John. "Breaking Rules: The Consequences of Self-Narration." *Biog-
raphy: an interdisciplinary quarterly* 24, no. 1 (winter 2001): 113–27.
Finnis, John. *Natural Law and Natural Rights*. Oxford: Clarendon Press, 1980.
Foucault, Michel. *Ethics, Subjectivity, and Truth*. Ed. Paul Rabinow. New York:
New Press, 1997.
Gosse, Edmund. *Father and Son: A Study of Two Temperaments*. Har-
mondsworth: Penguin. 1983.
Malone, Cynthia Northcutt. "The Struggle of *Father and Son*: Edmund Gosse's
Polemical Autobiography." *a/b: Auto/Biography Studies* 8, no. 1 (1993):
16–32.
Nagel, Thomas. *The View from Nowhere*. New York: Oxford University Press,
1986.
Parker, David. "Authenticity and Recognition in Intergenerational Auto/biog-
raphy: Carolyn Steedman's *Landscape for a Good Woman*." Paper presented
at the IABA Conference, Melbourne, July 2002.
———. "Locating the Self in Moral Space: Globalisation and Autobiography." In
Selves Crossing Cultures: Autobiography and Globalisation. Ed. Rosamund
Dalziell. Melbourne: Australian Scholarly Publishing, 2002. 3–21.
Peterson, Linda H. *Victorian Autobiography: The Tradition of Self-
interpretation*. New Haven: Yale University Press, 1986.
Steedman, Carolyn. *Landscape for a Good Woman*. London: Virago, 1986.
Taylor, Charles. *The Ethics of Authenticity*. Cambridge: Harvard University
Press, 1991.

——. *Sources of the Self: The Making of the Modern Identity.* Cambridge: Cambridge University Press, 1989.

Thwaite, Ann. *Edmund Gosse: A Literary Landscape, 1849–1928.* London: Secker and Warburg, 1984.

Williams, Bernard. *Ethics and the Limits of Philosophy.* Cambridge: Harvard University Press, 1985.

beyond his control, for instance, during childhood or times of great duress. A writer may recognize the limits of moral judgment for other reasons as well, including a desire to forgive and awareness of the danger of judgmentalism. Intergenerational autobiography is a matter of both judging and "not-judging." Moral judgment is not negated but made more complex by causal interpretations of behavior, by forgiveness, and by scruples about the appearance or reality of self-righteousness.

An unexplored issue is how moral assessment of parents is influenced by the experience of having children of one's own. On the one hand, raising children can make one aware of ways in which one's parents have made mistakes or could have done better. On the other hand, one's own failures may help one realize how difficult it is to be a good parent, and therefore may make one more understanding or forgiving of a father or mother. One knows that parents have a lot going on in their lives besides being parents, and that sometimes children suffer because they are not one's only responsibility. Many autobiographies focus on the writer's relationship to a father or mother. And, increasingly, life writers explore parenting, especially of children with health problems or in relation to controversial social issues such as homosexuality, mixed racial background, or a child's religious conversion. Very few works, however, explore how the writer's relationships to her parents and to her children influence each other, especially as these relationships are the focus of moral scrutiny. This is surprising, since assessment of one's parents and moral self-criticism must influence each other in important ways. The desire to protect one's children's privacy probably plays a large role in explaining the relative scarcity of reflection on the issues in which I am interested. Yet there are a few memoirs that explore these two ethical issues, which are often interrelated: the effect of the writer's own parenting experience on moral assessment of his parents, and the tension between judging and not judging. I discuss three autobiographical works in these terms: Paul Auster's *Invention of Solitude* (1982), John Wideman's *Fatheralong* (1994), and Kim Chernin's *In My Mother's House* (1983). Elsewhere I have written about the conscience of the autobiographer primarily in terms of the self-referential aspect of judgment; here I concentrate on the writer's scruples about judging others.

■

Paul Auster, in *The Invention of Solitude*, explores relationships between his father's enigmatic character, the meanings of solitude, and Auster's own career as a writer. In the first section, "Portrait of an

Invisible Man," Auster tries to understand his father, whom Auster presents as a man with no apparent inner life and little ability to be intimate with others. The father's coldness and remoteness created a lot of uneasiness and pain in his son. Like many recent autobiographers, Auster reveals the anger and grief of a child who never received his parent's love. Auster initially makes a very negative assessment of his father's character. Samuel Auster lacked self-knowledge and authenticity: "My father's capacity for evasion was almost limitless. Because the domain of the other was unreal to him, his incursions into that domain were made with a part of himself he considered to be equally unreal, another self he had trained as an actor to represent him in the empty comedy of the world-at-large" (15).

Auster describes his father's remoteness from others in terms of negative images of solitude: "He himself remained invisible, a puppeteer working the strings of his alter-ego from a dark, solitary place behind the curtain" (16). For Auster, solitude means more than physical separation from others, for he uses this term to describe emotional disconnection and inaccessibility in the presence of others. His father was always out of step with those around him; even the "clothes he wore seemed to be an expression of solitude, a concrete way of affirming his absence" (55). Hinting at the way in which he will formulate a more positive view of solitude, Auster presents his father's aloneness as an attempt to hide from both himself and others: "Solitary. But not in the sense of being alone. Not solitary in the way Thoreau was, for example, exiling himself in order to find out where he was; not solitary in the way Jonah was, praying for deliverance in the belly of the whale. Solitary in the sense of retreat. In the sense of not having to see himself, of not having to see himself being seen by anyone else" (16–17). His father's remoteness caused Auster a good deal of self-doubt, sadness, and anger. "You do not stop hungering for your father's love," he writes, "even after you are grown up" (19). His earliest memories are of his father's absence, the father's distracted unawareness of the son's needs. Auster's portrait of his father shows the destructive effects of aloneness both on the quality of life of a person who seeks solitude as an escape from others and on his family.

Auster's writing of the first section of The Invention of Solitude was prompted by his father's death. As he sorts through his father's belongings, he reconstructs Samuel Auster's mysterious past. He learns that at the age of nine, his father had witnessed his mother shoot and kill his father, Paul Auster's grandfather. This traumatic event and the sensational trial that followed explain a lot about Samuel: "A boy cannot live through this kind of thing without being affected by it as a man" (36). Auster believes that his father "learned never to trust anyone. Not even himself" (50). The scandalous murder and trial explain why Samuel worked hard all his life to make himself untouchable, inaccessible, invulnerable. Auster understands how family trauma influenced his father's incapacity for intimacy, but this insight does not lessen his continuing sense of having been damaged by his father's remoteness. His unhappy relationship to his father motivates the tasks he undertakes in the second part of the book: to establish a different relationship to his father, and to define a different meaning of solitude, by means of his writing. He interprets solitude in a more positive way by showing its potential role in fostering creativity and its very different place in Auster's relationship to his own young son.

In the second part of the memoir, "The Book of Memory," Auster writes about himself in the third person, referring to himself as A. His confessional tone and autobiographical meaning are explicit: "A. realizes, as he sits in his room writing The Book of Memory, he speaks of himself as another in order to tell the story of himself. He must make himself absent in order to find himself there. And so he says A., even as he means to say I" (154). The anecdotes in this section of the book explore several related themes, returning again and again to the role of solitude in creative work. Auster quotes Pascal: "All the unhappiness of man stems from one thing only: that he is incapable of staying quietly in his room" (76). Staying in one's room and using this time productively are surprisingly difficult, yet indispensable for creative work such as writing. Auster explores the meanings of aloneness in religious and literary exemplars such as Jonah, Robinson Crusoe, Emily Dickinson, and the paintings of Vermeer and van Gogh. He is especially fascinated by the tale of Pinocchio, largely because of the image of Gepetto, Pinocchio's father, in the belly of the whale. Because Pinocchio saves his father from being trapped in the whale, the story symbolizes Auster's desire to "save" his own father from solitude. *Pinocchio* is about a wooden toy who "becomes a real boy"; this idea expresses Auster's feelings of deadness and unreality in relation to his father, and his sense that, like Pinocchio, he will not "become a real boy . . . until he is reunited with his father" (132). The image of Pinocchio saving Gepetto has great power: "For this same incompetent little marionette, who is not even a real boy, to become a figure of redemption, the very being who saves his father from the grip of death, is a sublime moment of revelation" (134). How does the son save the father? In *Pinocchio*, by rescuing him from the whale. But Auster's father is dead; a reunion can come about only in a symbolic form. Auster's memoir represents a symbolic rescue and reunion with the author's father. In it he explores a bond he shares with his father: their common experience of solitude. Auster knows the pain of solitude, and this gives him, if not forgiveness, at least empathy for his father's isolation. Moreover, he "saves" not only his father but himself as well by giving solitude a new and positive meaning. He "becomes real" as he discerns in solitude not soul-destroying isolation, but an experience that can foster experiences of imagination, creativity, and even intimacy with his own son. Auster saves his father and himself by inventing a new meaning for solitude.

The Invention of Solitude redefines solitude in two ways, both of which involve the paradoxical idea that solitude can be shared with others. First, Auster interprets solitude as necessary for a writer's creativity. "Every book is an image of solitude" (136), the outcome of a great deal of time spent alone in a room. Literature is at once the product of an author's solitude and the means by which a reader reaches through his own and the author's solitude. In reading, the isolated individual becomes absorbed in something beyond his own preoccupations and communes with another mind. Auster's way of describing the writing and reading of literature strives to reconcile solitude and relationship to others. He tries to reconceive solitude not as solipsistic isolation but as the necessary condition for a more meaningful form of connection with others than is possible in normal social interaction. Writing is a redemptive act and a way out of solitude for Auster not only because it is ultimately aimed at communication with others, but also because the writer's exploration of language is a mode of discovery of the world. Writing is "a search for the world as it appears in language" (161). And the particular form of writing in which Auster engages, memoir, gives another redemptive meaning to solitude: "It is only in the darkness of solitude that the work of memory begins" (164). When one turns away from the present, and from immediate contact with others, one can recover one's past and save it from oblivion and meaninglessness. In the recollection of the past, especially childhood, the memoir writer finds a world that would otherwise be lost. In his conception of memory, Auster interprets solitude as a way out of isolation and a mode of access to the world, including other people. He realizes that "even alone, in the deepest solitude of his room, he was not alone, or, more precisely, that the moment he began to try to speak of that solitude, he had become more than just himself. Memory, therefore, not simply as the resurrection of one's private past, but an immersion in the past of others, which is to say: history" (139). By interpreting writing as a process of communication, and as a way of exploring the world, language, and memory, Auster gives solitude a very different meaning than it had in his father's life.

If solitude was a shell that enclosed Auster's father and undermined his relationship to his son, can Paul Auster pass on a different understanding of solitude to Daniel, his own young son? Is the positive, productive meaning of solitude that he invents in this book capable of being transmitted to the next generation? Auster's memoir does not clearly answer this question, but it shows him attempting to redefine solitude in a second way, as the basis for a bond between father and son. Already at three years old, Daniel takes great pleasure in imaginative experience and enjoys time alone. "I have to be alone to think," says the boy. In several scenes Auster portrays himself reading to Daniel. They gravitate toward the story of Pinocchio, both of them relishing the story of the separation and reunion of Gepetto and the boy who becomes real by saving his father. Children need stories, imaginative play, and the leap into fantasy. Following a fictional story is at once a movement into a private inner world and a shared experience that bonds father and son. A father lies down in the darkness and makes up a tale that takes his child into an imaginary world and into the aloneness of sleep. But the boy takes the father's voice with him: "And even as the boy closes his eyes and goes to sleep, his father's voice goes on speaking in the dark" (154). Auster's description of bedtime storytelling represents another attempt to reconcile togetherness and aloneness, intimacy and solitude. He depicts himself nourishing Daniel's capacity for solitude by sharing bedtime stories, transporting him into an imaginary world and into sleep with the assurance of his father's love. Behind Auster's depiction of this scene we sense his own childhood suffering, his anger at his father's failures to reach out to him, and his determination to do better as a father. Among the gifts of love that he wants to pass on to Daniel are intimacy and a capacity for solitude. These are not antithetical but deeply connected.

Yet it is not at all clear how Daniel will react to Paul Auster's orientation to aloneness and his rhythm of intimacy and detachment. Perhaps Daniel will need more or less solitude than his father, or will understand solitude in a completely different way, inventing his own version of aloneness. Perhaps he will experience his father's periods of solitary work as abandonment. The ending of the book raises the question of whether Auster will do a better job than his father did at nurturing his son's capacity for solitude and the "invention" or creativity and imagination that he hopes it can foster, while also being intimate, connected, and affirming. Auster's assessment of his father has become tied to the ambiguity of solitude, and to his awareness that how a child will react to his parent is always uncertain, and a matter of temperament and values.

Auster's memoir clearly shows and judges his father's failures as a parent and his superficial relationships with others. Yet the negative assessment of his father is tempered by three sets of considerations. First, Auster's detective work explores the causal influences that made his father so withdrawn. Understanding the effect of the traumatic murder and trial helps him to feel some empathy for his father, and to see how his father's attitude to other people was a self-protective, defensive way of coping with loss. Second, Auster realizes that the capacity for detachment and solitude can have positive as well as negative consequences. His career as a writer depends on his ability to use solitude productively, and so he cannot simply condemn isolation, detachment, or solitude as destructive states. Nor can he simply condemn his father, whose temperament and influence undoubtedly play a role in Auster's own capacity for solitude. Solitude is not intrinsically good or bad, and particular instances of solitude can be morally evaluated, as Auster does throughout the memoir. Third, because of Auster's own experience as a father, he wants to pass on to his son the capacity for solitude and the positive things that can grow out of it, such as imagination, memory, and creativity. He does not know whether he will succeed in this, for his son may choose for himself a very different rhythm of detachment from and engagement with others. Auster's reflections on his father's life, on the links between solitude and "invention," and on his role as a parent finally make for a far more nuanced and complex judgment on his father than the book's initial condemnation.

■

John Wideman's *Fatheralong* is subtitled *A Meditation on Fathers and Sons, Race and Society*. In this memoir Wideman describes his relationship to his father, narrating childhood experiences, their trip to South Carolina to search for family origins, and Wideman's frustrated efforts to transport his father to his son's wedding. The book articulates wide-ranging reflections on racism in America, the need for stories for the sake of survival and identity, and the author's grief for his son Jake, who is in prison for murder. Wideman's father, Edgar, has an aloof stance and a detached relationship to his family. While Wideman's mother assured him of her love, and affirmed that "you are not alone unless you let go of love" (52), his father's example taught Wideman that the world is not a friendly place, and all one can rely on is one's own inner strength: "The first rule of my father's world is that you stand alone" (50). Relentless self-discipline is necessary to survive: "your hardheaded power to deny, to withdraw, to remain detached" (51). His father seems to represent for Wideman the constant possibility of detachment, separation, and flight from pain and trouble. Edgar abandoned the family during John's teenage years, although he continued to support them financially and maintained contact with his children. At one point he tells Wideman that he left the family because he wanted "to do the things I wanted to do. Not worry about everybody and everything the way your mother does. Worry worry worry" (135). Pain and anger are evident in Wideman's comment that "*worry* included me, my mother, sister, and brothers. We were the flesh and blood stuffed into the words" (136). At the time of writing *Fatheralong*, Wideman was firmly committed to marriage and his three children.[1] His view of his father implies negative moral judgments about his father's emotional remoteness and his desertion of the family.

The main thrust of this memoir, however, is not condemnation of his father's character. Rather, the author's relation to his father is the springboard for three other forms of ethical reflection, all of which tend to soften Wideman's criticisms of his father. Most important is the indictment of American racism that runs through this book. According to Wideman, the history of racial oppression radically distorts the African American father-son relationship: "Arrayed against the possibility of conversation between fathers and sons is the country they inhabit, everywhere proclaiming the inadequacy of black fathers, their lack of manhood in almost every sense the term's understood here in America" (65). The distance between fathers and sons is attributed not primarily to individuals but to the culture and history that burden them with a sense of inadequacy: "This country, as it presently functions, stands between black fathers and sons, impeding communication, frustrating development, killing or destroying the bodies and minds of young men, short-circuiting the natural process of growth, maturity, the cycle of the generations" (66). Wideman's memoir addresses a long-standing American debate about racism and the relative importance of individual character and social environment in shaping an alternative future. At times Wideman presents racism as an inexorable, pervasive, and annihilating force in the lives of black people: "The bedrock issue raised by the paradigm of race ... is whether you can be someone other than a white person in this society and stay healthy, stay alive" (108). The effect of this kind of reflection is to remove most of the moral blame that could be assigned to his father, who seems essentially determined to act out the defensive strategies that black persons have developed in order to survive in America, such as wearing "a mask of not caring" and "the armor of

---

1. As indicated in *Hoop Roots*, Wideman's "thirty-odd years" marriage has since then "failed" (129).

his indifference" (133). Rather than blame his father for rarely visiting John's brother Robbie in prison, Wideman explains how African American males learn to protect themselves from shame. He does not address the question of whether America's destructive racial climate entirely exculpates his father, but the effect of this perspective is to remove some of his father's responsibility for the emotional distance within the family. This memoir leaves me thinking about whether the author's views undermine moral agency or help us to see that the ethical issues at stake involve more than simply matters of individual character. Wideman's work challenges the simple dichotomy of much of the debate about individual character and social determination; he tries to understand the sources of good and evil in both of these areas.

A second form of ethical reflection in *Fatheralong* is the discernment of positive dimensions in what initially seemed negative characteristics, similar to Auster's analysis of solitude. Wideman's father's love was not always readily apparent, and he was a stern disciplinarian: "He was part enforcer, part the physical embodiment of bad news: the world and people in it don't always love you" (85). But from such a father one can learn some valuable things, such as patience, toughness, and hope for the future. The stern and aloof father's love was never certain: "If he loved me, it definitely wasn't mother love, the love of my aunts and grandmothers" (85). Yet it gave Wideman something he needed: "It vexed me, kept me guessing, on my toes" (85). Wideman puts the best construction on his father's remoteness by asserting that it encouraged the development of certain desirable characteristics. Like Auster and Chernin, he tries to discern virtues in a parent who has some basic weaknesses.

Wideman's title alludes to "Farther Along," a traditional gospel song counseling forbearance and avowing faith in a coming peace and understanding of God's ways: "Farther along we'll understand you, farther along." He connects the religious meaning of this hymn with certain qualities of his father's character, of a man whom he asserts practiced a kind of love different from his mother's:

> Substituting father for farther, perhaps I blundered into the song's meaning in spite of myself. After all, isn't it about resignation, learning to wait and trust and endure? To love the imminent revelation, that great getting-up morning surely, surely coming, even though just as surely you won't know it till it hits you. By and by is when it arrives, by and by, the unbound Great Time of our African ancestors.
>
> Is suffering, bearing up under burdens, the only way to learn (earn) the Father's name, his dispensation? No path except a long arc of patience and suffering the Father resolves in his own good, by-and-by

time. On time. A snap and promise and sweetness in the music. My father's voice calling, "Get on board." Foretaste of peace and understanding. (86)

The religious language Wideman uses, referring both to imminent Christian revelation and the "Great Time" of African spiritual tradition, suggests that his father taught him an orientation to life that was of ultimate importance. Like the spiritual traditions that have sustained African Americans, Wideman insists on the inevitable suffering of human existence, counsels endurance, and yearns for release from pain and oppression. He has, however, less faith and trust in the certainty of eventual redemption and in a Christian understanding of God. Singing a gospel song at a time of despair, he says he "didn't believe in my mother and father's God so my song wasn't sent there" (143). In spite of conscious disbelief, however, Wideman feels that there is "a kind of prayer in the gospel song" and that he is searching for "some presence alive or dead with the power to release my imprisoned son, bear us across the waters home" (143). To anticipate a coming serenity and communion makes a difference to how life is lived, and may encourage several important virtues and the capacity for self-transcendence. Wideman learned this not from the church but from his father. In this way he compares his relationship to his father to religious faith and discerns a positive value in the qualities that made Edgar a difficult person with whom to be intimate. The reader may question, in all three of these memoirs, how much the author actually discerns virtues in a difficult parent, and how much the need to think well of a parent influences perception and judgment.

If Wideman asserts the value of patience and hope, he also expresses the anger of African Americans who for centuries have been told to postpone their demand for justice. At several points Wideman reveals the depth of his bitterness and anger at the treatment of black persons in the United States. Like his father, Wideman sometimes seems barely able to control his rage. As he researches family history in South Carolina, he is helped by an elderly white local historian. While he feels no personal animosity to his new friend, he experiences a wave of destructive anger and imagines cracking the skull of this gentle man who had enjoyed opportunities denied Wideman's father: "It was Professor Lomax's skull I had envisioned shattering, spilling all its learning, its intimate knowledge of these deeds that transferred in the same 'livestock' column as cows, horses, and mules, the bodies of my ancestors from one white owner to another. Hadn't the historian's career been one more mode of appropriation and exploitation of my father's bones, the pearls that were his eyes" (114). Wideman shows his struggle to restrain impulsive rage and suggests that some of his father's icy coldness reflected his own efforts to control similar emotions. This depiction of his anger shows a third way in which Wideman qualifies the judgment of his father: he shows himself struggling with the same unruly passions that his father lived with.

Wideman reveals in passing that Edgar "fathered at least one other set" of children and "a son about my age, upon women he never married" (35). Wideman, when he visits a strip bar, reveals the same sexual restlessness that probably led his father to leave his family. Escaping the constraints of domestic life, he is both fascinated and repulsed by the sexual display for sale. He can't justify this "thinly disguised self-destruction" (160), and often leaves in disgust. Yet two or three times a year he paid to have his "undomesticable erotic fantasies pumped up to virtual reality by live female bodies a few feet from where I sat" (161). Moral judgment of his father is complicated by Wideman's frank portrayal of his own erotic impulses, as well as his ambivalence about his ways of expressing and restraining these impulses. It seems to him significant that Edgar did not explain why he left the family until John was also a parent. Wideman speculates that his father may have "waited till I was a father so when I listened, his words weren't only about him but about the core of ego, ambivalence, potential for betrayal, hunger for the unknown few of us ever quell completely, no matter how character or fate lead us to behave" (137). He realizes that he cannot "blame, forgive, empathize, exonerate without implicating myself" (137). A similar self-recognition tempers his criticisms of his father's "hardness," for he admits that he, too, refuses to reach out, buries his feelings, keeps his distance, and can be charmingly evasive. Wideman discerns that in all this he is his father's son, and that "the part of him I dreaded [is] also the deepest bond" (134). Aggressive impulses, erotic desires, and an undemonstrative demeanor characterize both Wideman and his father; his assessment of these characteristics becomes less judgmental and more complex when he acknowledges their role in his own life.

Wideman's father is a man with powerful passions who can nevertheless control himself, usually by removing himself from other people. He seems always on the verge of separation or detachment. This can lead to evasion of responsibility, but it is also part of the repertoire of strategies that Wideman himself draws on to deal with pain. Wideman is deeply upset when his father misses the wedding of his son Dan. He copes with his sadness by imagining his father at a graveside, leaving behind his grief: "My father stuck somewhere losing this moment was lost to me. I mourned him. A sudden grief so strong it would have shut out the wonder of my son's wedding if I hadn't been able to call upon my father, retrieve the part of him inside myself that could bow, scatter a handful of dust, turn and walk away from the yawning grave" (174). By the end of *Fatheralong*, Wideman seems primarily interested in understanding and justifying the qualities that help father and son to cope with adversity and pain. Yet he shows that these qualities and defense mechanisms have a cost that needs to be reckoned.

In the final chapter, "Father Stories," Wideman turns to his own experience as a father. This brief chapter is addressed to his son Jake, who was imprisoned for murder in 1986 at the age of sixteen. Wideman expresses anguish at his son's bitter fate, but also says that he has had to conceal much of his grief from both himself and other people (193). Anger—like that which simmered in his father, like that which erupted when Jake murdered another boy—struggles with Wideman's need for self-control and his longing for acceptance, patience, and the hope that "farther along," in "the fullness of time," he will escape his grief and be reunited with his son. He shows how several virtues and emotions that seem to be in conflict all seem essential to a full response to tragedy. In particular, the tension between anger and the longing for acceptance and reconciliation runs throughout this memoir. *Fatheralong* explores how certain qualities of character, including patience, withdrawal, and anger, may function as either virtues or vices in the lives of African Americans, depending on a variety of circumstances. He shows how an individual's capacity for these attributes reflects individual temperament and choice, is affected by the history of black persons in the United States, and is also influenced by the lessons parents transmit to their children both deliberately and by example. "Father stories" name the characteristics that we inherit and may use for good or evil. "Father stories are about establishing origins and through them legitimizing claims of ownership, of occupancy and identity" (63). Understanding the sources of our character in our ancestors may help us to make better decisions about how we express inherited tendencies and capacities.

Fatheralong shows how ethical reflection on "fathers and sons, race and society," should encompass both moral judgments about individual character and understanding of the historical and cultural forces that condition it. Although there is a good deal of character assessment in this memoir, of both the author and his father, the book's final sentences convey the predominant tendency to criticize American racism for distorting the lives of black persons:

> A country and its practice of human bondage, its tradition of obscuring, stealing, or distorting black people's lives, begins to crowd out

the possibility of seeing my ancestors as human beings. The powers and principalities that originally restricted our access to the life free people naturally enjoy still rise like a shadow, a wall between my grandfathers and myself, my father and me, between the two of us, father and son, son and father.

So we must speak these stories to one another. (197)

Given the oppressive history of racism in the United States, the primary task for Wideman is not moral judgment of his father but simply understanding him as a human being. His memoir encompasses judgment of his father's actions and character within a larger perspective that qualifies and transforms those judgments, putting them in the context of the enormous pressures placed on black men in America.

■

Kim Chernin's *In My Mother's House* traces mother-daughter relationships across four generations, focusing on the author and her mother, Rose. Rose Chernin was born in a Jewish shtetl in Russia in 1903 and immigrated to the United States in 1914. Her life was dedicated to the Communist Party, and she put a lot of pressure on her daughter to share this commitment. Rose believed that the measure of any worthwhile life was one's fight for social justice: "The struggle of people against their conditions, that is where you find the meaning in life" (95). She was involved in many labor struggles of the 1930s, lived in the Soviet Union for several years, and was imprisoned for "un-American activities" during the 1950s. Rose was a determined and courageous woman, a leader of the Communist Party in California, and a person inspired with the Marxist vision of a just society. She shares her convictions with her daughter in no uncertain terms: "There's only one important fact about a life. . . . A woman who lives for a cause, a woman with dedication and unbreakable devotion—that's a woman who deserves the name of woman" (11). Rose is a person with firm moral commitments and no reluctance to make absolute moral judgments, and who often seems dogmatic and domineering.

In My Mother's House describes Kim Chernin's struggle to define her own life's meaning in dialogue with her mother's moral ideals. Although as an adolescent Kim was herself passionately committed to communism, a 1957 visit to the Soviet Union disillusioned her, with its secret microphones, its anti-Semitism and repression of religion, its ban on jazz and abstract painting, and other problems. She had already begun to be keenly interested in the arts, and to feel the need for a sacred dimension to life, and she regretted her parents' lack of interest in their Jewish heritage and faith. All of this set her at odds with her mother. *In My Mother's House* sorts out the values and qualities of her mother's character that Kim admires and the ways in which her life has led her to affirm different values. Chernin assimilates her mother's Jewishness and her rebellious spirit while rejecting communism: "She wanted me to acquire her dogma, she handed down to me her rebellious daring. And no doubt because Judaism can tolerate such a stance far better than Communism, I have remained Jewish where I have ceased to read Marx" (xx). Chernin judges her mother's "faith" in communism as inadequate for herself, even as she appreciates the heroic quality of Rose's life and believes that her own commitments to feminism, to writing, and to spirituality are analogous forms of taboo breaking.

In spite of Rose's tendency to make absolute moral judgments, there are several points in her story at which she realizes the danger of judging, and which seem to provide cautionary warnings to Chernin as she assesses her mother's character. In one of the stories Rose tells, titled "Wasn't I Once Also a Daughter?," she describes how a niece, Vida, stole her mother's savings. Although Kim and her daughter Larissa are willing to pass judgment on Vida, Rose warns against this: "Who am I to judge or forgive? I'm not God. I'm not a God of vengeance. And wasn't I once . . . also a daughter?" (115). For Rose, being a daughter means that one inevitably hurts one's parents in trying to become independent. When Rose left her quarreling parents, her mother, Perle, broke down, and her father committed Perle to an insane asylum. Rose asks: "Do you blame me? A young person doesn't think so much about these things. I never said to myself, Maybe I put myself before Mama so that Celia [her sister] and I could have our own life" (48). Rose believed that to become herself, she had to leave her parents and four younger siblings: "I put aside everything to go after my own life" (54). For once she seems to recognize that life can confront individuals with choices that are too complex to judge as simply right or wrong, for a person may have to choose between alternatives each of which would involve benefits and pain. Rose is therefore reluctant to judge Vida's theft. This conversation helps Kim realize that her negative view of Vida reflects not simply a moral judgment but her own psychological need to distance herself from her; she wishes that she could make a judgment that would "separate me out forever from the life choices of my cousin" (115).

Rose also acknowledges that her own earlier harsh judgments of her mother were too simple. Although she had always seen Perle as passive and weak, Rose now questions whether she "judged her by the wrong standards" (175) and says that in certain ways Perle was indeed a brave person. And when Rose recounts her crushing depression after the death of her eldest daughter, Nina, Kim begins to understand how her mother had reached a condition of despair culminating in attempted suicide. Rose's reservations about judging her own mother remind Kim to be cautious about her evaluations. *In My Mother's House* shows how the choice of one's own values involves ongoing assessment of parents' ideals, beliefs, and character, and how difficult it is to be fair in this evaluative process.

Chernin's memoir is instructively different from the books by Auster and Wideman, not only because of the different gender dynamics, but also because the writer is judging a parent who was a very strong moral influence rather than one who abandoned or failed the family. Rose did neglect Kim in childhood, because of both her all-absorbing political commitments and her incapacitating grief when Nina died. All three memoirs thus deal with parents who were absent in some way, but in Rose's case it was primarily because of her over-riding commitment to a moral cause. Kim has to justify—both to her mother and to herself—her choice of a different life project focused on feminism and writing. Although these commitments can also express deep moral convictions, during her adolescence her mother condemned Kim's interests as selfish, unrealistic, and, given urgent social problems, immoral. "Too busy for a meeting?" her mother asks. "The world in a state like this and she's too busy with her poetry?" (282). Chernin must judge her mother's commitments not as wrong or bad, but simply as not her own.

In My Mother's House raises other ethical issues because of the way in which Chernin narrates her mother's story by telling Rose's story in the first person. Paul John Eakin and Thomas Couser have examined the way that collaborative life writing raises the ethical question of how well the collaborator, editor, or "writer" represents the life of the subject. *In My Mother's House* was undertaken at the request of Rose Chernin, after initial reluctance on Kim Chernin's part. We do not know whether Rose was able to reject or modify passages, but Kim portrays her mother as generally pleased with and proud of the project as a whole. At the same time, Chernin shows how painful certain aspects of the story were for her mother, especially descriptions of Nina's death and Kim's feelings of abandonment and anger at her mother. The inclusion of passages depicting tensions between mother and daughter, their contrasting perspectives on many issues, and Rose's remarks that are critical of Kim make me relatively confident that Chernin has been successful and scrupulous in trying to render her mother's point of view accurately. This is not to say that the collaborative process is simple, but only that Chernin is aware of its ambiguities. In the 1994 foreword to the second edition of the memoir, Chernin explains that she did not simply transcribe tape recordings of her mother's stories but had to do extensive rewriting "to get my mother to sound like my mother on a page" (x). She refers to the process of fixing an oral story into a written text as a "betrayal" (xii). At a bookstore reading, Chernin finds that Rose's storytelling voice reflects the book's influence and her daughter's new power: "After that, my mother never, to my knowledge, told her stories again in her own voice. From that moment in the bookstore she had taken over, or been taken over by, the voice I had created for her" (xii–xiii). Paul John Eakin sees this passage as suggesting "a more distinctly imperialistic interpretation in which the domineering personality of the mother has been colonized by the resisting daughter" (180). He asks if Kim has appropriated her mother's voice in an ethically question-able way, violating its integrity. For me, Chernin's depiction of the ambiguities of the collaborative process is not troubling but reassur-ing, for I tend to trust an author who shows insight into the ethical issues at stake in life writing and indicates her scruples about the writing process.

Chernin finds herself recreating some of the same mother-daughter patterns in her relationship to her own child, Larissa, as she tries to influence her character: "I tried to cultivate in Larissa the qualities my mother disapproved of in me" (291). She describes herself as well as her mother in asserting that "secretly, we wish anyone we love will think exactly the way we do" (300). Kim's relationship to her daugh-ter is less conflicted than hers was to her mother because Kim largely approves of the artistic path Larissa has chosen. But she notes the similar dynamics as a mother pressures her child to share her values and a daughter asserts her independence. Can one blame one's parents for wanting to pass on what they most value? Can one forgive a parent who can't accept a child's right to choose her own values? Chernin's memoir raises these ethical questions as she evaluates her mother's character and values. Like Auster and Wideman, she offers not simply moral judgment but a self-critical assessment of the process of forming moral judgments.

The ending of *In My Mother's House* portrays a reconciliation and mutual affirmation between Rose and Kim. In the epilogue, set in 1981, Kim says of her mother to Larissa that "you can admire the life no matter what you feel about Soviet Communism," and asks: "Should you judge a life by the ideology that inspires it? Or by what that ideology, true or false, inspires the life to do?" (300–301). Clearly the latter is most important for Chernin, and her praise for her mother's character and relentless struggle for justice survives her rejection of communism. In a final tender moment, she asserts that "the distance between us, and all separation, heals over. We are touched by a single motion of forgiveness" (307). Kim's mother tells her she loves Kim more than life. Has Chernin passed beyond judgment to a love that overlooks faults? The ending of *In My Mother's House*, like *Fatheralong* and *The Invention of Solitude,* raises the question of whether the desire to forgive a parent can negate or distort accurate moral judgment. All these works show a writer struggling with a difficult parent, and finally affirming that there was much in the parent that was good. The difficult aspects of the parent are inextricably linked to the positive qualities, so that finally the author's love for a parent seems to affirm everything about the parent. At the end of each of these memoirs, the wish for reconcilation or forgiveness leads the authors to downplay the parent's faults that they have earlier disclosed. Idealization of a parent may be as great a danger to accurate discernment and assessment as harshly negative rejection. Is judgment distorted by the desire for forgiveness?

In *The Shadow Man*, Mary Gordon suggests the dangers of an idealized view of a parent and of the yearning to forgive when she criticizes an earlier essay she wrote about her father. That essay ended with "a promise of 'love that passes understanding.' In a way, I now see, it was a refusal to go further. A desire to be not the writer exploring my father but his loving child" (xx). *The Shadow Man* shows some of the same tendency Gordon criticizes, I think, as do the memoirs by Chernin, Wideman, and (to a lesser extent) Auster. Perhaps it is part of these works' significance that they demonstrate how difficult it is to separate moral judgment from the psychological needs of attachment, autonomy, and testy ongoing relationships with parents that must influence any life writing about parent-child bonds. I think that the final affirmations in these works, and their movement toward forgiveness, do not negate the work of moral assessment, or somehow move "beyond judgment," but rather display an integration of moral discernment and psychological understanding. And the writers show that whom we love, and why we love them, does not depend on the loved one's moral perfection or virtue.

■

What can we conclude about judging and not judging, based on the three memoirs I have discussed? How can we understand the apparent contradiction between the importance of forming clear moral judgments and the numerous reasons for cautiousness in judging others? I offer brief reflections on these autobiographies in relation to three issues: the limits of moral agency, the nature of forgiveness, and the relevance of religion.

As these writers interpret the various influences on their parents, they explore the murky areas where moral responsibility becomes unclear. A basic principle of moral agency is that a person can be held responsible only for that which is voluntary, for choices and actions that lie within the sphere of the will. Bernard Williams, Martha Nussbaum, and Thomas Nagel have analyzed how various forms of "moral luck" call into question a person's responsibility for his or her actions. For Nagel, there are several forms of luck or contingency that are outside a person's control, including constitutive luck ("the kind of person you are"), circumstantial luck ("the kind of problems and situations one faces"), and "luck in the way one's actions and projects turn out" (28). Although these factors are beyond a person's control, they affect moral evaluation of one's actions. Nagel describes how paying attention to all the factors that are beyond an agent's control poses a puzzle for ethics: "The area of genuine agency, and therefore of legitimate moral judgment, seems to shrink under this scrutiny to an extensionless point" (35). Richard Freadman draws on Nagel's ideas to analyze how Hemingway uses the idea of luck to evade moral responsibility for certain aspects of his life as described in *A Moveable Feast*. Even though the idea of luck can be used in dubious ways as a means of exculpation, this represents an attempt to recognize the genuinely ambiguous limits of moral responsibility.

Auster, Wideman, and Chernin explore the same indefiniteness in the sphere of moral agency. Although they do not introduce the notion of moral luck, each writer explores in depth how various influences shaped a parent's capacity for moral agency. Whether it is the traumatic impact on Auster's father of his own father's murder, or Wideman's portrayal of the effects of racism on African American males, or Chernin's analysis of her mother's Russian and Jewish heritage, these writers show how particular historical influences affected their parents' lives. Sometimes when the writers do not judge, or they explicitly reflect on their uncertainties in assessment, it is because they recognize that events can shape character in ways that individuals are virtually powerless to avoid. They do not simply excuse their parents from moral evaluation, however, or present them as passive victims of fate; rather they consider how their parents might have responded differently to the influences on them, what alternatives they had, and what it would have taken for them to act in other ways. They juxtapose interpretation of a parent as essentially determined by external causes with a moral viewpoint that assumes respon-

sibility. Their judgments are cautious, complex, qualified, and sometimes inconclusive; in short, they look a lot like not judging. These
autobiographers recognize the difficulty of determining a parent's
responsibility, given the role of many contingent factors in shaping
that life.

One way of explaining the tension between causal explanations of
human behavior and ethical assessment is to say that these are two
alternative frameworks for understanding human action, each necessary for different purposes but not mutually exclusive. Or one can
search for a theoretical resolution, such as a philosophical analysis of
free will and determinism. But these approaches are not of much help
when we face a concrete situation calling for moral assessment. Sometimes causal understanding and moral evaluation both seem necessary,
yet we are perplexed about what an agent can be held responsible for.
We need guidance in learning how to make such judgments wisely, and
it is here that I see one reason for the ethical value of autobiography.
A life writer can explore the interplay of luck and responsibility in his
or her own life, as Hemingway does in a way that Freadman challenges.
Or, as in the works I have discussed, the writer may reflect on the
limits of moral agency in another person, integrating moral judgment
of a parent and interpretation oriented toward understanding the determining influences that made that parent who he or she was.

Good judgment means trying to imagine the point of view of the
parent as well as taking an external observer's perspective; it calls for
ethical assessment that takes account of both what was within the
parent's voluntary choice and the ways in which he or she was constrained, pressured, or determined by things outside his or her control.
The life writer does not usually offer a theoretical account of how to
achieve this but rather constitutes a specific example, a case of constrained moral agency and ambiguous responsibility. A writer with
good judgment provides a practical instance of fairness to others,
imaginatively extending to another person the same considerations we
bring to bear in self-assessment. The writer recognizes that moral
agency is circumscribed, and that there is much in any life, including
how one's children will react to one's values, that is beyond one's
control, subject to the factors philosophers speak of as moral luck.
Certain actions may be neither simply voluntary nor involuntary, and
might provide moral excuses that diminish a person's responsibility
without entirely eliminating it, as we see in Wideman's analysis of his
father's ways of coping with racism. Because there are many gray areas
where the degree of responsibility cannot be measured exactly, good
judgment sometimes resembles not judging—that is, making assessments of responsibility with a good deal of caution, tentativeness, and

acknowledgment of ambiguity. I think that an ideal of good or fair judgment is a crucial intellectual tool for discussing the ethical questions at the heart of many autobiographies, because it is the standard in terms of which we criticize the actual practice of writers. I have tried to describe one characteristic of good judgment in a life writer: she considers searchingly and fairly the limits of moral agency in other persons as well as in her own life.

Not judging is often contrasted with harsh judging and linked to forgiveness. In Matthew's version of the Sermon on the Mount, the reason for not judging is the danger of hypocrisy, of judging others by a more rigorous standard than one would want to be judged by:

> Do not judge, so that you may not be judged. For with the judgment you make you will be judged, and the measure you give will be the measure you get. Why do you see the speck in your neighbor's eye, but do not notice the log in your own eye? Or how can you say to your neighbor, "Let me take the speck out of your eye," while the log is in your own eye? You hypocrite, first take the log out of your own eye, and then you will see clearly to take the speck out of your neighbor's eye. (Matthew 7:1–5)

Luke's version of this passage links not judging to forgiveness:

> Do not judge, and you will not be judged; do not condemn, and you will not be condemned. Forgive, and you will be forgiven; give, and it will be given to you. A good measure, pressed down, shaken together, running over, will be put into your lap; for the measure you give will be the measure you get back. (Luke 6:37–39)

While the three memoirs discussed do not refer to these Gospel passages, they reflect similar reservations about judging others. There is a long literary tradition that exposes the moral flaws of those who judge others harshly, including much of Greek tragedy and works such as *Measure for Measure*, *The Scarlet Letter*, Toni Morrison's *Paradise*, and Philip Roth's novel *The Human Stain*. Moral judgment—its purposes, forms of expression, and consequences—is itself subject to moral judgment in this literature.[2] Autobiographical works, too, sometimes analyze the shadow side of the moral will, such as the ways in which judgment can be used as a weapon, express unrecognized

---

2. The "moral realism" of the modern novel, according to Lionel Trilling, is "the perception of the dangers of the moral life itself," and the recognition that "the moral passions are even more willful and imperious and impatient than the self-seeking passions" (221, 222).

psychological motives, or selectively fail to consider all that should be relevant in ethical reflection. The memoirs by Auster, Chernin, and Wideman reveal their awareness of this dimension of morality and their consequent scruples about judging. Especially when they reflect about their own roles as parents, the three writers temper their more critical evaluations of their parents, for they are aware that they, too, will be judged as parents.[3]

I think that the desire to forgive a father or mother is one of the reasons why these authors examine a parent's character and history and struggle with the issue of how to judge the parent. As in the passage from Luke, and in Father Zosima's exhortations in *The Brothers Karamazov* (another work that strives to reconcile judgment of a parent with recognition of problems of judgment), forgiveness is often contrasted with judgment, as if to forgive someone means not to judge him. But forgiveness is not a refusal to judge; the idea that something needs to be forgiven reflects a normative judgment. Mary Midgely notes that when moral judgment is criticized, it is usually a particular form of judgment: an unfavorable judgment about others that is uncharitable and made from a detached position, without sympathy or allowance for circumstances (27). Rightly understood, Midgeley suggests, Jesus' words are a condemnation not of the whole faculty of judgment but only of vindictive blame and punishment:

> If we listen to what are used as anti-judgmental texts, we always find this sort of restriction built into them. Thus, what Jesus was talking about was punishment and denunciation. His message was: do not stone people, do not cast them out, do not write them off. His target was aggressive, punitive self-righteousness. His listeners were told not to regard themselves as a superior group, licensed to punish transgression. They were not told that there was no such thing as transgression ("Sin no more"). His moral spotlight was not on the original transgression at all, but on the evil response of the would-be punisher. (112)

The true nature of forgiveness is clarified by the Christian theologian Marjorie Suchocki, who criticizes two common misconceptions: that to forgive entails feelings of love, and that to forgive is to accept everything about another person. Suchocki sees these misconceptions

---

3. Nancy Miller remarks that a writer's children may constrain the expression of negative feelings about the writer's parents: "This awareness of the children to come as readers reins in the emotional violence of the family biographer. There are things you cannot tell your children about their parents or their grandparents, unless you want to model a hatred you might come in turn to inherit" (163).

of forgiveness as compromising the integrity of persons who have been violated and struggle to break the continuing power of violation. She defines forgiveness as "willing the well-being of victim(s) and violator(s) in the context of the fullest possible knowledge of the nature of the violation" (144). Forgiveness is an act of the will, not an emotion, and it requires memory, empathy, and imagination. It sometimes involves, but is not the same as, emotional warmth, acceptance of the violator, or the wish to share one's time or space with him in the future. Suchocki concentrates on overt forms of violence such as war, rape, and physical abuse, while the suffering described by Auster, Wideman, and Chernin encompasses less traumatic kinds of hurt and estrangement between parents and children. I find her analysis helpful, nonetheless, in clarifying how judgment may be related to, rather than the antithesis of, forgiveness. For instance, if one aspect of violence is its continuing power to affect a person harmfully through repeated remembering, forgiveness must mean not a denial that a moral wrong has been done but a new kind of memory:

> To be caught in the continuous repetition of violence within the psyche distorts memory, for it is a vivid making-present of the past as if it were *not* past, but still present. Transformative memory is that remembrance of the past as *past*, opening one to a new present. It does not eliminate the continuing pain of loss set in motion by the violation, for release cannot undo the past. However, transformative memory can allow the past to *be* the past for the sake of well-being. (150)

Forgiveness is "memory in the mode of self-transcendence" (151), not forgetting but reckoning fully with the past while one searches for a new future. To be released from one's view of the past and become open to a different future requires imagination and willingness to change. Forgiveness also involves the self-transcendence that comes from empathy, through which "one gains the ability to separate self from other and to see the other as fully other, even in relation to the self" (152).

Auster, Chernin, and Wideman strive for a forgiveness based on the fullest possible knowledge of a parent who caused them pain, an empathic imagination of the parent's point of view, and an attempt to break out of repetitive patterns of rehearsing past memories. Willing the well-being of the parent—or, in Auster's case, his father's memory—does not mean denying the parent's flaws, the author's continuing struggle with the influence of the past, or emotional gaps that will probably never be entirely bridged. Nonetheless, the author's desire to forgive a parent is one of the main motives for writing the memoir, and this horizon, distant goal, and hoped-for end result of writing colors judgments of a parent. Each author makes significant progress toward the goal of forgiveness, I think, and each has some distance still to go; forgiveness remains "farther along" even as its lure and appeal affect the writing of memoir. Both the plot and the ethical significance of these memoirs need to be understood in terms of an unsentimental conception of forgiveness that does not undercut the importance of moral judgment.

The three memoirs discussed here all begin with a fairly negative view of a parent and move to a more nuanced assessment, and to tentative, partial forgiveness. Do the dynamics of forgiveness shape and structure all family memoirs?[4] If so, even works of life writing dominated by bitterness or by cathartic expression of long-suppressed pain may be the necessary first stage in what could become a healing process of forgiveness. I am aware of the danger of imposing Christian assumptions on the genre of family memoir by making forgiveness the ethical norm by which we assess these works. And the nature of forgiveness is complex and ambiguous, both psychologically and ethically. For instance, the socially approved goal of forgiveness may authorize a writer's exposure of family secrets and emotional outpouring, which would otherwise look like vindictiveness or whining. With all its ambiguities, however, I think that the ideal of forgiveness plays a crucial role in many family memoirs, such as the three works discussed here. While the topic of forgiveness demands much fuller exploration, my central point here is that, rightly understood, forgiveness depends on accurate moral judgment.

Chernin, Auster, and Wideman do not invoke the Sermon on the Mount or other biblical norms. But it is significant that each of them turns to religious tradition in the course of assessing a parent. As he tries to understand the positive and negative aspects of solitude, Auster discusses the story of Jonah, Pascal's writing, and poets with spiritual concerns such as Hölderlin and Emily Dickinson. He explores how solitude has been understood in the myths of Western religious and

---

4. The tension between judging and not judging seems to me central in the family memoirs by two of the contributors to this volume, Richard Freadman and Nancy Miller, and also in the subject of David Parker's essay in this volume on Edmund Gosse's *Father and Son*. (I have not read Freadman's memoir but only his proposal for the essay in this book.) Gosse's and Freadman's works seem to me to move toward forgiveness of a father. Miller advocates acts of "realization," which she says lie between the poles of resentment and forgiveness and which she compares to the liberatory work of mourning. But in some ways realization resembles what I have called an unsentimental conception of forgiveness. For instance: "Realization entails understanding our parents' own unfinished business with their mothers and fathers: seeing it *as theirs*, finding the language in which to name it, and moving on" (6).

literary tradition, and this perspective affects his assessment of his father's and his own solitude. Wideman puts his relationship with his father in the context of African American religion, the title of his memoir connecting his meditation on his father's qualities with the spiritual orientation of a traditional gospel hymn. For Chernin, her struggles with her mother are inextricable from their ongoing debate about the meaning and significance of Jewish identity. In their efforts to judge fairly, these authors seek a religious perspective. They seek to guard against personal bias or judgmentalism by testing their perceptions and views against the wisdom of biblical tradition, which is for each of them a significant, though not the exclusive, source of ethical norms.

Biblical tradition claims an ultimate grounding for its moral norms yet holds that the final assessment of any action or life lies beyond any one human formulation. Christianity and Judaism seek to balance the need for moral judgment with the equally great importance of mercy, forgiveness, and readiness to love persons on grounds other than their moral goodness. As in the biblical tradition, these three writers seek to reconcile the need for clear moral judgments with several different reasons for caution about judging others. Underlying these writers' self-scrutiny in the process of judgment is their internalization of biblical insights about such threats to good judgment as self-righteousness and a punitive attitude. I do not want to overstate these writers' commitments to Judaism or Christianity; they are all, it appears, rather distantly related to religious communities, and there are many relevant biblical norms they do not consider, such as the commandment to honor one's parents. The religious dimension of these three memoirs is subtle but significant in two ways. First, biblical insights shape their scruples about judging. And second, while religious norms do not decisively determine how to judge the parent, references to Christian or Jewish texts and traditions serve to clarify for the authors some of the basic values that define their conflict with a parent, such as, for Auster, understandings of solitude, for Wideman, the virtues of self-discipline and patience, and for Chernin, the human needs for aesthetic beauty and religious experience as being equal in importance to her mother's insistence on social justice.

I have tried to describe some of the features of good judgment and to explain why this virtue sometimes resembles not judging, and why it should be central in discussions of the ethics of life writing. When autobiographers make complex and fair judgments, we recognize a paradigm of what moral deliberation ought to be in ordinary life, even when we differ from their substantive conclusions about particular issues. When we are troubled by or take issue with the memoir writer, it is usually for ethical reasons that focus on whether their judgments are fair, that is, conscientiously made. For us as readers, to understand and respond to this kind of life writing is to engage in acts of moral judgment that reflect our own values. The best (in this context, most ethically instructive) kind of autobiography can't simply be judged according to whether it fits our previous values. Rather, in it we encounter a perspective that makes us judge ourselves, helps us to reevaluate our moral practice or ideals. If this is so in the present case, then what these three memoirs disclose about judging and not judging should affect the way we think about our parents. What we have learned might also influence the way we read and assess these works of life writing, making us more self-conscious and deliberate about how we judge and do not judge them.

Given our awareness of the self-serving and vindictive tendencies in so many of our moral pronouncements, these autobiographers provide a crucial ethical perspective on the nature of good judgment. Along with biography that deliberately engages in ethical assessment and certain kinds of fiction, autobiography of this kind is the best vehicle in our culture for sustained, probing, and public examination of the process of moral judgment. While an autobiographer is no more infallible as a guide to morality than any other human being, I submit that writers such as Wideman, Auster, and Chernin provide a helpful critique of the moral judgments we make in everyday life and an incentive toward better ethical reflection.

WORKS CITED

Auster, Paul. *The Invention of Solitude.* New York: Penguin, 1982.
Barbour, John. *The Conscience of the Autobiographer: Ethical and Religious Dimensions of Autobiography.* New York: St. Martin's Press, 1992.
Chernin, Kim. *In My Mother's House: A Daughter's Story.* 1983. 2d ed. New York: HarperCollins, 1994.
Couser, G. Thomas. "Making, Taking, and Faking Lives: Ethical Problems in Collaborative Life Writing." In *Mapping the Ethical Turn: A Reader in Ethics, Culture, and Literary Theory.* Ed. Todd F. Davis and Kenneth Womack. Charlottesville: University Press of Virginia, 2001. 209–26.
Eakin, Paul John. *How Our Lives Become Stories: Making Selves.* Ithaca: Cornell University Press, 1999.
Freadman, Richard. *Threads of Life: Autobiography and the Will.* Chicago: University of Chicago Press, 2001.
Gordon, Mary. *The Shadow Man.* New York: Vintage, 1996.
Midgeley, Mary. *Can't We Make Moral Judgments?* New York: St. Martin's Press, 1991.
Miller, Nancy K. *Bequest and Betrayal: Memoirs of a Parent's Death.* 1996. Bloomington: Indiana University Press, 2000.

Nagel, Thomas. "Moral Luck." In *Mortal Questions*. Cambridge: Cambridge University Press, 1979. 24–38.
Nussbaum, Martha. *The Fragility of Virtue: Luck and Ethics in Greek Tragedy and Philosophy*. Cambridge: Cambridge University Press, 1986.
Suchocki, Marjorie. *The Fall to Violence*. New York: Continuum, 1995.
Trilling, Lionel. *The Liberal Imagination*. New York: Penguin, 1948.
Wideman, John Edgar. *Fatheralong: A Meditation on Fathers and Sons, Race and Society*. New York: Random House, 1994.
——. *Hoop Roots: Basketball, Race, and Love*. Boston: Houghton Mifflin, 2001.
Williams, Bernard. *Moral Luck*. Cambridge: Cambridge University Press, 1981.

Part III

REPRESENTING OTHERS: TRUST
AND BETRAYAL

Friendship, Fiction, and Memoir: Trust and Betrayal in Writing from One's Own Life

Claudia Mills

I once attended a writing conference for aspiring authors of books for children, at which one speaker enraged the audience by making the pronouncement that, in his view, parents were disqualified to be authors of children's fiction. His reason: parents have to protect themselves from the reality of their children's pain and so wouldn't be able to write about childhood traumas with sufficient awareness and honesty. To this the audience, largely composed of mothers, shot back that parents are especially qualified to write for children, for precisely the opposite reason: they live with children in a relationship of great intimacy and so know children in a way that non-parents do not.

But assuming, as I am inclined to do (as myself a writer of books for children who is also a parent), that the parents are correct here, or at least correct in asserting that they have a distinctive avenue of access to children on which they can draw to enrich the writing of their books, what ethical problems, if any, arise? If children do indeed provide their author parents with "material," is this material that the parents are entitled to use? If the children grow up themselves to be authors someday, will they be able to draw on their own childhoods— and their relationships with parents and siblings—to craft their novels or memoirs? (Flannery O'Connor is quoted as having said that no author need ever be at a loss for subject matter to write about: "All you need is a childhood.") Can friends write about friends, while still remaining friends and being true to the expectations and obligations of friendship?

In this essay I highlight—and then partially seek to dissolve, or resolve—the particular tensions that arise between the obligations of friendship (or family relationships) and the necessity for an author (of either fiction or memoirs) to draw on her own life—that is to say, her own relationships with friends and family—in her work. I have wrestled with these dilemmas in my own career as the author of children's fiction, where all my books are based either on memories of my own childhood (and so on my relationship with my parents, sister, and childhood friends) or on the ongoing experiences of my two school-age sons. I'm always having to agonize over how much of these memories and experiences to reveal in my fiction, and how to do this in a way that honors my obligations to my loved ones.

Let me begin by posing the two sources of tension most sharply.

Commitments of Friends

To be a friend is to stand in a certain kind of relationship to another person, one that is essentially noninstrumental, in which, as Aristotle tells us, we seek the good of the other for his own sake and not for our own. In books 8 and 9 of the *Nicomachean Ethics*, Aristotle contrasts the true friendship with the mere utility friendship, in which I pursue a relationship with you for what I can gain from that relationship for me. As Michael Stocker writes, in his critique of the instrumentalism of modern ethical theories: "It is essential to the very concept of love that one care for the beloved, that one be prepared to act for the sake of the beloved. More strongly, one must care for the beloved and act for that person's sake as a final goal; the beloved, or the beloved's welfare or interest, must be a final goal of one's concern and action" (69).

But this is not to say that one can never seek any benefits for oneself from a friendship or love relationship. Of course one can. Why, after all, would I choose to be a friend, or to get married, or to have children, if I weren't going to gain in some way from doing so? (Though I have one childhood friend who was told by her mother that she married her husband, my friend's future father, only because she felt sorry for him!) Why would I choose to spend my precious time and invest my limited energies in this way?

Some of the benefits I gain from intimate relationships are what Thomas Donaldson has called "value-intrinsic" to that relationship, values that are "logically unobtainable without the existence of the [relationship] itself"; benefits are "value-extrinsic" to "the extent to which [the ends in question] could be achieved by other means" (36).

Recasting his point for our purposes, we can say that it is at the very least permissible to be seeking from a relationship goods that are value-intrinsic to the relationship, goods that simply cannot be acquired in any other way: that is, the goods of participating in the relationship itself.

It is more problematic when we seek from a relationship goods that are value-extrinsic to it: money, prestige, family connections—and material to write about. But it is not clearly impermissible to seek or gain additional benefits for oneself. As the quip goes, "It's just as easy to love a rich man as a poor man." One thinks of Elizabeth Bennet realizing that there are certain desirable benefits to letting herself be wooed and won by the wealthy and socially well-established Mr. Darcy. Here one needs to be careful: the external benefits cannot be what drives the relationship; the relationship must be driven by the internal ("value-intrinsic") benefits and must always contain the central element of a desire to benefit the beloved for the beloved's own sake.

But in the case of writers who write about friends and family members, the external benefit of being provided with material to write about is never (I would think) what drives the relationship. Writers do not seek out difficult, stormy, heart-wrenching relationships so that we can write about them. We find ourselves in them and write our way out of their pain and perplexity. Journalists may occasionally undertake relationships for instrumental, career-related reasons, as Joe McGinniss cultivated a friendship with the convicted murderer Jeffrey MacDonald so that he could write about him, a relationship explored in Janet Malcolm's fascinating two-part *New Yorker* article "The Journalist and the Murderer." Writers of novels and memoirs, by and large, do not. So the issue becomes that of deriving some professional benefit for oneself after the fact of entering into the relationship for other reasons, on other grounds. Nor do these writers tend to be mere bystanders in their own lives, watching them unfold with pen in hand, as journalists have been known to do—allowing disasters to proceed before their very eyes just so that they could write about them afterward, or take a Pulitzer Prize–winning photo of the carnage. I have never heard of a real-life author deliberately disregarding the welfare of a loved one just to generate something to write about later. (A fictional exception here is Christina Schwarz's heroine of *All Is Vanity*, who encourages her closest friend to destroy her family in order to gather material for her novel-in-process, *The Rise and Fall of Lexie Langtree Smith*.) It doesn't seem to me that there is any problem simply with my deriving some external benefit for myself from my intimate relationships, so long as that benefit is not the dominant goal of the intimate relationship, and so long as I continue to value the loved one appropriately.

So now the issue is whether one can indeed value one's loved ones appropriately while also drawing on their lives as material for one's work. We have come to what is clearly the central issue when writers write about their loved ones: the public betrayal of trust.

Friendship and family relationships create a protected space in which I can "let my hair down" and "be myself," making myself vulnerable to another without fear of exposure to third parties. Even crusty old Kant wrote of friendship: "But if one finds a man of good disposition and understanding to whom he can open his heart with complete confidence . . . then he can give vent to his thoughts. Then he is not completely alone with his thoughts, as if in prison, but enjoys a freedom which he misses in the mass of men, among whom he must keep himself to himself" (138). Friends tell each other secrets without feeling any need to secure a pledge of confidentiality, for this is understood as a given, within the context of the friendship itself. The classic case of adolescent betrayal is when a supposed friend blabs embarrassing revelations about oneself to the entire seventh grade. Families, in particular, are often locations of deeply buried secrets, sometimes passed on for generations; every family, one suspects, has a skeleton in its closet somewhere, not to be exposed to prying public view. Those marrying into families gradually earn the right to be co-custodians of these family secrets. Such secrets are not to be blurted to outsiders, and especially not to be publicized in print, for financial gain. This clearly seems to pose a problem for writers drawing on family stories in their novels or memoirs.

Commitments of Writers

To be a writer is to be committed to telling the truth, sometimes the literal truth (for writers of nonfiction), sometimes a "deeper" truth which is more than mere factual accuracy but a kind of fidelity to what *is*. Writers can write only the truths that they know, which are often the truths drawn from their own friendships and family relationships. Now, the degree to which a writer draws from his own life varies: some write memoirs, or fiction only thinly disguised from their own life experiences; others may write about distant galaxies or Joan of Arc. But even those who write about far-flung places and long-ago times most likely draw on their own life experience as a means of understanding the human heart. Writers are famous for scouting for material wherever life places them. We write about our parents, our children, our colleagues, our friends. To eschew the richest of all veins of material—ourselves—would be tantamount to making writing altogether impossible. Moreover, writers often confront the most harrowing of life experiences with what sounds like a cynical question: "How can I use this in a book?"

Now, one might say that it's fine to write about one's friends and family members so long as one writes only the positive things, tells only the good parts. Even this may be problematic: what I think of as sweet and funny, you may think of as horribly embarrassing, or nonetheless as private. But in any case, writers cannot write only the good parts. The memoir writer Cathy Crimmins includes in her list of "10 Commandments for Writing a Memoir": "That shalt not honor thy mother" and "Thou shalt wreak revenge" (Lamb and Rold 5). In her wonderful manual on writing, *If You Want to Write*, Brenda Ueland cautions writers against self-censoring their less kind thoughts about family members. After thinking, "My goodness, how could I ever have such a mean thought about Auntie Mae!" the writer puts down, "She was just a dear, old lady with a roguish twinkle in her eyes." No, Ueland tells us: "Not from the true self and so no good" (91). We can't write sanitized, syrupy versions of our own lives. We have to write about problems, conflict, the dark night of the soul; we have to focus more on the bad than on the good. Tolstoy opens *Anna Karenina* with the famous observation, "Happy families are all alike; every unhappy family is unhappy in its own way." Jacqueline Jackson, in her guide on writing for young readers, advises, "Badness makes very good reading, I guess because we can empathize so well" (127), adding, "I find it hard to remember the good stories . . . while the bad ones are still fresh in my memory" (128). If we don't write about the hurtful, harmful, dark, dangerous things, we won't write anything anybody will want to read. And we won't get published, either. This is the complementary source of the tension in a writer's life: we can't use our most interesting family stories as material, but we can't give them up, either.

Thus, to be a friend is to stand to another in a relationship of trust, for the sake of one's friend; to be a writer is to stand ready to violate that trust for the sake of one's story.

Resolving the Tension

Can this tension be resolved? First, I want to set aside the special set of issues involved in revealing family secrets for publication—and for profit—and write toward those issues in what follows. There is a gradual continuum from telling one's stories to writing one's stories to publishing one's stories, with the distinctions along the continuum made increasingly blurry through the advent of the Internet. (Who among us has not had a private E-mail message to a friend broadcast far more widely, either deliberately or, too often, inadvertently?)[1] I begin by asking the more general question: In what contexts, if any, are we (prima facie) justified in sharing the stories of our most intimate associates with others?

Some moral rigorists may answer "None!" An (implicit) promise is (nonetheless) a promise; trust is trust. I do not. I simply couldn't live without sharing stories of my husband and children with my women friends, and they couldn't live without sharing stories of their husbands and children with me. At the very least, I couldn't continue as a participant in those relationships without occasionally talking about those relationships with others. I know that the husbands and children often feel uncomfortable about this, but most of us feel we couldn't survive marriage or parenthood, survive life itself, if we couldn't share our problems with others. Life is hard. Marriage is hard. Parenting is hard. Even friendship can sometimes be hard. For me, talking about my intimate relationships, especially the deepest and most enduring ones, is a condition of my being in those relationships at all. It wouldn't make sense to tell me, "Don't talk about the relationship at all to others outside the relationship." If I couldn't talk about my relationships, I simply couldn't have them. I believe that the conversations I have with female friends about my family members benefit me greatly, but they also benefit my family members, however much they might object to these conversations, because they give me the strength and wisdom and compassion to continue on as wife and mother, and to be a better wife and mother than I would be otherwise. I learn from the conversations, gaining in perspective, reawakening my sense of humor, deriving ideas for possible solutions to various problems. I benefit greatly, and my loved ones benefit as well.

Now, so far I haven't said anything to establish a benefit to my loved ones from my talking about them for intended publication. That is a more daunting task. To move in that direction, we have to look at the benefits I gain not only from talking to others about my family problems, but also in hearing what others have to say about *their* family problems, in reciprocal rather than one-sided conversations. For perhaps even more than I benefit from talking to friends about my loved ones, I benefit from hearing them talk about their loved ones— and how hard it can sometimes be to go on loving them. Whenever

1. The role of the Internet in blurring the distinctions among telling, writing, and publishing was brought to my attention by Craig Howes.

another wife admits a quarrel she has had with her husband, or another mother admits some secret disappointment she has in her children, I am strengthened, enormously relieved, blessed by the sense that I am not so utterly alone. I feel more ready both to accept my life as it is, as part of the human condition from which I am hardly exempt, and to take practical, proven steps to change it, drawing on the wisdom of others before me who have already invented the wheel.

Moving to the next step in the widening circle of conversation here: Do I feel betrayed if the friends with whom I have spoken talk about me to other friends, and perhaps pass on some of what I have told them to others? My answer is that it depends on how this is done. If a "friend" were simply to want to discredit and embarrass me before others, or to share a snide giggle at my expense, of course I would object. But if the friend needs to share with another the burden of a disturbing confidence that I've placed on her, to help her process what I've confided in her, I accept this as part of what she needs to do to continue to be my friend. And maybe my friend wants to make some other friend also feel not so utterly alone by letting her know the parallel difficulties others are facing: "I have this other friend. And she's going through some of the same things, too." I admit that it is preferable if the friend passes on my stories without including my name, giving me the protection of anonymity; but sometimes identity-revealing elements may be an important part of the story. And sometimes the other friend may have reason to care about me, too, and to want to know something of what I am struggling with. I've always subscribed to the unorthodox belief that a pledge of confidentiality (in other than a professional context) entails an implicit exception, to tell just *one* other person, who in turn is pledged to confidentiality, but permitted to tell just one other person. Thus, the circle of exposure continues to widen.

I have said that this is a good thing because of our need both to tell stories and to hear stories told. But I think that the gradual and growing light of exposure can also be a good thing because secrecy itself can be corrosive and damaging. "Good" secrets can be fun—savoring the news of a friend's pregnancy before this is yet public knowledge, planning a surprise birthday party—but "bad" secrets as often as not hurt those who are charged with keeping them. I grew up in a family full of secrets—probably all of us did—and keeping those secrets was one of the hardest parts of my childhood. I would venture the generalization that almost every "bad" secret involves a shame. And most of the secrets I was ashamed about, charged with never revealing, shouldn't have been viewed as shameful at all. One of my children's books, *The Secret Life of Bethany Barrett*, deals with a girl who feels that she has to keep secret from her mother the truth about who she is, the truth that she isn't the perfect child she thinks her mother needs to believe that she is; the book also deals with the mother's ongoing denial of Bethany's younger brother's learning disabilities. Oh, the relief, when those secrets can be faced and told! Kay Redfield Jamison writes in her memoir *An Unquiet Mind* about her lifelong journey through manic depression: "I have no idea what the long-term effects of discussing such issues so openly will be on my personal and professional life, but, whatever the consequences, they are bound to be better than continuing to be silent. I am tired of hiding, tired of misspent and knotted energies, tired of the hypocrisy, and tired of acting as though I have something to hide" (7). Thus, the secrecy protected by a certain view of familial privacy can be a crushing weight imposed on family members, so that the speaking of the truth, even the public proclamation of the truth, can be experienced as an act of liberation, and ultimately of love.

If there can be a great relief to me when finally I tell my secret, is there a great relief to me when finally *you* tell my secret? Or is there only a great sense of betrayal? Perhaps both. It can be a great benefit to me not to have to carry a secret any longer, not to have to hide and cower in the closet. And here it is important to note that there are also costs to others when one person hides in the closet, contributing to a public culture in which that secret is a source of shame. As Richard Mohr has argued, gays who hide their homosexuality from public view, to avoid social condemnation for who they are, cooperate with the forces that maintain that condemnation; closeted gays help to maintain social norms that assault their own individual dignity. Thus Mohr, controversially, endorses the "outing" of gays. A parallel conversation has taken place on newspapers' policies of not revealing the names of rape victims because it is perceived as so shameful, not to be a rapist, but to have been raped. By protecting one person's secret, we contribute to a climate of false shame surrounding that secret. The greater the climate of shame surrounding a secret, the more costly its revelation is to the subject of the secret. But the more some individuals are willing to—or forced to—bear those costs, the less those costs become for future others.

Of course, some things—not homosexuality, not being the victim of a sexual assault—really are shameful. What if it's a secret of this sort that I want to protect—my past as a pedophile, my violent criminal record? Where shameful secrets pose dangers to others, it's arguable that these secrets should be revealed—though even as I say this, I have to admit that I feel sick when past offenders are labeled for life and denied any opportunity, ever, at public redemption. Still, I'm inclined here to state the exposure quandary in this way. Either the secret is truly shameful or it's not. If it is, perhaps the secret should be exposed for the protection of others. If it's not, perhaps its exposure can help reduce the unwarranted shame attached to secrets of this kind.

I recognize that in real life the alternatives are seldom so starkly posed. Different stories are shameful to different persons in different contexts, perhaps as a result of their different social positions. It has been pointed out to me that individuals in a socially oppressed group may have good reason to fear the dissemination of certain stories about themselves to those in the socially dominant group, who may use these stories to reinforce their own prejudices and stereotypes.[2] And yet, I'm still drawn to the view that in the end the truth helps to make us free. A recent young-adult novel, *Chill Wind*, by Janet McDonald, an African American author who grew up in the Brooklyn projects, depicts a teenaged black welfare mother who has no intention whatsoever of working or taking any real responsibility for her life. Does the novel reinforce racial stereotypes? In my view, no, because its heroine has so much sass and in-your-face attitude and humor and warmth that instead it shows me the real person behind the stereotype in a way that a pious treatment of a "perfect" black character would not, and could not, do.

Still, the consequences of one's exposure of another's non-shameful secret can in some cases be devastating. Alice Wexler, in her essay for this volume, calls attention to the crushing material consequences individuals may face in terms of loss of livelihood and loss of health or life insurance when stigmatizing genetic or medical information about them is revealed. These are serious repercussions from disclosure that cannot be dismissed lightly, nor would I want to dismiss them. I am arguing only that the sharing of revelatory stories is at least sometimes prima facie justified; I leave open the possibility that in certain contexts, for certain individuals, the costs of sharing may simply be too great.

At this point we've moved beyond the benefits of disclosing one's stories to only a few select friends, toward the benefits of a wider, public disclosure. We're also closing in on the benefits of the published sharing of stories. To return to my need to hear others' stories, I have benefited greatly not only from one-on-one confidences shared with friends but also from reading others' stories, both in fiction and in memoir. The same relief I get from feeling not so utterly alone in the universe comes to me from literature as well as life, and sometimes

2. I owe this objection to Alison Jaggar.

more forcefully or poignantly from literature, if the writer is more skilled and articulate than my lunchtime friends might be, more able to distill the core of his or her experience or that of the characters he or she has created. Some of us don't have a rich and varied circle of friends to share our stories with, and our only access to the experience of others will come through the media—literature, film, television.

The sharing of published stories generally means the sharing of stories for financial profit. Should this additional element of the storyteller's financial gain make a difference to my conclusions here? I would say no. I think that we can accept the legitimacy of seeking some extrinsic benefits from friendship. We can also accept the legitimacy of trying to make a living through the use of one's talents and gifts. If I'm benefiting the world through sharing my published stories, it's appropriate that I be recompensed for doing so. It takes an enormous amount of developed ability and sustained effort to write a readable and publishable memoir or novel; it is natural that writers should write as a profession, for which they expect to be paid. Thus, the last piece of the puzzle falls into place.

I'm ready now to lay out my formal argument for why it is at least sometimes permissible for me to share the stories of my friends and family members, not just with other intimates in confidential confession, but even in print, for profit. I will then consider several objections to this argument and some qualifications and caveats regarding it.

I need to *tell* stories about my intimate relationships; I derive great benefit from this. Those in my intimate relationships benefit, too, because telling the stories helps me perform my role in these relationships better. I need to *hear* others' stories, I derive great benefit from this, and those in my intimate relationships benefit as well, for the same reason. Furthermore, in the same way, I benefit, and they benefit, from my hearing the published stories of others. (And presumably my intimates are also primary benefiting consumers of these stories themselves.) Now, all of this benefit is possible only at the cost of somebody's stories getting told. I have suggested that there are some benefits even to those whose secrets are shared—the lifting of the crushing burden of "shameful" secrecy—but there are also undeniable costs as well. Still, if these costs were not incurred by somebody, the great benefits I've listed could not be generated.

While this argument as stated has a utilitarian flavor in its reckoning of costs and benefits, I find myself drawn to a quasi-Kantian approach here (although Kant would be rolling over in his grave at my thoughts about the permissibility of breaking promises of confidentiality: "The strictest friendship requires an understanding and trusted friend who considers himself bound not to share without express permission a secret entrusted to him with anyone else" [139]). I cannot will a world in which nobody shares intimate stories. And so, if I'm going to act only on that maxim which I could will to be a universal law, I cannot exempt my own stories from being shared by others. "Yes, share stories, but not mine" isn't a fit item of legislation in the kingdom of ends. If I am unable to forgo the crucial benefits to be reaped from others' stories, I must make myself vulnerable to the sharing of my own.

Objections and Replies

Now, our goal must be to achieve the great benefits of the sharing of stories while minimizing the costs to those whose stories are shared. But before I turn to some thoughts about how to approach this, I want to consider several sweeping objections to the argument itself.

First, my argument turns on the importance of being able to share stories and to tell secrets. The objection could be raised that we live right now in a culture of too much story sharing, too little secret keeping, shaped by the talk show and Internet culture of baring our souls, "letting it all hang out," in front of 30 million viewers/voyeurs. My argument implies that we have too much false shame; the counterargument charges that we have too little true shame. Complete strangers blurt out their intimate secrets to one another on the subway, and to the whole world on *Oprah*, or on their own tell-all Web sites. Far from a dearth of stories, we have a cultural surfeit. The issues raised here concern shame and modesty, coarseness and crassness, self-absorption and narcissism. Indeed, the rise of memoir as a literary genre has sometimes been linked with a growing culture of narcissism: "And now for some more about me . . ."

My response here is twofold. First, even in the United States of America in the early years of the new millennium, I myself still experience an almost bottomless hunger for story, and for connection with others through story. I still can't stop talking with friends and can't stop reading books by strangers. Moreover, I still feel crushed and burdened by the effort of trying to hide my own imperfections from others. As a mother, I fall into the arms of any other mother struggling with issues similar to my own, eager to share our tales and draw strength from them. Social critics may mock the proliferation of support groups for every affliction under the sun—but I still need and crave support. I repeat my earlier point: life is hard, relationships are hard. I continue to welcome all the help I can get.

Second, we need to draw distinctions among stories. Part of the objection I raised earlier is not to the sharing of stories per se but to the glib, shallow, sound-bite way in which they are shared, and to the overly sexual content on which they are focused. The true sharing of stories takes some time for both telling and listening. The beauty of sharing stories from friends, or stories through literature, is that we get a chance to know, or at least try to know, at least catch a glimpse of, the "whole person" whose story it is. To read, for example, Jane Hamilton's novel *A Map of the World* is to see how unspeakable disaster can come to a mother very much like me from a moment of carelessness of the kind of which I am completely capable. To see a talk-show segment on "mothers who accidentally killed other mothers' children!" would just be sensational; what would be lost is the individual person behind the shocking story line. And a friend pointed out to me that when stories are shared through literature, one still has the sense of a secret confided from one individual to another, from writer alone at her desk to reader alone in her bed. Even the sharing of stories through film takes place in a darkened theater, with the intimacy that darkness provides. But the sharing of stories on television is the willy-nilly broadcasting of those stories to anyone who can casually pick up the remote control and click on the tube.[3]

Moreover, while I have a hunger for story generally, my own prudish, modest self doesn't have a hunger for stories about other people's sexual proclivities and performances. These are not stories I share with my friends over lunch, whatever other deep personal stories we share. I've always hated biographies that tell us too much graphic detail about, for example, Abraham Lincoln's sex life. I don't want to know! Despite our undeniable public interest in sex, evidenced by the content of most prime-time TV shows, I would say that stories about sex itself are inherently uninteresting. What Richard Mohr calls our sexual "fumblings" are, in the end, all largely the same (16).

Thus, my reply to the first objection raised to my argument is that it impugns not the sharing of stories generally but the sharing of certain kinds of stories in a certain glib and shallow way. The need for sharing deep, meaningful stories emerges unscathed.

A second general objection to my argument is that, because I have grounded it in a deep human need to tell stories, I have provided at best an *excuse* for the sharing of stories, not a *justification* for doing so.[4] We are excused for telling stories because we can't help ourselves; as Aristotle would say, in drawing his own similar distinction between

3. Catherine Altman shared this insight with me.
4. I am grateful to David Boonin for this point.

excuse and justification: "In some cases there is no praise, but there is pardon, whenever someone does a wrong action because of conditions of a sort that overstrain human nature, and that no one would endure" (31). On this view, it's wrong to betray others' confidences and share their stories, but we (sometimes) forgive those who do so, because, according to my argument, it would have been too hard for them, given human nature, to have refrained.

I disagree. I don't think the telling of stories is something that we should generally try our best to avoid doing or regret having done. I think a world where we didn't share stories would be poorer world— a *morally* poorer one. If saints are those who could somehow keep the stories of their loved ones bottled up within their own hearts—that is, if saints can even *have* loved ones in any sense the rest of us can understand—then, with Susan Wolf, I am glad that I, and my friends, fall short of saintliness. So I think I've offered not merely an excuse for the sharing of stories but a prima facie justification for doing so—where, by "prima facie" justification, I mean that the practice is justified "on its face," though not necessarily justified all things considered.

The third and final objection I want to raise to my account is, if successful, the most damaging. It is that I have drastically dismissed or discounted the importance each of us places on having control over our own stories. Control over information about ourselves is central to the right to privacy, and the human dignity that right protects. I offered earlier the quasi-Kantian argument that I couldn't will a world in which stories were not shared. But could I really will a world in which everyone's stories would be completely up for grabs, in which there was no sense in which *my* story was respected as *mine*, in which it was simply seized for the telling by whoever felt like telling it? It seems that a maxim of utterly careless and heedless storytelling, if universalized as law, would completely self-destruct, for no one would be willing to tell stories in a world such as that. And without this initial telling of stories, there would be no common stock of stories to retell.[5]

I find myself moved by this objection. This is how I would reply. I do believe that even in such a world people would tell their stories, simply because, as I have argued, we can't help ourselves; telling stories is a condition of our continuing to live, or at least interacting socially with others, at all. And I don't think my argument has tried to establish even a prima facie justification for the sharing of all stories, at any time, to anyone. I reject storytelling that violates professional codes of confidentiality, storytelling motivated by malice (with

5. This alternative Kantian maxim was suggested to me by Jackie Colby.

exceptions to which I'll return shortly), storytelling that fails to exhibit appropriate care and respect for the stories told (as in the talk show broadcasting of stories). Storytelling must be done with sensitivity and concern both for the stories themselves and even more for the persons, for the human beings, whose stories these are.

Minimizing the Costs

How, then, can we share stories in a way that exhibits appropriate care and respect for persons and for the stories of their lives? How can we reap the great benefits of story sharing while minimizing the costs to those whose stories are told?

First we need to know what kind of "costs" we're talking about here. If the cost is simply the sheer fact of having one's story told, however it is told, and whether or not one ever knows that it was told or incurs any adverse effects from having it told, that cost is inescapable, on my argument. My argument, if it is successful, gives us grounds for being willing to accept this kind of cost: the sharing of stories does require that stories be shared. So we need to look at other kinds of costs: the lack of respect or sensitivity or kindness revealed in certain modes or contexts of storytelling; the pain the person may experience from embarrassment at the revelation; the pain she may experience from discovering what the storyteller really thinks about her; loss of reputation or standing in another's eyes.

The best but hardest way to reduce these costs is simply to be a great writer, with a wise, compassionate view of your characters in all their enormous complexity. Brenda Ueland praises the great Russian authors for their "honesty, earnestness, and extraordinarily clear vision" (124). She continues:

> Now every word they write in a mysterious way is autobiographical and *true* and yet when they write about repulsive people, whom no doubt they knew well, there is nothing caddish or reprehensible about it, as there is when other writers describe living people in their books. Why is that? Is it because Tolstoi and Chekhov and Dostoyevsky and Gorky were so serious, so impassioned, so truthful about everything and would never let themselves show off or jeer or exaggerate? If you are serious in describing bad people and not mean or derisive or superior . . . even the bad people will be grateful. I would never resent being described by Chekhov, no matter how repellent the picture. I would try to be better. If Sinclair Lewis did it, or D. H. Lawrence or H. L. Mencken I would sue for libel,—a million dollars. (130–31)

If we can write about our loved ones, or even our hated ones, while doing full justice to their unique and distinctive and suffering and joyful personhood, they, like Ueland, may view their portrait as a gift.[6]

Another, less daunting way to reduce the costs to those whom we write about is to protect their identity in various ways: to share a person's story but withhold the person's name, changing revelatory (but irrelevant) details whenever possible. This points us toward sharing stories through fiction rather than through nonfiction. This has been my own choice in writing about my friends and family members. I write fiction, changing the names, making up most of the events that take place, so that only the emotional core remains.

In my Gus and Grandpa books, focusing on the relationship between a little boy and his grandfather, the grandfather is almost entirely like my boys' real-life Grandpa, my father-in-law—who recognizes himself so much in the books that he actually grew a mustache to match the illustrator's portrayal of Grandpa more closely! The portrait of Grandpa is a very idealized and positive one, so that I had little to fear in drawing so liberally on Grandpa's real-life character and mannerisms— which isn't to say that I didn't tremble when I gave the first book to him. ("People pay money for this?" he asked, incredulously.) Gus himself is less idealized, however, and here I made the crucial change of collapsing both my boys into the one character of Gus, who in different books struggles with some of the same issues that have faced my boys: being the last kid in the neighborhood to ride a two-wheel bike without training wheels, getting confused on the basketball court, hating piano lessons. Our real-life perfect neighbor boy makes an appearance in the books as Gus's nemesis, perfect neighbor boy Ryan Mason—with his name changed and his identity additionally shielded by the fact that the illustrator, in an effort to promote diversity, has drawn Ryan as African American. Much of what actually happens in the books is completely fabricated; for example, our real-life ninety-two-year-old Grandpa was not the one who taught our boys how to ride a bike, nor would he ever, in a million years, attend their noisy, chaotic basketball games.

The Gus and Grandpa books are sweet and basically unthreatening to my boys, so I've disguised our lives the least here. In my books that deal with issues closer to the painful realities of our lives, I disguise my characters more liberally. In 7 × 9 = *Trouble!* a third-grade boy, Wilson, struggles with learning the times tables—as my older son struggled. In the book, he has a gifted younger brother, Kipper, who shines at math—as my younger son shines. But just about every scene

6. I develop this point more extensively in my essay "Appropriating Others' Stories."

in the book is a product of imagination, including a subplot about a classroom hamster, and I obtained my younger son's permission to use, in dialogue, two actual lines that he once uttered. My book *You're a Brave Man, Julius Zimmerman* deals with the relationship between a mother and son; the mother is disappointed in her son for not being more of an academic success and for preferring television to reading. I am close enough to the mother in the book to have felt quite threatened when my writing group critiqued the first scene in which she appears: "This mother is a witch! She's so mean to poor Julius!" But again, as every single scene and line in the entire book is the product of imagination (Julius's summer French class, his babysitting job—all of it), I felt at a safe distance from my own family situation in writing it.

I don't think I could publish a memoir about my family, either my childhood family or my family now. For me, it would be too much of a betrayal; it would cross the line I have drawn for myself. Maybe this is because I've established a career as a writer of children's fiction, and so I'm able to achieve my own story-sharing goals in this way. (And so many mothers of boys have come up to me at conferences to tell me they see themselves in Julius's "witchy" but nonetheless loving mother.) I'm mentioning my family here only safe in the knowledge that this essay isn't likely to be widely read (!), and so my boys are unlikely to hear me say any of this about them. And I've taken pains not to say anything *too* terrible, as well.

So, fiction is a choice for story sharing that provides more protection for those whose stories are told. That said, the strength of memoir is precisely its claim of literal truth. If what I am seeking, as a reader, is real stories of other real people who share my struggles in a way that illuminates my world, there is no substitute for reality. Memoir provides the crucial possibility of witness: "This happened to me."[7] Moreover, memoir is arguably more direct and honest as a choice here than fiction, which can involve deliberate distortions of someone's life presented as thinly disguised fictionalization, and which lacks memoir's accountability, its public declaration that it offers at least an attempt at the truth.[8] Thus, on my balance sheet, against the greater protection to loved ones provided by fiction is opposed the witness and accountability gained from the presentation of literal, actual truth— or, at least, literal, actual truth as distilled by the subjective, fallible,

7. This objection to the choice of fiction over memoir was made persuasively to me by Art Frank.

8. This is one of the issues raised by Diane Middlebrook in her analysis of *Sylvia and Ted*, the fictionalization of the lives of Sylvia Plath and Ted Hughes, in this volume.

overinvested human being writing it. Here I'll say only that the writing of memoirs is the riskier choice—with greater potential benefits from the story sharing, but greater potential harm to loved ones as well. By saying this, am I retreating from my central argument that purports to justify the widespread sharing of *real* stories?[9] I don't think so. I think I'm offering a compromise that recognizes that while the sharing of stories has great value, it also has painful costs, which a responsible moral agent will seek, if possible, to minimize. Fictionalization is one possible way of accomplishing this.

Given the kind of costs I'm focusing on—the harms suffered by the living person in having his stories told, rather than the sheer fact of having those stories told—it is somewhat less morally problematic to write a memoir after the death of the key persons whose stories are told in it. The dead feel no pain (although novels like *The Lovely Bones* by Alice Sebold do make me worry that the dead may be somehow present still, to witness how we, the survivors, process our grief). Now, while the dead can no longer experience conscious pain, it still seems important to respect at least some of the interests they expressed when they were still living. Joel Feinberg, exploring the puzzle of posthumous interests, writes: "We can think of some of a person's interests as surviving his death, just as some of the debts and claims of his estate do. . . . The final tally book on a person's life is not closed until some time after his death" (83). Thus, we carry out the terms of the deceased's last will and testament and try to fulfill his stated wishes for burial—even though he would never know if we failed him here. Likewise, it seems important to protect someone's posthumous interest in protecting her reputation and legacy: "The desire to maintain a good reputation . . . can be the basis of interests that survive their owner's death, in a manner of speaking, and can be promoted or harmed by events subsequent to that death. Fulfillment and thwarting of interest, after all, may be possible, even when it is too late for satisfaction or disappointment" (Feinberg 86). That others will read what we write, and judge our loved ones accordingly, gives us some reason at the least to write carefully, constantly weighing the need to tell what we are telling against the costs, in some sense, to the loved one, even post mortem, of having it told.

My own choices to write about my friends and family as I do have been formed by the fact that I do love them dearly and want to protect them as I proceed in the storytelling which is my passion, and my livelihood. How would my deliberations change if in fact I didn't love them, or loved them only in some qualified way, with love equally

---

9. Thanks to Ray Hedin for pressing me on this point.

mixed with anger or hurt of my own? I don't think bad people deserve the protections that good people do. I once read a quote that thrilled me, that the task of the historian was to hold up evil deeds "for the reprobation of posterity." That is certainly part of the fitting punishment for evildoers, that their evil deeds are no longer hidden—but instead documented, dissected, despised. In my sharing of stories with friends, one of my delights is to tell the truth about bad people. Bad people deserve to be known for who and what they are.

And yet . . . I am not perfect either, and perhaps my moral condemnation of others is too hasty and short-sighted, warped by my tendency to magnify my own grievances and minimize my own moral failings. All women had awful ex-boyfriends; they think they had awful ex-girlfriends. We all had difficult, problematic parents; they think they had difficult, problematic children. The rush to judgment here can be too quick and easy. Our ex-lovers and parents are probably not the monsters we imagine them to be; for the most part, they are flawed, sad human beings who did the best they could in difficult circumstances. All parents, in particular, need to be viewed through the lens of pity. When I read the noted children's author Beverly Cleary's autobiography A Girl from Yamhill, I was struck by her lack of any forgiveness at all for a mother who seemed not that much worse than the run of mothers, not that much worse than I am myself. Overly harsh judgment of others tends only to make those who judge seem unattractively self-righteous.

For these reasons there are special dangers in kiss-and-tell memoirs, for all lovers scorned are unreliable witnesses to the true character of those who have scorned them. Moreover, sex is special. As I have noted, sex is an area of life in which all stories are so strange and bizarre, and yet so utterly familiar, that we don't really benefit from the telling of them. As Richard Mohr writes, in defense of privacy regarding specific sexual behavior (as opposed to general sexual orientation), "The success of sex in our unedited lives presupposes the creation of sanctuary, a presumption that what one is doing is not being watched and subjected to judgment—even or especially through the indirect agency of one's partner himself" (16). And the dangers in Mommie Dearest memoirs are signaled by the fact that the genre even now has its own disparaging name. This is not to say that we shouldn't write about our parents—as I said earlier, the best stories most of us have to tell are the stories of our childhoods. But we probably shouldn't tell these until time has given us some perspective and healing distance and some ability to forgive.[10]

10. The essays by John Barbour and Richard Freadman in this volume both address the kind of forgiveness and compassion that one should strive toward in writing about one's family members.

∎

I have argued for the importance of sharing the stories in our lives, first for the need for friends to share stories with one another, and then for the need for all of us to have access to a wider circle of stories, in the great storehouse of world literature. For stories to be heard, stories must be told. I have tried to give a prima facie, qualified justification for the telling of at least some of those stories. Although one may choose to minimize the cost of story sharing through fictionalization of the stories shared, there remains a distinctive and irreplaceable value in the sharing of "real" stories, with their inescapably flawed but nonetheless valiant attempt at witness. The truth *does* make us free. At least that is what I have argued here.

WORKS CITED

Aristotle, *Nicomachean Ethics*. Trans. Terence Irwin. 2d ed. Indianapolis: Hackett, 1999.

Cleary, Beverly. *A Girl from Yamhill*. New York: William Morrow, 1988.

Donaldson, Thomas. "Morally Privileged Relationships." In *Kindred Matters: Rethinking the Philosophy of the Family*. Ed. Diana Tietjens Meyers et al. Ithaca: Cornell University Press, 1993. 21–40.

Feinberg, Joel. *Harm to Others*. Vol. 1 of *The Moral Limits of the Criminal Law*. New York: Oxford University Press, 1984.

Hamilton, Jane. *A Map of the World*. New York: Random House, 1994.

Jackson, Jacqueline. *Turn Not Pale, Beloved Snail: A Book about Writing among Other Things*. Boston: Little, Brown, 1974.

Jamison, Kay Redfield. *An Unquiet Mind: A Memoir of Moods and Madness*. New York: Alfred K. Knopf, 1985.

Kant, Immanuel. *Elements of Ethics*. Trans. James W. Ellington. Indianapolis: Hackett, 1983.

Lamb, Sandra E., and Cindy Rold. "Should You Be Writing a Memoir?" *InPrint*, March 2002, 5.

McDonald, Janet. *Chill Wind*. New York: Farrar, Straus and Giroux/Frances Foster, 2002.

Malcolm, Janet. "The Journalist and the Murderer." *New Yorker*, March 13 and 20, 1989, 38–73, 49–82.

Mills, Claudia. "Appropriating Others' Stories: Some Questions about the Ethics of Writing Fiction." *Journal of Social Philosophy* 21, no. 2 (spring 2000): 195–206.

——. *The Secret Life of Bethany Barrett*. New York: Farrar, Straus and Giroux, 1994.

——. *7 × 9 = Trouble!* New York: Farrar, Straus and Giroux, 2002.

——. *You're a Brave Man, Julius Zimmerman*. New York: Farrar, Straus and Giroux, 1999.

Mohr, Richard D. *Gay Ideas: Outing and Other Controversies*. Boston: Beacon Press, 1992.

Schwarz, Christina. *All Is Vanity*. New York: Random House, 2002.

Sebold, Alice. *The Lovely Bones*. Boston: Little, Brown, 2002.
Stocker, Michael. "The Schizophrenia of Modern Ethical Theories." In *Virtue Ethics*. Ed. Roger Crisp and Michael Slote. New York: Oxford University Press, 1997. 66–78.
Ueland, Brenda. *If You Want to Write: A Book about Art, Independence, and Spirit*. Saint Paul: Gray Wolf Press, 1987.
Wolf, Susan. "Moral Saints." In *Virtue Ethics*. Ed. Roger Crisp and Michael Slote. New York: Oxford University Press, 1997. 79–98.

CHAPTER 6

Decent and Indecent: Writing My Father's Life

Richard Freadman

After my father died in 1993, it occurred to me that I might write something about his life. Over the next few years, I made several attempts to do so. I got as far as an introductory scene and a couple of outlines, but for one reason or another I couldn't get further. When I'd try intermittently to resume the narrative, I'd encounter a curiously vague inner resistance. Sometimes it felt like apathy; at others like lack of confidence, a doubt about my ability to write narrative; most often the feeling was one of muted fear: I knew that writing the book would hurt, and I shied away from that. It was much easier to shelve it and to go on with less threatening academic work.

In 2002 something changed. I was now fifty; I had a son of six, with whom I have a close bond. My father had been dead almost ten years. Having written a book about autobiography and the will, I decided to steel my own will, set other projects aside, and write the book about my father. I immersed myself in his letters, his academic and other writings, my correspondence with him, magazines from his school days, and much else. I interviewed his brother, my mother, surviving friends and acquaintances. Quite suddenly, I got a picture of how the book might go. I wrote the first, eighty-thousand-word draft in about two months. The last section of the draft was an essay—a sort of coda—on the ethical complexities of the project. I'd been so disturbed by what I was doing that, about a third of the way through, I suspended work on the narrative and wrote the coda on ethics in an attempt to

121

decide whether the project was morally acceptable. Because I'd often been frustrated by impressionistic debate about the ethics of particular works of life writing, I wanted the coda to be philosophically informed and argued; but in making it so I produced an extension of the narrative that, in some parts at least, did not sit well with what had gone before. So I decided to detach the coda and publish it separately. This essay is that coda, slightly adapted for the current volume.

The book I wrote is part biography and part autobiography. It's about my father's life, but also about my relationship with him, and about what it has meant to be the son of such a man. I think of it as an example of what I term the subgenre of the Son's Book of the Father. Some notable examples of this subgenre are Gosse's *Father and Son*, J. A. Ackerley's *My Father and Myself*, Philip Roth's *Patrimony*, Geoffrey Wolff's *Duke of Deception: Memories of My Father*, Sidney Offit's *Memoir of the Bookie's Son*, Larry Lockridge's *Shade of the Raintree*, Art Spiegleman's *Maus*, and in Australia, which has produced a striking number of such volumes, Raimond Gaita's *Romulus, My Father*.

My father, Paul Freadman, was not a glitteringly successful person; nor was he very well known. He was a fine man who had what most would regard as quite a successful career as a teacher of political science at a business school, a political commentator, and an exemplary citizen. He was a navigator in the Australian air force during the Second World War—an experience that seems to have left deep emotional scars. On the face of it, he was a successful family man: married to Fleur for forty-five years, two children (I have a brother, Andrew, a lawyer, who is three years my junior), both of whom have families and satisfactory professional lives. Though not a religious man, Paul came from a quite observant Jewish family (his father, a jeweler, was bankrupted by the Great Depression), and his Jewishness ran very deep in his sense of himself and of his world. Although his distant roots were east European, most branches of his family arrived in Australia in the mid-nineteenth century. In style he was a highly assimilated "Anglo-Jew." As with Jews everywhere, no matter how assimilated, no matter how far from Europe, his sense of the world was decisively shaped by the Holocaust.

My father was a thoroughly decent man, and in this his life and personality reflected one of the most powerful conditioning moral norms of the Australian culture that shaped him: the ideal, the virtue, of Decency. Decency brings with it protocols about privacy: what one can reasonably reveal about others, and indeed about one's self. The decent person doesn't often probe the dark psychological places—not even his or her own "desert places," as Robert Frost calls them—and tends to be shy about the inner life.

To a considerable degree this was true of my father; and so, immediately, writing his life raised ethical problems. I knew that he would not have wanted aspects of his troubled inner life set on the public record. Nevertheless, he had a craving for recognition, and my book, which is fond, admiring, but also frank about his difficulties, puts on record his fine qualities, his many talents, his estimable achievements. In thinking about the ethical complexities of the project, I had to weigh his needs and rights against my own. His emotional patrimony was mixed: he gave me a lot, but being the son of a disappointed and increasingly depressed man was a burden to bear. The book's title, *Shadow of Doubt: My Father and Myself*, refers principally to the corrosive self-doubt that shadowed his life. Some of this shadow fell across my own path, my own self. His sense of disappointment and failure weighed on me, complicating my emotional life as a young man, and to some extent beyond.

I was puzzled by a deep paradox in my father's life and character: to many, especially in his earlier days, he seemed a man of great ability and energy who was determined to make something of life. He wanted to live well, both in the sense of being a good moral being and in the sense of flourishing, fulfilling his potential. In this respect he seemed an impressive man on a quest. Yet there was his dangerously low self-esteem and treacherous self-doubt. Increasingly, self-doubt became ascendant. He made damagingly cautious career decisions, became depressed, and underachieved in his own eyes. The situation was compounded by the fact that his best friend was to become one of the most successful and famous Australians of their generation.

I needed to write my father's story in order to "work through" his legacy. I'd taken on aspects of his incomplete life task, and with it some of his complexities. My next-generational emergence from some of the shadows he'd cast seemed to require that I put him and our relationship on the record—for myself, for my children, but also for a wider audience, both "literary" and "general." I believe that my father's life, and its influence over mine, reflect some widely occurring sociological and psychological patterns, and that others—fathers and sons particularly—might profit from reading "our" story. What's more, I am a writer, and I knew that a powerful and revealing story was there to be written. Writers have a right to write. But how far into the privacy of others does that right extend?

There is, I believe, no single or general answer to that question. There are some rough guidelines, and philosophical analysis can help to discern and elaborate these; but each case has to be taken on its merits, has to be considered in context and with respect to the rights, wishes, and feelings of those involved. Here, too, philosophy can assist, but only in concert with appropriate attention to context. I could give a fairly considered account of how I felt and of how I saw my rights in the situation. But what of my father? He had been dead eight years. How was I to assess *his* rights, the feelings he might have had, the attitude he might have taken to my project? I decided to write an essay that was part philosophy, but also part imagined encounter with the subject of my narrative.

■

I presume that few would question the propriety of my writing but not publishing the book, given that, at most, it would then be read by a small circle of family and friends. But publication is another matter. In a piece titled "A Man's Own Household His Enemies," an attack on what she sees as betrayals of trust by some recent memoirists, Gertrude Himmelfarb quotes this passage from the Talmud:

> Rabbi Eliezer the Great said: As the footsteps of the messiah approach, shamelessness will spread. . . . Schoolrooms will be used for lechery, . . . scholarship will degenerate, those who shun sin will be despised, and truth will be banished. Boys will insult the elderly and the elderly will defer to children—"son spurning father, daughter rising up against mother, daughter-in-law against mother-in-law—a man's household his enemies" [Micah 7:6]. The face of that generation will be like a dog's face, men not being abashed before their fathers. (34)

Her particular targets are John Bayley and James Trilling. In *Iris: A Memoir of Iris Murdoch*, Bayley graphically describes how his wife, the novelist and philosopher Iris Murdoch, declined into Alzheimer's disease. James Trilling, the son of the famous literary scholar Lionel Trilling, had just published an article in which he documents what he construes as his father's symptoms of ADD (attention deficit disorder). As various genres of life writing boom and the boundaries of privacy become more porous, such attacks are inevitable—and important. But at this point we need more than vituperative denunciations of alleged ethical travesties. We need to work these problems through carefully, both in general terms and with respect to particular examples. As Annette Baier says in a classic discussion of trust: "We need a morality to guide us in our dealings with those who either cannot or should not achieve equality of power (animals, the ill, the dying, children while still young) with those with whom they have unavoidable and often intimate relationships" ("Trust and Antitrust" 249). So let's go back to basics.

I presume that those who endorse the sort of position Himmelfarb holds believe that in close relationships one is privy to certain things that should never be made public. There's an initial problem with this: one can imagine situations in which it would be perfectly legitimate— say, in the "common interest"—to breach such confidentiality. Would we condemn the wife of a genocidal political leader who revealed very private things about her late husband in order to aid understanding of the sort of psychopathology he exhibited and thereby, perhaps, reduce the risk of similar genocidal behavior by others? I think not. This of course is an extreme case, and far removed from the sort Himmelfarb has in mind; but one of its aspects—the notion of a wider public good or common interest—is relevant to less extreme cases, including, arguably, the ones she does have in mind.

Her position seems to turn principally on two notions: trust and loyalty. The first is predominantly a psychological concept; the second may be partly that, but it is most obviously an ethical concept. Let's leave aside questions pertaining to the sorts of responsibilities that we might—or might not—have to the living and concentrate on the elusive but profound notion that we often owe loyalty to the dead. What values and assumptions are at work here? The principal assumption in a case like the one I'm discussing here is that a *relationship of trust* existed between the deceased person and myself, and that my loyalty is to that person, but, as it were, *via that trust*. My loyalty is to the person I knew, and one implication of this is that the character of my loyalty will be shaped by the relationship in which that knowledge evolved. Trust seems to function at several levels in a case like this. The nature and degree of trust present may help a third party who so wishes to categorize the relationship in question. Longstanding mutual interpersonal trust will be characteristic of close friendships; in the relationship of trust we have with, say, a new physician, the trust will have shallower interpersonal roots and will be heavily conditioned by professional roles and protocols. The notion of trust also helps characterize what the relationship felt like from the inside: my friend and I had a *feeling of trust* toward each other. That feeling of trust would have been quite a nonspecific feeling, but it could also translate into—or, to adapt one of Baier's terms, be "relativized to" ("Trust and Antitrust" 237)—trust about particular things: "I trust you to do so-and-so."[1] I see my departed friend's trust as an expression of him, specifically of his wishes, attitudes, outlook, and so

---

1. It seems to me that Baier is somewhat equivocal as to whether trust is constitutively open-ended, gratuitous, on the one hand, or susceptible of relativization, on the other. In this respect, as in some others, I find Jones's criticism of Baier's "three-place predicate" "entrustment" model convincing. See Jones 17.

on. As Lawrence C. Becker says of particularly generous trust: "Trust of this sort is not only a way of handling uncertainty; it is also a way of being, a way of going, in uncertain or certain terrain" (50). Being loyal to that friend entails, perhaps necessarily takes the form of, being loyal to his trust.

Let's consider some of these points with reference to an example that is relevant to the ethical problems that have confronted me in writing my book. Suppose that the deceased, knowing that I am, say, a novelist or autobiographer, has actually wagged a finger in my face and said: "Don't you ever dare write about me. I'd regard that as a gross betrayal, whether you did it when I was alive or dead." This is pretty clear, so far as it goes: he has appealed to our relationship of trust, and has done so in a way that tells me how that trust should be interpreted with respect to a particular imagined activity—my writing about him. In his mind, to write thus would be a breach of our trust. In some respects, however, his action is hard to characterize. In a way it would be more accurate to say that in aggressively wagging his finger, he is showing me that his trust is not unconditional. He is signaling the limits of his trust in me and implying that beyond a specific domain of trust, his trust modulates into distrust. In principle, at least, I think he's right about this. Trust isn't an absolute; as Trudy Govier suggests, there are "degrees of trust and distrust" (18), and trust can be domain-specific: it can apply to some areas but not to others.

In wagging his finger, then, my friend seems to be appealing to our relationship of trust, but also to be seeking a degree of security that his levels of trust in me don't provide. Implicitly he seems to be seeking some sort of verbal contract, a promise from me to the effect that I will not write about him. While early philosophical discussions of trust tended to be contractarian in nature, the more recent philosophical literature on the subject often sees "contract" and "trust" as contrastive—perhaps even contrary—terms.[2] For them, trust is in essence something we feel without needing assurances. Trust, in this sense, is intrinsically gratuitous, open-ended; it does not require formal

2. Philosophical attempts to elucidate a notion such as trust are subject to all manner of methodological and epistemological complications. For instance, if one's method is aimed at conceptually differentiating between trust and proximate concepts such as, say, reliance, then one will be inclined to conceptualize trust as an unqualified thing. Where the phenomenon seems to be qualified, say, by elements of distrust, the tendency will be to call it by another name, say, distrust or reliance or dependence. But if one takes an "affective" approach to trust, if, that is, one tries to grasp it empirically, as an *emotion*, then it makes sense to speak of degrees of trust, qualified trust, and so on. Because, as we know, speaking phenomenologically, the emotions are generally impure, imperfect. I take the view that our conceptualizing should accommodate, not eliminate, these phenomenological impurities.

undertakings, evidence of reliability, and other forms of guarantee. As Karen Jones puts it, "Roughly, to trust someone is to have an attitude of optimism about her good will and to have the confident expectation that, when the need arises, the one trusted will be directly and favorably moved by the thought that you are counting on her" (5–6). Less trusting analysts of trust, such as Bernard Williams, are apt to discern strong traces of "egoistic" motivation in trust behavior (13).

How might I respond to the finger-wagger? If he succeeds in extracting the desired promise from me, then, promises being what they are, I would do as I promise. I would refrain from writing about him. But it's possible to imagine a situation in which, having weighed all the circumstances, I might conclude that his threatening exhortation need not be binding on me. It could be, for instance, that I remained noncommittal in the face of his pressure; that I gave no undertaking, whether explicit or otherwise, not to write about him. Additionally, I might believe that my friend was in an anomalous state of mind when he applied that pressure, or in a situation that in some respect qualifies the assumptions and/or terms under which the injunction was made. I might say: "He'd just lost his youngest son and was 'not himself' at the time. In general he was a very open person—he'd even written a very self-revealing column for the Sunday papers—and wouldn't have minded being written about. But he died before he could withdraw his injunction, as I'm sure he would have done had he lived." In saying this I might be rationalizing the situation, but not necessarily. I could be entirely sincere, and indeed correct, in saying such a thing; and in reaching this conclusion I might be exercising a margin of discretion that often accompanies the bestowing of trust. If I really believed this, I might go ahead and publish something quite revealing about the deceased. In so doing, I'd be making a context-specific judgment that, all things considered, I was not breaching trust in an unacceptable way.

In most instances, of course, the finger is never wagged. My father had some slight reason to think that I might write about him one day: in 1976 I asked him to keep my letters so that I could refer to them in sorting out my relationship to my past and to Australia. He was probably in his usual agitated, well-meaning rush when he received the letter containing my request, and simply did as I had asked. Had he stopped to think about it (perhaps he did), it could have occurred to him that I might write about these matters someday; such a thought would have been consistent with the kind of person he took me to be. He knew enough about autobiography to know that parents generally figure prominently therein. He was also sensitive to the fact that he loomed large in my life, not least on account of his own difficulties.

But even if he had stopped to think about it, and wondered whether I might someday write about him, he could not have envisaged anything quite like the current memoir. My memoir is partly modeled on books that constitute a subgenre of life writing: books by sons about their fathers, but also about *their relationships with their fathers*. Such books attempt a sort of fusion of autobiography and biography. They are perhaps best termed *relational auto/biography*.[3] Unlike me, my father probably hadn't read examples of this subgenre, though he'd almost certainly have read John Stuart Mill's pained account of his relationship with his father in his *Autobiography*. It's also possible that he'd read Gosse's *Father and Son*, though I don't recall his ever mentioning it. All of this is to say that even if it occurred to my father that I might one day write autobiography, he would have seen little reason in terms of what might be called detailed *projective anticipations*, that is, detailed previsions of what such a life narrative by me might look like, to wag the finger at me. But common sense and his reading of Mill would have told him that, however well intended, books about family are bound to involve *some* degree of compromise of the sensibilities of others, some measure of *indecency*. Self-revelation just does entail revelations about others. The moral issue is where to draw the line.

Even if he had seen reason to wag the finger, I rather doubt that he would have done it. So deep was his desire to see me have a good life that, in principle at least, he'd have wanted to concede my right to write—and publish—if I felt that this would help bring the desired good life about. The notion that writing about one's life can improve it in this way was very familiar to him. He accepted it, and would almost certainly have accepted my judgment that such writing would help me. In spirit he'd probably have concurred with Annette Baier's contention that "parental and filial responsibility does not rest on deals, actual or virtual, between parent and child" ("Trust and Antitrust" 244). One would have to qualify this, however, by saying that my father's propensity to anxiety was so great that "deals," whether with me or anyone else, always had a certain appeal for him. Like many anxious people, he was risk-averse, and the appeal of deals lies in their apparent ability to minimize risk and uncertainty. To quote Baier again, "Trust and distrust are feelings, but like many feelings they are what Hume called 'impressions of reflexion,' feeling responses to how we take our situation to be" ("Trust" 111).

---

3. I discuss this issue at greater length in " 'Heddy and I': Relational Life-Writing in Susan Varga's *Heddy and Me*." On relational auto/biography, see also Eakin, esp. chap. 2.

In a case like this, the trust that obtains, and the ethical requirements that might follow from it, are of a rather implicit kind. There was what we call a relationship of trust between the two people concerned, and it would have been assumed, certainly by both parties to the relationship, and probably by a third party looking on, that the obligations associated with that trust would be ongoing in the event that either of those involved in that "relationship of trust" died. Given that my father was thirty-five years older than me, initial projections about what might happen in the event of a death would be based on the assumption that my father would predecease me. In the event that one of us died, it would seem that something that had been present in the relationship, something I call an *implicit trust provision*, could now kick in. The condition had—and has—something like the following force: "Neither of us will reveal anything in a given medium about the other when he is dead that he would not have wanted to have been revealed in that medium while he was alive." On the face of it, this would seem to be a pretty reasonable and widely applicable kind of implicit provision (but qualified by the sort of case involving the genocidal murderer's wife). And so in many instances it is. Many, but not all, because in fact it sometimes seems appropriate for someone to breach this kind of guideline. For instance, I may discover something posthumously about another person with whom I shared a relationship of trust that I think needs to be revealed because it's in the "public interest"; or I may feel, on reflection, that there has been something inappropriate about the relational environment in which my trust, and the expectation of loyalty to which it gave rise, took shape—something I didn't perceive at the time. Under such circumstances I may reasonably breach the implicit trust provision, though not, I would hope, without careful consideration.

In fact, we speak of people trusting one another, or some other, "implicitly." This notion seems to mean something like: "Whether I'm alive or dead, you know me well enough to judge whether, in a given but unspecified instance, I would want or not want something about me to be revealed in a certain medium." Not everyone who is so trusted is aware of the nature or extent of the trust vested in him; and not everyone who is aware of being the recipient of such trust would welcome it or act at its behest; but in general terms, and within reason, most of us would want to honor such trust, would want to be *loyal* to it. And I'd hope that others would take the same view of my sensitivities when I died. But that qualifier "within reason" requires further consideration. For a start, there is what Baier calls "the pathologies of trust" ("Trust" 117): some people confer trust in dysfunctional ways, and for dysfunctional reasons. We may feel that, for various reasons, we are not bound to be loyal to trust of this kind.

Now, consider the following case. If my best friend and I are both dog lovers, and have enjoyed many walks in the park with our dogs, it would be natural and unproblematic for my friend to trust—without having even to mention it—that, in the event of her death, and unless some dire exigency intervened, I would not allow her beloved dog to be put down. This is relatively straightforward because the parameters, so to speak, of trust are in this instance clearly continuous with the parameters of the relationship in which the trust obtained: the love of dogs has been part of the very currency of our relationship, indeed, one of the bases of our bond; and my friend knows that I love her dog. Moreover, there's a sense in which the notion that a dog might be put down after its owner's death is easily grasped in conceptual terms (though, for a dog lover, not in emotional terms). Certainly, a "doggy" person knows what it would mean, in pragmatic terms, to have a dog put down. So when such a person vests in me the implicit trust that I would not allow her dog to be put down if she died, there's little ambiguity about what it is she trusts me not to do.

But not all examples are this clear-cut. Even the simple example I've just given involves an element of what might be called *imaginative modeling*. In order to trust with respect to some issue, to trust in a "relativized" way, I need to have an imaginative picture of what that issue (say, putting a dog down) entails. The more generalized, nonspecific, the trust, the less this kind of modeling is involved. If I trust you, pure and simple, not to do the wrong thing by me when I'm dead, I'm not modeling any particular possibility when I vest that trust in you. What I'm conferring on you is a kind of *blanket trust* that would apply to all situations, whether conceivable to me or not. Although she does not concede the possibility of trust that is wholly free of domain specification, Baier sees this discretionary function as integral to trust: "*For to trust is to give discretionary powers to the trusted, to let the trusted decide how, on a given matter, one's welfare is best advanced*" ("Trust" 117). Precisely because it can be vested without modeling particular situations to which it might apply, blanket trust is a complicated matter. What sense does it make to say, "I trust Jim not to do *anything* that I would not want done when I'm dead, and this includes possibilities that would never even cross my mind?" What it means, I suppose, it that I've got such trust in Jim—in the sort of moral and deliberative being he is—that I'm happy to leave it to his judgment to determine what would be okay, and what would not be, if I died. In Jones's terms, I'd be "optimistic" about his "good will" toward me and his "competence" to enact that good will in appropriate ways (7). I trust not only in his loyalty but in his discernment as well, his fitness to operate as a sort of proxy for me, even in situations I could not have foreseen. In many cases this kind of trust would be fine: if your moral estimate of the trusted person is right, and if bizarre contingencies don't intrude, you'll probably be okay.

But this situation puts an enormous onus on Jim, at least potentially. Deciding about the deceased dog owner isn't so hard (for reasons I've already stated); but what about deciding on situations that were way beyond the imaginative purview of the deceased? One such situation might be the prospect of life writing that involves him or her. Here Jim would have to act on the basis of what Williams calls "non-egoistic micro-motivations" (13), that is, context-sensitive under-standings of and intuitions about the particular individual in question. Suppose for a moment that the deceased didn't like reading, wasn't reflective, and didn't ponder issues pertaining to privacy. He was a fairly private person, but would never have modeled a situation in which aspects of his life might be put on record. Indeed, he'd have had little sense of what this might involve. For instance, because he'd never read a sophisticated biography, and had never seen probing discussion of such texts, he'd have had no idea who might read a probing book about him, and with what effects on perceptions of him and his life. Jim, who for present purposes can now become a biographer, has to figure out how someone who never thought about biography would feel about becoming a posthumous biographical subject. On the one hand, he may think that he can guess with some confidence. On the other hand, he may not. An instance of the sort of complication that might nag at Jim is this: "Yes, my subject was very private, and this might suggest that he wouldn't have wanted his life story published; but he was also one of those people who never really adjusted to the anonymity that characterizes most lives, and would have given a lot to be widely remembered. If it came to a decision, would he have pre-ferred to be revealed and remembered, or concealed and forgotten?" It might be hard to say.

So, it's one thing to be loyal to what I'll term *relativized trust* (you won't allow my dog to be put down), another to be loyal to blanket trust. Note, too, that precisely because blanket trust puts so much onus on the person in whom the trust is vested, it carries a risk that relativized trust is less likely to involve: the risk that the trusted person will feel put-upon, subject to a kind of moral or pragmatic presumption, even coercion.

As I've shown, my father was an intellectually sophisticated man who was quite well versed in biography and would have been sensi-tive to the ethical issues it raises. Indeed, he'd tried his hand at a reveal-

ing form of family narrative in his own auto/biographical fragments
about his father-in-law, Roy Isles. So, while he never wagged the finger
at me and said, "Don't write about me," and though he couldn't have
entertained a detailed anticipatory projection of what my auto/biogra-
phical narrative would look like, he'd have had an informed general
sense of the sorts of revelations that tend to occur in post-Freudian
autobiographical and biographical narrative. He'd have realized that
our interpersonal modes of trust are heavily shaped by cultural factors:
a pre-Freudian society might regard intimate sexual revelations about
a biographical subject as a breach of trust, while a post-Freudian
one might regard such disclosures as morally unexceptionable. To that
extent, I think I can imaginatively model the way he might have imaginatively modeled a situation in which I was to write a memoir about
him of the kind I have in fact written. Moreover, because I knew him
so well, I'd have a fair sense of what issues would have most exercised
him if such a memoir were in prospect.

As I've tried to show, there was a profound relationship of trust
between my father and myself. (I speak here of moral trust: because
his tendencies to high anxiety and irrational caution caused him to
make a series of bad life decisions, I had limited trust in many of his
judgments about pragmatic matters.) I'd say that, even allowing for the
impingement of his anxieties, for him this trust was of both the *relativized* and the *blanket* kind. There were particular things he could
model and reckon—that is, trust—I would not do; but he would also
have trusted me to use what he saw as my considerable powers of
judgment were a situation to arise that he could not have foreseen
(for whatever reason). Let me qualify this by saying that he trusted
in what might be termed my powers of *decency-informed judgment*,
because the implicit trust in question was based on the assumption
that I would act in accordance with the ethos of decency to which he
subscribed, and which he believed we shared. He trusted, that is, in
my *trustworthiness*. So he would have trusted me to act *in a certain
spirit* in situations that required complex ethical decisions, even
where he could not predict what precisely those situations would be.
This suggests that trust and decency can be quite intimately linked,
as when Annette Baier urges that we need to assess whether a given
instance of trust "is sensible and morally decent" ("Trust and
Antitrust" 240).

Here some further complications enter the picture. First, with
respect to decency, I hope that the foregoing narrative makes plain my
respect for Paul Freadman's fundamental decency as a human being,
and my respect for the ethos of decency more generally. It will be clear,
however, that I don't therefore endorse that ethos, or indeed my

father's version of it, unconditionally, in all particulars. One of my reservations about it is, precisely, that it needlessly, and at times harmfully, conflates the notion of decency with the notion of privacy: it seems to suggest that to reveal one's inner self is to do something *indecent*. My skepticism about this conflation arises, in part at least, from what I saw of my father's life. I think that life would have been more satisfying, less disappointing, to him had he been less guarded, better able to reveal and pursue his inner needs. Second, it's sometimes the case that those who bestow blanket trust actually set in train a kind of circularity that takes the moral anguish out of what might otherwise be vexed situations. In order to bestow such trust, people have, often at a quite subliminal level, made the assessment that "Jill is utterly trustworthy." Having done so, they're inclined to trust Jill unreservedly. If Jill does something that unsettles their trust, they may be troubled for a while but resolve the matter by saying: "She's entirely trustworthy, so I must be wrong to see what she did as morally dubious. If it were morally dubious, she wouldn't have done it." This leaves open the possibility that Jill could in fact have breached trust in a dubious way, but without the person whose trust is in question acknowledging that she had done so. In this direction lie complex issues about the perspective from which acts-in-trust-contexts are assessed. In this essay I'm not just reviewing the sort of trust my father had in me; I'm also reviewing, even monitoring, my own trustworthiness. I'm asking whether I'm a fit—a decent—recipient of his trust, and how I would need to act in order to be such a recipient. This suggests that I don't wholly trust myself, and in this, as in so many other ways, I am my father's son. But it also confirms Baier's claim that "we need a morality to guide us" in such matters. Whether I trust myself or not, these issues are too complex for simple, unchecked, intuitive "gut" resolution.

Because it probably never occurred to my father that I would publish this sort of auto/biographical book about him and me, I have to try to figure out how he as a man with a fairly informed understanding of life writing modes in general would have felt if I'd proposed to him that I publish such a book. If I can do this, at least to my satisfaction, then I have some idea of what kinds of *trust parameters* (as I'll call them) on his part I should be loyal to. Note here that the loyalty (or lack thereof) in question is of at least two kinds. First, there is loyalty to a moral ideal—loyalty itself—a feature that Josiah Royce in his renowned study *The Philosophy of Loyalty* sees as central to ethical conduct (60). Second, there is loyalty to an individual: my father. And there is this further dimension: he was himself an intensely loyal man, and my own commitment, such as it is, to the virtue of loyalty is something I learned in large part from him. This is part of the story of father and son I've tried to narrate in the book. To breach his trust in a disloyal way would be to subvert the fine moral legacy, as well as to betray his trust. It's notable, however, that my sense of loyalty to my father has much more to do with the kind of person I take him to have been than to the fact that he occupied the position of Father. In other words, there is little in me of earlier conceptions of loyalty that link it closely to matters of position or social standing, as in the pre-Enlightenment idea of the "loyal subject," nor of the traditional Jewish precept "Honor thy father." Perhaps I am one of those sons foreseen by Rabbi Eliezer who are not "abashed before their fathers." The English word *loyalty* derives from the French *loi*, meaning something like "legality," or what is warranted by existing social provisions. Modern loyalty is more democratic, more rooted in individual judgment. Someone like me believes that, in large part, I can and should choose the persons and values to which I will be loyal. Of course, the fact that someone may trust me is likely to influence my choice, as are a range of other, often emotional factors.

The sort of loyalty—call it *blind loyalty*—that holds regardless of context can, as we know, be dangerous: we want a concentration camp guard who suddenly sees what Nazism is really about to forget his loyalty to Hitler and help inmates escape. This again is an extreme example, but it makes a point that can have more nuanced application. The fact is that, as we have seen, trust and loyalty assessments can be very hard to make. Aristotle, perhaps still the greatest authority on practical ethical conduct, says: "Matters concerned with conduct and questions of what is good for us have no fixity, any more than matters of health. The general account being of this nature, the account of particular cases is yet more lacking in exactness; for they do not fall under any art or set of precepts, but the agents themselves must in each case consider what is appropriate to the occasion, as happens also in the art of medicine or navigation" (1754). In other words, "general rules" can provide provisional guidance, but one can't just "read off" a rule and fully grasp a particular moral situation. The specifics, the "micro-motivations," of that situation have to be gone into. Let me now take this process a step further and try to model a situation that might assist with my ethical dilemma: Should I or should I not publish this manuscript?

■

Let's suppose that my father came back to life for a day and that this gave me the opportunity to talk with him about the as yet unpublished manuscript of *Shadow of Doubt*. Forgetting for the moment about other circumstantial details, I'll set us down in an environment we used to enjoy together. I'll say that we've come to the MCG (Melbourne Cricket Ground) to watch a one-day cricket international. The game starts at 2.30 P.M. We've arrived at 11.30 A.M. in order to get a good seat—looking right down the wicket, so that we can see what the ball is "doing" in the air and off the pitch—and to leave time for a long liquid lunch in one of the dining rooms in the Members' Stand. Putting our bags and cushions on the seats in the stand to keep our places, we adjourn to the dining room and sit down with salmon bagels and one of Paul's favorite reds. A couple of sips in, I start putting the cards on the table.

"Look, I've got something complex I want to put to you, and I'd rather do it now, before the red takes too much of a hold."

"Okay. Fire away."

"Well, I've written a book about you, really about you and me, and I want your blessing to publish it."

"About *me!* You'd better buy an A4 envelope, because you won't fit my deeds on the back of anything smaller! What's there to say?"

"More than you think, which is one of the reasons I want to write it. You lived a more significant life than you ever gave yourself credit for, and I'd like to put that on record."

"*Really?* How so?"

"Well, you started a bit behind the eight ball because the family business was poleaxed by the depression; yet you went on to get a first in politics and history, writing a very strong thesis, which I've read, and then made a series of very good contributions: at the ABC [Australian Broadcasting Commission], Gas and Fuel [the Gas and Fuel Corporation], CAE [the Council of Adult Education], the College [the Australian Administrative Staff College], not to mention charitable activities and kindly dealings with various individuals."

"It's nice of you to say so, son, but, really, it wasn't that much. I mean, compared to Zelman [his best friend and former governor general of Australia] . . ."

"Bugger Zelman! How many people have a career like that? It's really not the issue. Let's stay with you."

"Okay, let's. Back to my brilliant career!"

"You know what I'm saying is more complicated than that. And I don't want to give you the impression that I'm writing a flower arrangement. The manuscript is warts 'n' all, and you did have the odd wart or three."

"I had so many warts you could hardly see the rest of me! But which ones in particular do you reveal?"

"Well, some fairly confronting ones, to be honest. Your bad career decisions, your breakdowns, depressions, anxieties, even your Alzheimer's."

"Oh, *fair go, son!* That's not on. Sorry, but that's way over the odds! I can't possibly agree to that."

He's looking drained and anxious, the fingers of his right hand gripping the stem of his wine glass hard. He's stopped drinking for the moment.

"Okay. I didn't expect you to jump for joy, any more than I would in your shoes. But it's a more complex issue than it seems at first. Please hear me out."

Raising his eyebrows he nods dubious permission for me to continue.

"What I really want to do is take an overall view of your life. That means looking at its various facets, and also at how it sits in its context. You know, yourself as a pre- and post-Holocaust Melbourne Jew of a generation of Australian men who lived through the depression, went to war, and were raised on a sort of ethos of decency."

"Well, I was certainly raised to be decent. The word was constantly on my parents' lips. That's true."

"I put a fair bit of weight on the Jewish aspect. I mean, [his father] Henry's family were religious; you and your generation assimilated but still identified with Jewishness. Then there was the Holocaust. But I also put weight on the traditional Jewish notion that what really matters is the ethical quality of the earthly life one lives. There you stand out: you lived with great integrity, and I've interviewed a lot of people who have been only too pleased to put their appreciation of your loyalty and kindness to them on record. And there were lots of others, dead now, who said similar things to me and [my mother] Fleur. You were a kind guy, and most people who knew you valued you very highly."

"Go on—I'm warming to this!" He refills his glass.

"With pleasure. The book shows that you were a highly talented, even charismatic young man before the war. But it also shows that after the war you made some lousy decisions and lost a fair bit of confidence. One result was that you didn't achieve what you might have done in print. That's a pity, and it's surprising because I've found an offprint of a good academic article you published around 1950. More to the point, I've found some really good unpublished stuff in your files and I've quoted them at length in the book."

"Really? Such as?"

"Well, there's some excellent material in your honors thesis, including really prescient passages about Australia's resistance to constitutional change. Some equally good stuff in your ABC research material about the role of the national broadcaster in Australian public life. Hard-hitting and persuasive analyses in many of those Radio Australia scripts, in occasional pamphlets, and so on. Throw in the fact that you were a fine teacher and strong on academic policy making and a visionary when it came to Australia's place in the [Southeast Asian] region, and you have a pretty fair record as what I've called a public intellectual."

"That's nice to hear."

"Yep, and there's more. But first I have to tell you that you were a shithouse poet. Lisa Brodribb [a woman he dated as a young man] gave me a couple of poems you wrote to her during the war. They were unremarkable, I can tell you, even by the standard of what gets done in bunks by navigators after long bombing missions."

"God! I'd forgotten I ever wrote poetry!"

"But you also wrote autobiography. Those fragments you wrote about meeting Fleur, and then about [Fleur's father] Roy. They are *really* good. I'm not having you on. I was thrilled when I found them in your files, because they confirmed something I always believed and told you—that you were an exceptionally good prose writer."

"*Really!* But I never finished those things. No one ever saw them. Not even Fleur. What's good about them?"

"I surmise in the book that you lacked the confidence to finish them."

"True."

"What's good about them is, well, several things. The actual writing style is firm but subtle and supple. Something about the sentence rhythms, the phrasing. The prose is poised, deft, but it can go deep, can achieve real power. And you get beautifully the quizzical quality of looking back on one's earlier self: the sense that the person back there is, yet is not, me; that those events are long-past but still strangely present. It's got a kind of burnished, slightly estranged quality that you often find in really good autobiographical writing."

"Gosh. You mean it might have been publishable?"

"It needs a bit of work, and a lot of filling out so that the fragments add up to something a bit more substantial. But if you'd done that, I'm sure you could have published the stuff. I've seen much lesser material in print. I like the idea of putting them in print now, even in their preliminary form."

He's warming to the idea now; but still he worries.

"This sounds tempting, but it's all very well. . . . What about the Alzheimer's and the breakdowns? That's something else altogether. Is *nothing* private?! It's obscene, it's indecent, to show people at their lowest ebb like that."

"I know what you're saying, but traditionally life writers have tended to reveal more than the mores of their time would approve of. And nowadays there's nothing unusual about writing about someone with, say, Alzheimer's. John Bayley has written three books dealing with Iris Murdoch's decline and death from it."

"You mean the guy who was so kind to you at Oxford?"

"Yup."

"How did people react to his writing about his wife in that state?"

"There were a few hostile reviews, but on the whole people found it moving and morally appropriate. They assumed that Bayley would know what was consistent with the sort of trust he and his wife shared, and they welcomed what he had to tell about the experience of the disease and caring for a loved one who has it. I guess, also, that many people would realize that when Alzheimer's takes hold, it carries the victims away long before they die. At one point you asked me whose son I was. The moment was shocking, for all sorts of reasons. But one of them was that it hit me like a train that the Paul we'd known all those years was no longer with us."

"*Jesus!* What about the breakdowns?"

"Same thing, really. Donald Horne writes about his father being confined to a mental hospital after a breakdown and what a changed man he was as a result. The philosopher Raimond Gaita also writes about his father having a breakdown. Both of these fathers were in worse shape than you. Then there's an American called Larry Lockridge whose father was a successful novelist but committed suicide. You can imagine the kind of probing he goes in for, trying to figure out why the man killed himself."

"As usual, you've got an answer for everything, haven't you! What about my cancer?"

"There's a whole genre now called 'pathography'—writing about death and dying. There must be hundreds of such books. One of the ones that influenced what I've written about you and me is by Philip Roth. It's called *Patrimony*. His father dies from a brain tumor. Roth tracks the illness, but also changes that happen in their relationship because of it. Turns out that the 'patrimony' Roth comes to value most isn't material. It's cleaning up shit."

"*What!!!!*"

"Late on in his illness, his father beshats himself and Roth cleans up the toilet area. Nothing's left to the imagination. His point is that this is what it means to have your place in the generations. Not the patrimonial savings and share portfolio, but acknowledging the 'dust to dust' life we pass on and receive. Not shirking that, or being too uptight about opening up to the messy tragedy of things. It's actually a beautiful book."

"Christ! Is there anything like that in your book?"

"No, but there's some pretty rugged stuff. I describe the way you went downhill, physically, psychologically, confidence-wise."

"And what about things that might hurt family? Do you say why I had that breakdown in 1968?"

"No. I say that you told me the cause, but I don't say what it was."

"And the family rifts, problems in the marriage, that kind of thing?"

"Not a word about the rifts you've got in mind. I say as little as I can about the marriage, but it's impossible to write your life, and our relationship, without acknowledging that the marriage had its tensions—especially around child rearing. But I also make clear that you and Fleur had a very deep bond."

"We did. So you don't write harshly about Fleur, because you could be terribly hard on her?"

"No, the portrait of Fleur, like the portrait of you, is basically affectionate and admiring, though I do say that her volatility was problematical and that she lacked common sense."

"And you've talked to her about the book?"

"Yes, I interviewed her and spoke to her all along and gave her the manuscript to read. There are things she disputes and things she doesn't welcome, but nothing too major. Basically she's okay about it."

We're about talked out for the moment. The cricket is due to start in a quarter of an hour. The TV monitor in the dining room posts the teams in batting order. Australia is to bat first. I tell Paul that I'm really pleased because I want him to see Damien Martyn, who's to bat at 4, play sooner rather than later.

"He's the most cultured Aussie bat since Mark Waugh came into the team. Clean and balanced through the leg side; and he plays that late cut that Bradman [the greatest Australian batsman] scored so many runs from. And his driving through the off side—it's magnificent."

"Good. Let's hope he gets runs. Let me think about the book business for a while."

"Okay."

■

We take our seats in the stand and, behold, Martyn obliges with a cultured hundred.[4] Since I'm in charge of this narrative, I can see to it that

---

4. Good batsmen can score one hundred or more runs in an innings.

a shot Martyn played in the summer of 2002 against New Zealand at the MCG is replayed before my father's eyes. It's a square drive, the specialty of great West Indian players like Sobers, Fredericks, Richardson, and Lara. But whereas they played it with a high sweeping flourish of the bat and a wicked late flick of the wrists, Martyn's all smooth economy of movement as he eases into the creamy shot and glides the ball to the distant point boundary.[5] It's beautiful to watch, and we're cooking with gas now. We're having fun.

The Australian innings ends and I get sandwiches, thermos, and a Coke bottle, the contents spiked with rum, out of my bag. We've got an hour before the next innings.

Paul says, "Getting back to this here book of yours—what's in it for you?"

"Well, I guess a lot of things; a strange mixture. Part of it is to pay a kind of tribute to you. To say that even though you were disappointed in yourself, there was a lot to like about you and what you did with your life and that you gave me a lot as your son."

"I know you mean that, and I appreciate it."

"I guess, too, that part of me wanted to spare you the indignity of oblivion. I mean, it seems insane, indecent, an utter scandal, the way we pour ourselves into our lives, the way we strive to flourish, to make a difference, leave a mark—and then it's all over. For a generation or two we're a few faded snaps in a family album, the odd reference in a library catalogue. Then we just vanish."

"Don't I know it! It stings like buggery."

"You were too good a bloke for that. I wanted more for you—and I guess for me."

"I'm very touched."

"Well, good; but another part is more selfish. Being your son has been, shall we say, a challenge. The book's called *Shadow of Doubt: My Father and Myself*. The shadow refers mainly to the self-doubt that haunted you. Being the son of a self-doubter isn't all roses. The shadow falls on the son as well. The book helps me feel more resolved about the pain in your life, some of which got passed on to me. If you say that everyone has a core story to tell, a story that lies at the heart of all the stories they're capable of telling, then maybe my relationship with you is my core story. Get that out into public view and I feel better. It's as if you find your voice in telling your core story, and find you're yourself in finding your voice. And of course, I've got your need for success, your drive to do things and be respected for them."

5. For the ball to reach the point boundary, the batsman, stepping out toward the oncoming ball, must redirect it at an angle of about ninety degrees. If he is right-handed, the ball will travel to his right, and the contrary for a left-hander.

"So ambition comes into it?"

"No question. I've read enough life writing to know that there's a compelling narrative in your life and in our relationship, and I don't want to pass up the opportunity. I want to make a good book of it and be admired for having done so. So it's an impure tribute I'm paying you."

"Life's impure."

"Yup."

"And what about your career? What effect would publishing the book have on your reputation? What if the sort of people who criticize John Bayley get stuck into you?"

"Too bad. I'm fifty, and at some point you've got to do what you feel you need to do, and to hell with the consequences. And anyway, I think there'll be plenty of people who'll feel that they can learn something of real use from the story."

"Such as?"

"Well, things about how attitudes to manliness in Australia affect particular people, and how they get passed down. About relationships between Australian fathers and their sons. About ambition, choice making, depression, anxiety, the impact of the Holocaust, Australian Jewish life, decency. Even about the impact of Alzheimer's."

"I'm not sure that I want to be Exhibit A, but it would be nice to help, if only by negative example."

"You know that right in the middle of this I'm saying that your example was positive in crucial ways. That's why it's a tribute. An affectionate, albeit warts 'n' all, tribute."

"So where do we go from here?"

"Well, what say I give you the manuscript to read. I don't promise to be bound by what you decide, but obviously I'll take whatever you say very seriously."

"Done—like a dinner."

And South Africa come out to bat.

What would my father have decided once he'd heard me read the manuscript? The short answer is that I don't know for sure. But I'm pretty confident that there wouldn't have been a categorical no, and to that extent I don't think he'd have felt betrayed by me. He would have regretted some of what's in the book, and perhaps felt let down by, even temporarily angry at me on that score; but he'd have welcomed other parts of the narrative. I don't think there'd have been a long-term change in his basic feelings toward me, not even in his trust. I think that he'd admire the complexity of the undertaking, and would understand that it involved some inevitable infringement of the privacy of others. I feel that he'd appreciate the trouble I'd taken to research and bring him back to life in print, and that he'd like the idea of being remembered via the book. After all, one of his great regrets was that he hadn't been better known. That feeling often links to a fear of vanishing from memory. I'd guess that he had this in good measure, as many do.

Of course, this piece of fictive modeling is so deeply artificial that the procedure itself raises all sorts of questions. Some of these, however, shed interesting light on the core problems I'm discussing. Thus, you might ask, which Paul Freadman are you at the cricket with? It proves to be an intriguing question. If it was the Paul of, say, 1960, a man who, despite knocking back a great career opportunity (a scholarship to Harvard), still seems to have been fairly resilient and open to new possibilities, he might look quite favorably on the idea I was putting to him. But it can't be him, because I was only nine at the time and we didn't have the adult relationship of trust that provides the framework for this set of ethical reflections. In order to reconstruct that framework, we need to move forward to, say, 1980, at which point I'm twenty-nine and he's sixty-four. By this stage he's shared a good deal of his anguish with me, and the inversion in the relationship whereby I become the senior partner, so to speak, has basically occurred. But by this time he's become a profoundly cautious, anxious, depressed man. His judgment about a range of things suffers. Should I then feel bound by his judgment about what should or should not be revealed in the life narrative I write? I find that a very difficult question to answer. Clearly, his feelings matter deeply, but I'm not sure that, provided the book I write withholds the most sensitive things and reads as a genuine, if qualified, tribute, I should decline to publish simply on account of doubts he might have had when he was depressed.

In a variety of ways he delegated a lot of discretionary responsibility to me—responsibility to make appropriate decisions in respect to him and his well-being. So it's consistent with the terms of the later relationship he did much to bring into being that I should see fit to exercise my judgment in deciding whether or not to publish this book. Here again, though, his depression and anxiety must be taken into account. Highly anxious people find it hard to bestow blanket or blind trust. It leaves them vulnerable to too much uncertainty. While my father's depression and anxiety made him increasingly dependent on me, and disposed to trust me, his state must in some instances have compromised his capacity to trust unconditionally. There were signs that this was so, particularly in respect to "hot" issues like money: for instance, his anxiety about when I would repay a $5,000 loan he and

Fleur gave Diane and myself as a wedding present. His state, then, might at times cause him to doubt my trustworthiness; but, here again, I need to make a hardheaded assessment of these doubts. If I'm satisfied that they were irrational, I'm entitled to set them aside—but only after I've made the most hardheaded assessment of my own motives I can.

The decision whether to publish or not is hard in part because loyalty doesn't pertain only to others, or to ideals and so on. We speak so often of being "loyal to myself" that there must be something in the notion of loyalty to self. "Unto thine own self be true . . ." But what does it mean? It seems to spring from the fact that, day in and day out, sometimes consciously, sometimes not, we in effect *profile ourselves to ourselves*. We carry around a narrative account of "who we are," and we rerun, amend, and otherwise attend to this narrative continually. This *self-image*, as I'll call it, includes aspects of moral self-imagining, and some of what I think about myself as a moral being may take precedence, may be ascribed higher value, in my self-image than my desires, wishes, and so on. In this sense it can be an image not just of self but of *my best self*. Of this self I have a high(er) moral valuation, and the notion of truth—or loyalty—to self seems to make maximal sense when applied to the self understood in this way, that is, as loyalty to my best self. It may even make sense to bring trust in here. We all know ourselves to have "egoistic" wishes, desires, and so on, which are not morally laudable; but to have a certain kind of *moral trust in self* would mean being confident that I'd act in accordance with my best, not my morally dubious "lower," self. This would be to see myself as fundamentally trustworthy.

How might my need to publish this book look in the light of these considerations? The "need" alone doesn't seem sufficient to justify publication. There has to be the additional feeling that the book that was published as a consequence of this need was acceptable, that its inevitable traces of indecency aren't gratuitous with respect to my father's and my own moral entitlements in the situation. To honor what I took to be my father's moral entitlements would also involve being true, loyal, to my self—that is, to my best self. The notion of "best self," however, isn't just static. It refers not simply to the self I may have attained now but to the self I may become. It is something I have still to uncover, perhaps bring about through processes of exploration, further experience, and so on. This book about my father and myself is in part a narrative of exploration, an attempt to give the fullest—and the most morally consequential—answer to the question Who am I? My father would certainly have understood and endorsed such a search. He'd also have recognized that such a quest changes the person who embarks on it, and that, provided it's undertaken with integrity, chances are that the changes will be for the best.

So I think I can justifiably cite "loyalty to self" as one source of justification for publishing this book. But that wouldn't suffice if loyalty to my father were clearly being set aside. I need to ask again: Which father is it that I aim to be loyal to? I emphasized shifts in his mood during the cricket sequence because my father was a moody man. If Damien Martyn played that square drive, and if Paul had a bottle of red in him, if there were ninety thousand people at the "G" on a lovely Melbourne summer's afternoon—he might agree to something that he'd see as unacceptable if he were doing his taxes on a messy desk with winter rain pelting at the windows. In trying to figure out what "he" would really have wished in respect of this book, I find myself having recourse to a sense of him that is, as it were, *distilled*, from many moments, phases, facets of an extremely complex human being. The trust to which I want to be loyal (without prejudice, if possible, to my own needs) is in this sense a curious, in some ways heterogeneous, thing. It's trust that I'd want him to have vested in me when he was in really good shape. Why? Because then I feel reassured that he really "knew what he was doing" when he reposed that trust in me. It would then follow that I could, as it were, trust in the trust, and this would help me sort out what my loyalty to him should look like. But in fact by the time he reposed really extensive, responsibility-delegating trust in me, he was well past his best and often not thinking clearly. In this sense, there are at least two trusting fathers present here: the one who could have made astute trust choices but didn't need to because he was still largely in command of his own life; and the man who was no longer in command of his own life and therefore needed to make trust choices but wasn't in good enough condition to do so.

In fact, these Pauls are just two among many down the years and through the spectrum of his moods. It seems that what I have to do is to sort out what *his best self* would have felt about my publishing this book. The father I ask permission of, then, has the confidence and daring of youth, the middle-aged man's balanced perspective on his young adult son's needs, and the old (pre-Alzheimer's) man's wisdom of hindsight. In truth, there never was such a man; yet the distillation I have fashioned here doesn't seem wholly fictitious. Much of what we "know" of others, be they alive or dead, is a distillation of something like this.

I'd like to think that in putting many facets of my father on record, as I have done here, I have brought a fine man back to life for the contemplation of others. In the end, I have to leave it to the reader of the book to decide where, if anywhere, the essential Paul Freadman resides, and what he would have felt about this book. I hope I haven't subjected a profoundly decent man to unreasonable narrative indecency. I hope I have done the right thing in publishing this auto/biography. I *think* I probably have.

> He was a man, take him for all in all,
> I shall not look upon his like again.[6]

WORKS CITED

Ackerley, J. A. *My Father and Myself.* New York: Poseidon, 1968.
Aristotle. *Nicomachean Ethics* 3.1104a5–9. In *The Complete Works of Aristotle.* Ed. Jonathan Barnes. 2 vols. Princeton: Princeton University Press, 1984.
Baier, Annette. "Trust." Tanner Lectures on Human Value, no. 13. Ed. Grethe B. Peterson. Salt Lake City: University of Utah Press, 1992. 109–74.
——. "Trust and Antitrust." *Ethics* 96, no. 2 (January 1986): 231–60.
Bayley, John. *Iris: A Memoir of Iris Murdoch.* London: Duckworth, 1998.
Becker, Lawrence C. "Trust as Noncognitive Security about Motives." "Symposium on Trust." *Ethics* 107, no. 1 (October 1996): 43–61.
Eakin, Paul John. *How Our Lives Become Stories: Making Selves.* Ithaca: Cornell University Press, 1999.
Freadman, Richard. "'Heddy and I': Relational Life-Writing in Susan Varga's *Heddy and Me.*" *Australian Book Review* (February 2002): 20–23.
——. *Shadow of Doubt: My Father and Myself.* Melbourne: Bystander, 2003.
——. *Threads of Life: Autobiography and the Will.* Chicago: University of Chicago Press, 2001.
Gaita, Rai. *Romulus, My Father.* Melbourne: Text, 1998.
Gosse, Edmund. *Father and Son: A Study of Two Temperaments.* Harmondsworth: Penguin, 1983.
Govier, Trudy. "Trust, Distrust, and Feminist Theory." *Hypatia* 7, no. 1 (winter 1992): 17–33.
Himmelfarb, Gertrude. "A Man's Own Household His Enemies." *Commentary* 108, no. 1 (July–August 1997): 34–38.
Horne, Donald. *The Education of Young Donald.* Melbourne: Penguin, 1975.
Jones, Karen. "Trust as an Affective Attitude." "Symposium on Trust." *Ethics* 107, no. 1 (October 1996): 4–25.
Lockridge, Larry. *Shade of the Raintree: The Life and Death of Ross Lockridge Jr.* New York: Viking, 1994.
Mill, John Stuart. *Autobiography.* Oxford: Oxford University Press, 1971.
Offit, Sidney. *Memoir of the Bookie's Son.* New York: St. Martin's Griffin, 1995.
Roth, Philip. *Patrimony: A True Story.* London: Vintage, 1991.
Royce, Josiah. *The Philosophy of Loyalty.* Nashville: Vanderbilt University Press, 1995.

6. *Hamlet* 1.2.87.

Spiegleman, Art. *Maus I and II*. New York: Random House, 1993.

Trilling, James. "My Father and the Weak-Eyed Devils." *American Scholar* (spring 1999): 17–41.

Williams, Bernard. "Trust Considered: Formal Structures and Social Reality." In *Trust: Making and Breaking Cooperative Relations*. Ed. Diego Gambetta. New York: Blackwell, 1988. 3–13.

Wolff, Geoffrey. *The Duke of Deception: Memories of My Father*. London: Vintage, 1990.

CHAPTER 7

The Ethics of Betrayal: Diary of a Memoirist

Nancy K. Miller

July 14, 2002

In the opening pages of her autobiography, George Sand complained about Rousseau, "Who can forgive him for having confessed Mme de Warens while confessing himself?" It was hard for Sand to blame Rousseau because she was otherwise a huge fan of his *Confessions*. But as every autobiographer knows, you can't tell your own story, especially your love life, as though it were a solo event. George Sand, of course, did her own share of confessing others, which was something of a tradition among nineteenth-century French novelists. Not that she saw her autobiography as a novel. Just the opposite, in fact. Which was her point about the ethics involved. Autobiography is a form that comes with responsibilities; just as our lives exist in human solidarity, all of us inextricably "bound up with one another," so too, Sand believed, does the genre (1:13).

July 20, 2002

The end of Mme de Warens's story, which details her lovers and her "unlimited extravagance" (198), coincides with the end of the first six books (the first part) of *Les Confessions*, as Rousseau brings the curtain down on his revelations with an uncharacteristic salute to future discretion: "Such were the errors and faults of my youth. I have related the story of them with a fidelity that brings pleasure to my heart. If, in later years, I have amassed any virtues to grace my maturity, I should have declared them with equal frankness, for such was my purpose. But I must stop here. Time may lift many veils; and if my memory descends to posterity perhaps one day it will learn what there was in me to say. Then it will be understood why I am silent" (257). More typically, Rousseau, the bad-boy precursor whom French women writers both shun and admire, sets no limits on revelation: "I have only one thing to fear in this enterprise; not that I may say too much or tell untruths, but that I may not tell everything and may conceal the truth" (170). But even with tell-all Rousseau, it seems, there is telling and telling. Not to say *enough* may betray as much as saying too much.

August 10, 2002

Philippe Lejeune has somewhere made the claim that all theorists of autobiography are closet, or at least crypto-, autobiographers. In this he generalizes from himself (a familiar autobiographical principle: me too!). Explaining his obsession with autobiography in his witty essay "The Autobiographical Pact (bis)," Lejeune declares: "The aberrant form that my idolatry has assumed is the desire to write. I chose to work, academically, *on* autobiography, because in a parallel direction I wanted to work *on* my own autobiography" (132). Although I can't quite say that, like Lejeune, in working academically *on* autobiography I knew that I wanted to work on my *own* autobiography, it's certainly true that the more I worked on autobiography as a critic, the more I was tempted to write one. But I could only go there step by step (like the heroine of an eighteenth-century novel about to lose her virtue), never fully realizing where I was going. In hints. In fragments. In the margins of criticism.

August 24, 2002

Like George Sand, Simone de Beauvoir marked off her difference from Rousseau's confessional model when she undertook her vast autobiographical project. In the preface to *The Prime of Life*, the second volume of her memoirs, for instance, Beauvoir confronts both the inevitability of telling other people's stories in sorting out the meaning of a life and her personal resistance to telling certain ones.

It may be objected that such an inquiry concerns no one but myself. Not so; if any individual—a Pepys or a Rousseau, an exceptional or a run-of-the-mill character—reveals himself honestly, everyone, more or less, becomes involved. It is impossible for him to shed light on his own life without at some point illuminating the lives of others. . . .

I described my childhood and my adolescence without any omissions. . . . I cannot treat the years of my maturity in the same detached way—nor do I enjoy a similar freedom when discussing them. I have no intention of filling these pages with spiteful gossip about myself and my friends; I lack the instincts of a scandalmonger. There are many things which I firmly intend to leave in obscurity. (10)

Until well into the second half of the twentieth century, French women writers continued to demonstrate a Beauvoir-like reticence about revealing the details of their private adult lives—and for the most part, like Colette, blurred the boundaries between autobiography and fiction. That discretion has been shattered by Catherine Millet's best-selling erotic confession *The Sexual Life of Catherine M.*[1] But why should we assume that the truth of sex—if it *is* the truth—might not still leave "many things . . . in obscurity" (could the initial M. signal an eighteenth-century veil of decency)?

September 2, 2002

As a theorist of autobiography I was always kind of a literalist. Naïve, even. I took the "autobiographical pact" seriously, to the letter.[2] I believed that autobiographers could and should reach unequivocally for the verifiable truth that corresponded to the events they signed their names to; that strategies of fictionalization were antithetical to autobiography. When I began my memoir, I still believed in telling a true story, but I also began to realize that there were gaps that could be filled in only by leaps of the imagination, and scenes that I could recreate through dialogues that were anything but verifiable. I could write down what I remembered; or I could craft a memoir. One *might* be the truth; the other, a good story. I'm not saying that these

1. Asked about her relationship to the libertine model in a *New York Times* interview, Millet takes her distance from Laclos's novel: "I'm not like the characters in Laclos's 'Dangerous Liaisons,' who risk hurting people to give free rein to their instincts" (Camhi E1). The paperback edition displayed in Paris (January 2003) on a bookstore table with the author full frontally naked on the cover would have made Rousseau blush. The trend toward the explicit representation of sexuality in the first person by contemporary French women writers dates from Marguerite Duras's *L'Amant* in 1974 and Annie Ernaux's *Passion simple* in 1991.

2. See Philippe Lejeune, "The Autobiographical Pact," in *On Autobiography*.

two processes are mutually exclusive. In fact, the two pulls are equally strong. When I sit down to reconstruct my past, I call on memory; but when memory fails, I let language lead. The words take me where I need to go.

My memory of the period I want to evoke has been complicated by what I have found in letters I wrote to my parents. The letters offer me concrete evidence of the sort that Rousseau said he wanted to help make his "soul transparent to the reader's eye": it is not enough, he explains, for his "story to be truthful, it must be detailed as well" (169). Rousseau wasn't talking about letters, of course, but about memories; the details of the correspondence help me ground the story; they make *me* believe in the truthfulness of my story. Often for the readers of my memoir, though, I've learned that what sccms most truthful to them is what I least remember, or rather what I am least able to document: the dialogues.

Sometimes I think it's harder for me to be transparent to myself than to appear so to the reader.

September 9, 2002

Twenty-odd years ago a middle-aged French academic, who had been romantically involved with a close friend of mine, came upon a packet of letters my friend had received from me during a sabbatical abroad and appropriated them to construct an ending for a thinly disguised autobiographical novel he had written about their relationship and its demise. Hijacking my letters without, of course, acknowledging the theft to the reader was how the wounded author chose to document the woman's change of heart toward him; it was as if the letters proved that he was justified in taking revenge in print against someone he had once loved in life.

The violation of my privacy was not without effect on my life outside the text; the stain of revelation spread, embarrassing, in particular, the man I was soon to marry. While I *might* one day have told him about aspects of my secret history chronicled in the correspondence, his discovering them in print during the early days of a new relationship, in a book friends and colleagues were bound to read, was a rather different matter. I view the appropriation of my letters to be as unforgivable an act of plagarism today as I did then, but now that I myself am writing a memoir about a love story gone wrong—my first marriage—I better understand (while still regretting) a writer's temptation to put the material before the person, as though the letter were no more than words on paper (a mistake well understood by eighteenth-century novelists, and belatedly by their characters), as though the words no longer carried, were no longer attached to, the sender's emotions.

In addition to my letters home, I have in my possession letters written by my ex-husband to me and also, as I've said, to my parents, who are now dead. I can't help feeling that the letters are mine, that they belong to me, and most of all to my *story*. I want to tell that story as I remember it, fully aware that I might be getting some of the details wrong. But if this is how I remember it, and it feels like my truth, then shouldn't I have the right to put it out there? Yes, but. When as writers we expose other people, for whom are these revelations really intended? How do we justify them? Does it matter whether the person is an unknown, as in the case of my ex-husband, or a celebrity (as in the case of Ted Hughes and Sylvia Plath, which Diane Middlebrook addresses in her chapter in this book), or me, known within a small academic circle? What, moreover, is the nature of harm in the context of a story motivated by disappointed love or sexual betrayal? Beyond the excuse of Art (I need it for my story), or Truth (it's what really happened), on what grounds is it possible to argue that readers can be served, not soiled, by the expansion of the domain subjected to the glare of publicity? What is important for a given community, at a given historical moment, to know? If it is sometimes possible to justify violating the privacy of others by telling, whom can we trust to adjudicate these acts of exposure? How can we tell whether to trust the teller?

September 16, 2002

Couldn't you have sued, you ask? Yes. But beyond the expense, someone in my case would have had to "publicly identify herself as the author of the letters," as Philippe Lejeune points out in a discussion of juridical privacy and autobiography, and thus "complete with her own hands," as he puts it, "the author's crime" (*Pour l'autobiographie* 73).

Perhaps betrayal is contagious; I cannot name my own betrayal without producing another.

September 20, 2002

All betrayals are not sexual, of course. Several years ago when I was doing readings from my book *Bequest and Betrayal*, a work that dealt with the death of parents—my own and that of others as described in memoirs (Philip Roth's *Patrimony* is probably the best-known example)—someone in the audience asked me about the meaning of the word betrayal for me. While the question was being asked, I was thinking about how I had betrayed my parents by revealing family secrets. But that was obvious. The question was much smarter and more insidious. Did I think that by betraying my parents I was telling the truth? Was *betrayal* the truth? I had worked on this book for several years and never once asked myself that question. As I continue with various projects of life writing, I find myself tripping over the assumption I had unconsciously made that my truthfulness *required* betrayal. This is almost the autobiographer's credo: better to push the envelope, bring the dark into the light, than to conceal. The ethics, if you like, of betrayal. " 'You must not tell anyone,' my mother said, 'what I am about to tell you' ": this is the first line of Maxine Hong Kingston's *Woman Warrior: Memoirs of a Girlhood among Ghosts* (3), whose narrative flows directly from the refusal to obey that injunction. My questioner was making me wonder whether *not* telling (not telling the truth—the *whole* truth) would make for a stronger ethics. What would *Patrimony* be without the scene of Roth cleaning up his father's shit (which is at the heart of "patrimony")? "Don't tell Claire," Roth senior begs, referring to his son's wife. "Nobody," Philip promises, as he details the mortification, making the scene of his father's disgrace the centerpiece of his memoir (173). Roth—as author—includes the acknowledgment of his betrayal at the end of the memoir through a dream that stands as a metaphor for his self-consciousness about his acts as a writer. He dreams that he has dressed his father "for eternity in the wrong clothes" (237). Roth recognizes that in his dreams, he would forever be his father's "little son"—subject to his father's judgment—just as Kingston's memoir is marked by her debt to her mother's stories. Kingston may have become a writer; she is still her mother's daughter—and judged by her. The mother's gift for "talk-story" is her bequest to her daughter, a girl whose name in English sounds like "ink" in Chinese (131). We autobiographers hate giving up on the really good material. *The Woman Warrior* and *Patrimony* would be much less exciting literary texts if their authors had obeyed their parents and kept silent.

September 22, 2002

Whose story is it? However uncomfortable, the truth of human relations resides in the fact of relationship—and to say relation is to say relative.[3] Add memory and we can begin to see how delicate our notions about describing a relationship have to be. Any form of life writing must weigh the mix of competing interests. (The publication of my letters without permission in itself tipped the scale of ethical standards, I think.) If, moreover, every account of the self includes relations with others, how can an autobiographer tell a story without betraying the other, without violating the other's privacy (Sand's problem with Rousseau), without doing harm, but nonetheless telling the story *from one's own perspective*, which by virtue of being a published text exerts a certain power? You—the person whose life is being written about—enter willy-nilly into the public domain. Faithfully recorded or maliciously distorted, your story circulates, utterly outside your control. Can such publication ever be fair? Can ethics share the side of power? Can we imagine—would we want to—an ethics of betrayal? An ethical betrayal?

I don't know, even less because I find myself grappling with these questions now as a memoir writer.

"My Dangerous Relations." As the title of my memoir (in progress) suggests, I'm looking back at my life through the literary legacy of eighteenth-century France, not with Rousseau's confessions but with Laclos's epistolary novel. Something about seizing the world through letters imprinted on me at a vulnerable moment in my intellectual development—sex, letters, and a rage for freedom combined to confuse and excite me. I went to Paris at age twenty after graduating from college. Away from home for the first time and entranced by *nouvelle vague* movies, I tried to live what I took to be a life of total sophistication. Roger Vadim made a movie, *Les Liaisons dangereuses 1960* from Laclos's novel. The movie wasn't very good, and the complications of its erotic plots spelled doom for everyone (as it did in the novel, too, of course), but I still found it hard to resist the pull of the glamour, updated for what was not yet *les sixties*. I wanted—but what did I want?—to leave my nice New York Jewish girl self behind and become . . . Jeanne Moreau (no less). Failing my reincarnation as a French movie star—or even an American one like Jean Seberg (in *Breathless*, Godard's heroine represented another kind of unattainable ideal)—I went to graduate school, studied French literature, wrote a master's essay on the *Liaisons dangereuses*, taught English, ate cheap food in bad restaurants, had adventures, and got married.

---

3. On the interrelated questions of harm, ethics, boundaries of the self, and life writing, see John Eakin's exemplary *How Our Lives Become Stories*.

I was a fifties girl living on the cusp of the sixties and badly in need of a feminism that had yet to be invented—an analysis, or more simply a story that would help me make sense of my life.

The memoir deals with my brief marriage to a much older man I'm calling Patrick. Our second wedding anniversary was approaching. In my letters home, I had been telling my parents how happy I was, how I had really made the right decision in choosing Patrick; Patrick wrote too.

Suddenly, in March, after raving endlessly about how wonderful everything in my life now is, I mention, as if in passing, that I've decided to spend Easter break in New York. "I need a change of scene," I announce. All plans for the future are off, including the notion that Patrick and I would spend part of the summer with my parents ("Go to the Orient," I say, "don't count on us, I'm not sure how much money we have"). My letter explains nothing. In his letter, Patrick fleshes out the picture. He complains about the contractor, Erich, and the slow pace of renovations on the new apartment, offers details about the book I'm translating for a Sorbonne professor (in his view, a waste of my time), reports on a scheme recording classical music he wanted my father to invest in, comments on the generosity of my aunt's birthday check to me, on Peter Gay's winning the National Book Award, requests copies of the Saturday Review *and* Business Week, *informs my father of my weight (in kilos), my health, fine, except for my being "nervous" (especially when I'm driving our car), and finally the "good news": that I'm planning a trip home. Writing separately to my mother and my father, my husband offers his diagnosis of my condition. He tells my father (paternally) that I'm having a* crise. *I need someone to confide in, Patrick thinks. I need days of sleeping until noon, rest. I've developed a cleanliness mania, he writes, taking showers all the time, in draughty conditions, and now I have a cough, aggravated by my obsessive smoking. Parisian* grisaille *is getting me down; we should have taken a winter holiday in the snow, as the French say, but the money wasn't available. Maybe I need a vacation from him.*

Uxorious *is the word I want. Excessive concern for a wife.*

Even with the distance of time, I feel ventriloquized. My husband is telling my story in my place. Three letters written on our second anniversary (Patrick asks to borrow $100 from my father to buy me an anniversary present). What happened between us that's left out of these letters—his and mine?

I remember thinking back to this moment in my life when I read Sylvia Plath's letters to her mother in Letters Home—*that sense of how what appears to happen suddenly always turns out to have been* building insidiously. Aurelia Plath describes a car trip the mother and daughter took while Aurelia was visiting Sylvia in England: "I have everything in life I've ever wanted," Sylvia declared, "a wonderful husband, two adorable children, a lovely home, and my writing" (458). But to help the readers of the diary, Aurelia Plath fills in editorially the missing information that all was not well in the marriage. Ted was involved with another woman. On August 27, 1962, less than a month after her mother returned home, Sylvia wrote: "I hope you will not be too surprised or shocked when I say I am going to try and get a legal separation from Ted. . . . I simply cannot go on living the degraded and agonized life I have been living" (460). The readers of Letters Home were even more surprised, since the letters had given no hint of the strains in the marriage.

How do you "have" everything you want and at the same time find the life you lead unendurable, degraded? Aurelia asks the reader to recognize that Sylvia was only telling one side of a complicated situation (459). Two sides always exist. That's the definition of marriage. What matters is that corrosive contradiction between having and being.

What do I want? Don't I have what I want? I wanted to stay in Paris. I'm there. I wanted to get married. I'm married. I wanted to teach. I'm a teacher. So what is the problem? Suddenly, nothing adds up. Could this marriage have been saved? Did I want to save it? Patrick said he did.

I confess to being surprised, occasionally touched, by Patrick's recognition that he might have played a role in my crise—an acknowledgment entirely missing from our conversations as I remember them. He even imagines in these letters the need for his greater self-knowledge and possible change. But toward the end, the blame shifts. With a touch of irony, Patrick reminds my mother of a conversation they had in Paris, walking from the Hôtel d'Angleterre on the rue de Rennes toward our apartment after we were just married. "She's your problem now," my mother said to him with a cynical laugh. He thought he had solved the problem, he sighs, reaching for complicity; now he sees how abysmally he has failed. He spirals into a litany of abjection—citing his ignorance, rigidity, self-delusion. Still, whatever his faults, whatever difficulties inherent in the situation—life in France, distance from friends and family, financial constraints— somehow I am the problem.

In a way, I still seem to be the problem—this time, to me the auto-biographer. I remember, sometimes in great detail, the scenes I describe, the affair, my despair, the trip to New York. What I have trouble understanding—and then writing about—is in a way the same thing that bewildered Patrick. How did this happen? What's in my memory that's not in our letters? As a writer, I need to figure out what must have happened; I need to create a narrative that works on its own terms. That means representing Patrick according to the demands of my story as I reconstruct it. I want to be fair to him in my memoir, yet I doubt very much that I'll make him happy when I describe our relationship. I confess that I fear the reaction of this man (with whom I've had no contact since the breakup, though I've seen his wife, who was a friend, and I occasionally have news of him through her or a mutual friend). He is not a public figure about whom American law allows just about anything to be said. I've changed his name, of course, but some people—including himself—are bound to recognize him however much I disguise his traits. Patrick is in the position that I was in when my letters were stolen and I was fictionalized as the entirely recognizable object of a narrative of another's self-justification, which is the essence of all autobiographical writing.

October 1, 2002

At the suggestion of a friend who has dealt at length with problems of legal privacy, I decided to reproduce a letter—experimentally—to see what the effect would be of using the actual letters as opposed to paraphrasing them as I have done here.[4] I discovered that I had to fight interjecting snide comments as I typed Patrick's letter. He *sounds* so understanding and self-critical, but let's not forget that in a world before the term existed, there was nothing he couldn't spin in his favor. Besides, he is constructing a self-portrait designed to please my parents: the sympathetic husband. And, of course, the letters are much too long to be included in the memoir. It's *not* the eighteenth century; I'm not writing an epistolary novel. The letters would have to be excerpted or else broken up with commentary, as I do with my own letters to my parents and their letters to me and to Patrick. Once you cut into a letter, though, you necessarily distort its integrity, change its effect on the reader—for whom it was not destined in the first place (that distortion ranks above all the others).

Paradoxically, were I to flout the rule of intellectual copyright, I would betray the letter writer *less* rather than more. Patrick, the bewildered husband, sounds quite appealing in his own words minus the

---

4. Deborah Nelson. See her *Pursuing Privacy in Cold War America*.

edge of caricature that I create through my paraphrase; even I feel that. So perhaps there really is such a thing as an ethical betrayal: publish the letters and let the man speak for himself.[5] But setting aside the legal privacy conundrum, I face another, more intractable problem. As I confessed awhile back, I am no longer entirely sure about what happened thirty-five years ago. What caused the collapse of everything I had been building toward and indeed believed in—forging a life in France with a man I thought I was in love with—I still don't know. Isn't that in part why I've written the memoir: to find out? So I ask myself the harder question: What is the truth in the name of which I choose to betray another person by revealing intimate details about his life? For me as a writer, the answer to the question of what "really" happened is literary—or at least textual. I will know only when I write it. When I write it, the truth will lie in the writing. But the writing may not be the truth; it may only look like it. To me.

November 13, 2002

It is not my wish to do harm, but I am forced to acknowledge that I may well cause pain—or embarrassment to others—if I also believe, as I do, in my right to tell my story. I can engage to make the memoir as honest as I can (respecting, as I started out to do, the "autobiographical pact"); but by the rules—or, rather, the realities—of the genre, I can't promise not to impinge on the lives of others in the process. This problem of boundaries extends even to this exercise in life writing, which contains analogous ethical constraints. I can't in fact write freely about writing the memoir. Sometimes I have the uncomfortable feeling that the truest ethical position is closely related to silence, to self-silencing.

---

5. John Eakin has reminded me that in the United States, the letter writer (or her estate) retains the right to the *contents* of her own letter, even if the letter is in someone else's possession (this is true in France as well). If *mine* (in my possession), Patrick's letters are nonetheless not mine to quote—without permission (which I'm certain would not be granted). What to do? Eakin pointed me (without recommending that I follow it) to the example of Melanie Thernstrom in *The Dead Girl*, the true story of the author's relationship with a friend who was murdered. Faced with the refusal of the dead girl's parents to allow her to reproduce the actual letters, Thernstrom ended up composing "imaginary letters," acknowledging her creation in a postscript to the book. If I were to make up Patrick's letters, would I be able to resist making him (even more) unsympathetic in order to justify my side of the story—to make my suffering plausible to the reader, to bind the reader to my side?

January 4, 2003

Among the many questions that I've left hanging there's one—from October 1—I want to return to in closing. "What is the truth in the name of which I choose to betray another person by revealing intimate details about his life?" More modestly, how do I justify telling the story of my marriage, and what do the letters have to do with it? It would be easier to deal with my question if I stopped using the words betrayal and truth, as though I (or any of us) knew what either of them really meant in any absolute way. Telling my story truthfully does not necessarily constitute a betrayal of the people who shared in it, even if in the telling I illuminate some of the darker moments from my point of view. Scenes from a marriage are always just that: scenes.

The letters from my ex-husband, I've come to feel, are just a shorthand for my difficulty as a writer, as a critic of autobiography turning memoirist, her head filled with theories of autobiography; and as a woman who has inherited the legacy of women writers reluctant to go public with certain stories. True, the actual language of the letters is a temptation, but I can paraphrase or invent, if need be, now that I understand the law. The issue, finally, is not whether I should quote from the letters but whether I have a story worth telling—and for whom. Who decides, author or reader?

January 5, 2003

Looking back at the coming-of-age story that I'm trying to transform into a memoir, I wish it were a better—nobler—tale. I wish that my younger self had been less lost, more self-reflective; I wish she had aimed higher than the seductions of a Françoise Sagan novel, that she wanted to be a writer and not merely a heroine. If only she had had an idea of someone to become.

In their introduction to *The Feminist Memoir Project*, the editors comment on the work of memoir in accounting for the recent feminist past, in the value of memoir as a gesture toward "making an honest and ethical attempt to restore a sense of history's specifics." Their view of what any one memoir can do, however, is neither nostalgic nor naïve: "There will always be unbridgeable space between the story of the one and of the many; highlighting one memory often casts another in shadow. The past is inside us in flickering and mysterious ways that can never be fully acknowledged nor easily represented" (23). Part of what set the second wave of feminism in motion was the belief that if only our stories could be shared, our world could change. Telling those stories autobiographically required overcoming the kind of self-censorship Sand, Beauvoir, and even Colette practiced and recommended for other women writers—though it's true that they also offered in fiction clear windows onto women's and indeed their own lives.

In "My Dangerous Relations" I am the narrator of a kind of female quest whose first movement is set in the 1960s just before the explosive effects of feminist consciousness which in the 1970s changed the stories of many lives, including my own. My emotional style then, I've come to think, was a kind of desperate unknowing as I stumbled through love affairs and their disappointments, intense hopes and devastating betrayals; as I looked for something I could not have named. (However perversely, was this not my struggle as a very young woman to answer the question "What is it good to be?" which David Parker, echoing Charles Taylor, suggests in his essay occupies the heart of life writing?) Like the heroines of so many women writers I've dealt with as a critic, I wanted to be happy and to live in the world. I tried to do that with Patrick and fell for (or into) the marriage plot. Unfortunately, things didn't quite work out the way I had imagined.

January 7, 2003

After listening to me read a much earlier version of this account, a seminar participant asked (with a slight edge of disdain, or was it incredulity) why he should care about "these people"? I can't say I know better now how to answer that question. If not "these people," then which people do (or should) readers of life writing care about? For some in the seminar, the people readers (like writers) should care about are, in G. Thomas Couser's phrase, "vulnerable subjects," people who suffer from grave and multiple medical disabilities. True. But ethical as well as aesthetic dilemmas arise in the telling of any narrative, no matter how unsavory a story—not to say life—they emerge from.

When we expose the narratives of our lives to others through the forms of life writing, do we not all become vulnerable subjects?

WORKS CITED

Beauvoir, Simone de. *The Prime of Life.* Trans. Peter Green. New York: Paragon House, 1992.
Camhi, Leslie. "Sex Obsession by the Numbers." *New York Times*, June 22, 2002, E 1, 9.

Du Plessis, Rachel Blau, and Ann Snitow, eds. *The Feminist Memoir Project.* New York: Three Rivers Press, 1998.

Eakin, Paul John. *How Our Lives Become Stories: Making Selves.* Ithaca: Cornell University Press, 1999.

Kingston, Maxine Hong. *The Woman Warrior: Memoirs of a Girlhood among Ghosts.* New York: Vintage, 1976.

Lejeune, Philippe. *On Autobiography.* Trans. Katherine Leary. Ed. Paul John Eakin. Minneapolis: University of Minnesota Press, 1989.

——. *Pour l'autobiographie.* Paris: Le Seuil, 1998.

Miller, Nancy K. *Bequest and Betrayal: Memoirs of a Parent's Death.* Bloomington: Indiana University Press, 2000.

——. "My Dangerous Relations: Paris in the 1960s." Unpublished ms.

Millet, Catherine. *The Sexual Life of Catherine M.* Trans. Adriana Hunter. New York: Grove Press, 2002.

Nelson, Deborah. *Pursuing Privacy in Cold War America.* New York: Columbia University Press, 2002.

Plath, Aurelia, ed. *Letters Home: By Sylvia Plath, Correspondence, 1950–63.* New York: HarperPerennial, 1992.

Roth, Philip. *Patrimony: A True Story.* New York: Simon and Schuster, 1991.

Rousseau, Jean-Jacques. *Les Confessions.* Trans. J. M. Cohen. Harmonsdsworth: Penguin, 1953.

Sand, George. *Histoire de ma vie.* In *Oeuvres autobiographiques.* 2 vols. Paris: Gallimard, 1970.

Thernstrom, Melanie. *The Dead Girl.* New York: Simon and Schuster, 1990.

Part IV

ACTS OF RESISTANCE:
TELLING COUNTERSTORIES

CHAPTER 8

Mapping Lives: "Truth," Life Writing, and DNA

Alice Wexler

In the summer of 1983, scientists' success in mapping a DNA marker for Huntington's disease (HD) sent me off on a mapping journey of my own. The fact that my sister, Nancy Wexler, was one of the researchers responsible for finding the marker meant that I had a sense of family pride in this work. And because my sister and I were both at 50 percent risk for this genetic disease, I also had a strong emotional stake in the outcome of the research. In addition, my sister and father presided over a biomedical organization—the Hereditary Disease Foundation—that had recruited and partly funded the researchers. These ties gave me a powerful motivation for writing about the discovery. But such connections also threatened to undermine the very story I wished to tell.

Huntington's disease—formerly called Huntington's chorea, and sometimes popularly referred to as St. Vitus' dance or magrums—is a fatal inherited movement and mental disorder that develops usually in a person's thirties or forties and may last through ten to twenty years of slow, inexorable decline. Characterized by involuntary movements of the body, cognitive loss, and emotional disturbance, it gradually robs the sufferer of memory, speech, and physical and emotional control, leaving him or her "a wreck of his former self," as George Huntington wrote in his classic 1872 description of the disease. Each child of an affected parent, moreover, has a 50–50 chance of inheriting the disease gene.[1] The disease is above all a family affair, and the diagnosis of any

---

1. The Huntington's disease gene is an autosomal dominant mutation of nearly 100 percent penetrance. This means that both men and women are vulnerable, that just a single copy of the gene passed on from one parent can cause the disease, and that those who possess the disease mutation will inevitably develop the symptoms if they live into the age range of the disease. See Huntington 317–21.

one individual in a family inevitably shapes the lives of the others, not only emotionally and socially but often biologically as well, since the diagnosis of a parent reveals the 50–50 risk of each child. The identification of a genetic marker in 1983 meant that, for the first time, those at 50 percent risk could find out whether they had inherited the deadly mutation that would one day lead to the disease.

It was partly this possibility of finding out my "genetic identity" through predictive genetic testing that inspired my desire to write *Mapping Fate*. I had learned about Huntington's disease in my family in 1968, when I was twenty-six, at the time my fifty-three-year old mother was diagnosed with the disease. Although her father, three brothers, and other relatives had all died of Huntington's, prior to 1968 she and my father had chosen not to tell my sister and me. Her diagnosis that year brought the disease into the open. On one August afternoon, four months after Martin Luther King Jr. was assassinated in Memphis, and two months after Robert Kennedy was gunned down at the Ambassador Hotel in Los Angeles, in my father's bedroom on Manning Avenue on the west side of Los Angeles, in the space of about five minutes, the hopes of my sister and me for our mother, ourselves, and our future children were smashed. At least, that was how it felt at the time.

I could not have written about these events at that time, nor any time soon after. Indeed, in the midst of graduate school at Indiana University, where I was about to embark on a Ph.D. dissertation on the history of the Argentine tango, I abruptly decided to change my topic and never return to Latin America again. (The right-wing Argentine generals had just taken over, and the "dirty war" against the left would soon begin, so in retrospect I realize there were other factors at work as well.) My first dissertation adviser (I had three) was dismayed and, unbeknownst to me at the time, put a damning letter in my file stating that while he classed me among the outstanding graduate students he had known, my record was "somewhat spotty." He doubted that I would become "a productive or on-going scholar-writer." Nonetheless, I managed to complete a dissertation on the comparative historiography of the 1898 war in Cuba and miraculously got a teaching job at Sonoma State University in northern California. I tried not to think about Huntington's.

My father and sister did think about Huntington's. My father organized multidisciplinary workshops for scientists and raised money for research, first through the California chapter of the national Committee to Combat Huntington's Disease, and later through the Hereditary Disease Foundation, which he started in 1974. Nancy completed a Ph.D. dissertation at the University of Michigan titled "The Psychology of Being at Risk for Huntington's Disease," went on to teach at the New School for Social Research in New York City, and eventually took a two-year post in Washington, D.C., as executive director of a congressionally mandated commission to study the needs of families with Huntington's. Soon after, she began the remarkable international Venezuela research project that would lead in 1983 to identification of the genetic marker.

Although I had kept my distance from the world of Huntington's disease until that time, the finding of the marker was a turning point. By 1983 I had quit my job at Sonoma, feeling as I turned forty that if my life was to be limited by Huntington's disease, I wanted to use it to write. I enjoyed teaching, but I felt more passionate about writing, and I wanted to write books, or at least to complete the biography of the anarchist Emma Goldman which I was working on. I also had another ambition, supported by a generous husband at the time.

In the euphoric atmosphere sparked by the marker discovery, I began to imagine documenting the scientific research on HD, which had used a revolutionary new approach to locating genes. I started this new project even before I'd finished the Goldman biography, interviewing scientists, studying basic genetics, and attending as many scientific meetings on Huntington's disease as I could. As I began writing, however, I realized that I could not exclude personal issues, since my family was so centrally involved in this research. Moreover, in the context of this new optimism about the possibilities for a cure, I felt empowered to look back on the painful parts of my life in relation to the disease, to try to sort out the ways in which Huntington's had shaped my own sense of self and influenced our family history.

As the book project advanced, I also became aware of the eugenics discourse that had informed many discussions of Huntington's chorea, as it was then called, in both the scientific and medical literature. Huntington's chorea had been a favorite topic of one of the United States' leading eugenicists, Dr. Charles B. Davenport, founder of the Eugenics Record Office (ERO), director of Cold Spring Harbor Biological Laboratory, and sponsor of the first large field study of Huntington's chorea families, carried out by a eugenics worker at the ERO, Dr. Elizabeth B. Muncey. In 1916 Davenport had published an influential paper based on Muncey's data. He concluded that "a state that knows who are its choreics and knows that half of the children of every one of such (on the average) become choreic and does not do the obvious thing to prevent the spread of this dire inheritable disease is impotent, stupid and blind and invites disaster" (215). Davenport was not an extremist on the margins of respectable scholarly discourse. He was a highly respected mainstream scientist, a member of the National

Academy of Science. He published in major scientific and medical journals such as the *Proceedings of the National Academy of Science* and the *Journal of Nervous and Mental Diseases*. His views were influential in shaping medical thinking about Huntington's chorea. Yet while many medical researchers cited Davenport's work, few noted his eugenic perspective. Nor did they acknowledge that his claims were based on a field study carried out much like other eugenic family studies, in which the families were usually portrayed in negative and stigmatizing ways and generally represented as if their own views of themselves had no importance whatsoever.[2]

I decided to show one such family, my own, from the inside, rather than as viewed through a clinical or eugenic lens. While we were more privileged than many, or perhaps most, families with this disease, we shared with other families the burden of secrecy, problems of caregiving, and feelings of betrayal, anger, and shame. I hoped to use my experience as a sort of case study, writing both emotionally and critically about our encounter with the disease. In this context, then, I set out to write the book that became *Mapping Fate*, taking as my structural metaphor the double helix of DNA. That is, I envisioned two narratives, one of science, the other of family, intertwined in the manner of DNA. As I began writing, however, I immediately confronted several issues relating to privacy, confidentiality, and disclosure. And it is the relationship between genetic identity and ethical issues in life writing that I wish to address here, although I realize that this project risks sounding defensive and accusatory: a platform purporting to show how I was right and everyone else was wrong. Nonetheless, exploring the process of ethical decision making may be useful in illuminating some of the pitfalls and pleasures of life writing.

■

Because Huntington's disease had been so stigmatized, I felt it was essential to write as honestly as I could, neither idealizing nor overly pathologizing our own family experience. If I was writing in part for other families with Huntington's, then I needed to be as truthful as possible. But what precisely did it mean to be "truthful" in this context? How could I balance my commitment to "truth" with respect for the needs of others for privacy? The first dilemma I encountered was whether to disclose my father's lengthy extramarital relationship, now long past. The woman in question had been a professional colleague of my father's, and my sister and I also knew her from child-

---

2. See Rafter.

hood as a family friend. She had been, as my father and even my sister said, almost a "second mother." When we were in our early twenties, we learned that she had been more than a family friend for many years.

Initially I felt that I needed to disclose the relationship, since my sister and I had learned about it just a few years before our mother's diagnosis with Huntington's, and it formed the emotional context for our—or my—understanding of the disease. In effect, it was the secret behind the secret of Huntington's disease. I thought that readers would not grasp the full meaning of Huntington's for my sister and me if they did not know that this was the second major secret to be disclosed in our family, and that, in my case at least, anger from the one informed my responses to the other.

I also felt that I could not fully portray my mother's life without showing that, in addition to her worry about Huntington's disease, she undoubtedly suffered from the knowledge of her husband's other relationship. At the very least, it must have contributed to her growing withdrawal and depression, perhaps preventing her from confronting the fact directly and leaving the marriage of her own accord. There were multiple possible causes for her depression and passivity. To reduce everything to Huntington's disease would have been yet another betrayal of her reality.

The woman in question, however, strongly opposed any disclosure of her relationship to my father, which she felt would constitute a "ruthless" invasion of her privacy. My father's response was more moderate, but he too opposed any disclosure. They both shared a sense that I was motivated by hostility and anger. In one unguarded moment of rage, my father even claimed that I wished to destroy him. He suggested that I indicate that there were "problems" in his marriage and leave it at that. When I protested that such vagueness would undermine the book, he eventually backed down, though he made it clear he did not accept my "rationalization," as he called it, regarding it as "bullshit."

My sister, too, opposed such disclosure, though she was gentler in her opposition and listened to my side of the story with more understanding. She was concerned that such disclosure would have devastating effects on the two older people, both in their eighties and in fragile health at the time. Nancy was not convinced that disclosure was essential to the story, and she felt that the potential for harm, especially to the other woman in violating her deep sense of privacy, was too great to justify the story I proposed to tell.

I wrestled with this issue for several years. I would include the disclosure in the manuscript and then remove it a few months later. After a while I would put it back, but then, overtaken by guilt, I would scratch it out again. Meanwhile I was reading and talking to friends about the dilemma. Sometime during this process I discovered *The Illness Narratives: Suffering, Healing, and the Human Condition*, by the medical anthropologist Arthur Kleinman, who described how the contexts of disease—familial, social, cultural—define its meaning for the sufferer. As Kleinman put it, "Understanding the influence of illness on the family necessitates understanding the family itself, not just the illness" (185). I took to heart his statement that "acting like a sponge, illness soaks up personal and social significance from the world of the sick person." (31). Kleinman's analysis had a powerful impact on my thinking. How could I convey the meanings of Huntington's disease in our family if I excluded a critical part of the "world of the sick person"? And yet, as Nancy Miller asked at the seminar that gave rise to this volume (and in her essay included here), did my truthfulness require betrayal?

Ultimately, I decided that I could not portray all that Huntington's disease meant in our family, and in my life, if I excluded a relationship that had been so central to all of us. I felt, against the wishes of my family, that truthfulness did require such disclosure. That relationship had helped shape the power dynamic of the family, since even before our mother became sick, her marriage was already destroyed. To be female, or at least a certain kind of female, was perilous indeed. I wanted to show, not merely assert, how the disease had entered into a preexisting constellation of relationships, exacerbating patterns of power and powerlessness. Since all families involve complex power relationships, and most have multiple secrets and tensions that shape the meanings of any genetic disease—or any serious illness, for that matter—I felt that describing one case in all its specificity would illuminate the larger point for others.

One further consideration influenced me as well, although I could not have formulated it clearly until after the seminar. As I was writing, I had kept in mind a potential audience of families with Huntington's disease, and I felt deeply responsible to them in my writing. But Thomas Couser's discussion in the seminar of what he called "vulnerable subjects, such as minors, members of disadvantaged minorities, and people with certain kinds of illnesses and disabilities— especially mental illness and cognitive or neurological impairments," clarified for me another reason why I had felt so strongly bound to reveal the story of my father's affair. Families with Huntington's usually have so many tremendous problems that omitting the story seemed a betrayal of trust with readers who needed to know that even a family such as ours, with many professional and personal resources, was not free from confusion and despair. As I saw it, my responsibility to this community of vulnerable subjects outweighed my commitments to both my father and the woman involved.

In retrospect, of course, it is difficult to know whether these ethical considerations actually shaped my choices at the time or were more the product of subsequent reflection or even rationalization and self-justification. Nor do I know why my sister, who grew up in the same family, developed a different autobiographical narrative. But perhaps the most important question is whether my choice did harm to the people involved. As it happened, the woman in question decided eventually to grant me "permission" to write what I chose, since her family had all died, and she was, as she said, "the last leaf upon the tree." She suggested that we needed to talk about this. But we never did. To my regret, my heart remained hardened against her, and I could not bring myself to renew our relationship. Others told me, however, that when the book appeared, she gave it to all her friends and kept a copy on view in her living room. Perhaps she found that readers were most impressed not by her secret affair with my father but by the way she assisted my mother in her illness, and her many years of support, including financial contributions, for Huntington's disease research.

My father, too, was relieved to learn that readers did not judge him harshly. They were touched by the fact that he continued to support my mother after their divorce and all through her years of illness, while working on behalf of HD research. Whatever else he did, he did not abandon her. And he made curing her illness the great mission of his life. When the book was published, my father invited all his friends to a reading I gave at a Los Angeles bookstore. It seemed that disclosure of the secrets ultimately had a healing effect on our family, since I was able to express my anger about the affair, while my father, perhaps, was relieved of the burden of secrecy.

■

There were several other issues that posed challenges to writing. One of these was whether I had an ethical responsibility to disclose the choice my sister and I had made about the predictive genetic test which Nancy herself had helped to develop. Beginning in 1986, the year such testing became available, we had many long discussions in the family about the pros and cons of testing. I decided to incorporate sections from a diary I kept during those years relating to these discussions, which had been highly emotional and fraught with tensions. I hoped to show that even a family that included several professional psychologists found the implications of predictive genetic testing extremely difficult to untangle. I decided, however, not to disclose whether we had chosen to take the test.

Some readers later complained that I had let them down by not revealing our decision. They felt frustrated by the ambiguity of the book's ending. Indeed, they wanted to know not only whether we had chosen to take the test but also the results. It was as if they could not stand the lack of closure in the text and wanted a definitive answer as to whether either one or both of us carried the Huntington's gene. But lack of closure was precisely the point. I wanted readers to experience the uncertainty and anxiety of the person at risk for Huntington's; I wanted to frustrate their expectations for a tidy ending.

In this case, I felt that I had no ethical obligation to disclose information that might be harmful to our own lives—risking loss of health insurance, jobs, and social relationships. After the book was published, however, I decided to state publicly that in fact I had chosen not to be tested—at least not yet. I wanted to validate this decision as a legitimate and reasonable choice for some people in the face of not-so-subtle pressure for testing in the media and even from health professionals, who often depicted those who chose not to be tested as remaining "in denial," or as choosing "ignorance," while those who got tested were seen as "courageous" and willing to "confront the truth." Since there is still no medical benefit to taking the test and significant social risk of discrimination in insurance and employment, I wanted to emphasize that those who chose not to be tested had rational grounds for their decision, and perhaps even psychological strengths—such as tolerance for ambiguity and a capacity to live with uncertainty—that should be acknowledged as well.

■

A third issue that came up as I was writing *Mapping Fate* was whether to disclose my own coming out as a lesbian during the years I was writing, in the early 1990s. In most respects this issue lay outside the time period of the book, which dealt only briefly with the years after 1986. But I also felt that if I was willing to disclose the intimate facts of my father's life, I should be willing to reveal my own as well. As a feminist I understood that coming out was an important political statement, and since this process was occurring as I was in the midst of writing the book, it offered a challenge to engage in a more self-reflexive and experimental form of writing.

Once again, I asked myself how this information might illuminate the issue of Huntington's disease in our family, the question that I held up to myself as a central rule or algorithm guiding my writing. I worried that simply dropping this information into the narrative without being able to analyze or contextualize it adequately would distract at best, and at worst would encourage arm-chair psychoanalyzing. My sister also feared that a "lesbian paragraph" would have a sensational effect, stealing attention away from the central aspects of the scientific story.

I finally decided to exclude this complicated issue, telling myself that I was still too close to the question to represent it adequately. I was not ready for such self-revelation. Still, I asked myself if I had chosen to protect my own privacy while not respecting that of others. Were I to write the book today, I would probably make a different choice.

■

There was one privacy issue that did not come up in the writing of *Mapping Fate* but would have had we been a larger family. To reveal genetic information about one member of the family has potential implications for others. Indeed, that is the meaning of genetic identity, which differentiates it from the individual identity so dear to Americans. Genetic identity is shared with the family. To identify those in our family who had Huntington's disease could have had medical and social implications for their children and grandchildren, if indeed there had been any. The fact that my mother's family was small and that her brothers had no children meant that my disclosure of their illness did not have wider implications. But what if it had? Would I then have had an ethical responsibility not to reveal their genetic status, even if not doing so compromised my ability to tell my own family story?

This issue emerged recently in a historical article I wrote about the history of Huntington's disease in East Hampton, New York, where the original Dr. Huntington, author of the classic 1872 description of the disease, had observed the condition local people called St. Vitus' dance.[3] It was not difficult to find the names of individuals from the late eighteenth and nineteenth centuries—in newspapers, in family papers in the library, in eugenics records—who had been identified by their neighbors as having this disease. But identifying them by name in 2002, even though others had previously made such identification in publicly available sources and even in print, could pose dangers to their descendants. There was no question of legal liability, since all the individuals involved were deceased. But what was my ethical responsibility in this case? Diane Middlebrook tells us, the dead belong to

3. See Wexler, "Chorea."

the living. We the living have a right to make what we will of the dead. But the new genetics means that the dead are more closely related than ever to the living—or, more accurately, the living are ever more closely related to the dead. What if a genetic truth about the dead can do harm to the living?

Disciplinary practices clearly come into play here. Anthropologists routinely change the the names of their informants in community studies to protect confidentiality. Psychologists and psychiatrists change the names of patients and clients in published clinical accounts. Historians using hospital records are usually required to omit or change names as well. But historians using publicly available records from earlier eras when standards of confidentiality were much looser face a more complicated dilemma. If I change or omit names, how do I cite archival records that might contain the real names of my subjects? How do I protect a subject's privacy if he held local office, for instance, and his name is in the town records that I must cite among my sources? How do I refer to a newspaper obituary from 1800 that contains the real name of the person whose name I have changed in my article? But if, as most historians advocate, I use the real names of my nineteenth-century subjects with "St. Vitus' dance" or "Huntington's chorea," I may be putting their descendants—or even non-descendants with the same surname—at risk of gossip, social stigma, or worse. These dilemmas have emerged with increased urgency in the context of both the new genetics and the tremendous explosion in information that makes tracing individuals on the Internet so much easier.

Finally, the new genetics has also reintroduced the ghost of early-twentieth-century eugenics, which haunts at least some contemporary life writing, including my own. Even my own father was influenced by eugenic ideology. To have knowingly had children at risk for Huntington's disease was, in his mind, even in the 1990s, morally unacceptable. Even to raise the question whether he had known before they had children that the disease ran in his wife's family was to him an outrageous affront.

Shadowed by the history of eugenics, the genetic revolution of the present day has given a particular poignancy to life writing by members of the families targeted by early-twentieth-century eugenicists. In some ways, *Mapping Fate* represented my effort to disrupt an old eugenic narrative by telling a story of genetics from the inside, up close and personal rather than at a distance, revealing the humanity of those of us who happen to be unlucky in our genes. Indeed, many members of families with Huntington's disease are writing their stories, self-publishing them or posting them on the Internet where others can read them. Such narratives are playing an important role in the discourse of genetic testing, since people considering predictive testing can read about the experiences of those who have gone through the process. Such "peer counseling," as it were, is one of the most valuable aspects of the life writing of genetic narratives.

The new era of DNA raises the stakes in such truth-telling narratives, since the possibilities for surveillance and discrimination are much greater than in the past. Yet the possibilities for insight, knowledge, justice, and independence are also greater. Whereas the old eugenics mapped a story of failure, misery, and degeneracy onto families with Huntington's disease, the new genetic activism—and I include life writing as a form of activism—has already created a different kind of map. Whether or not the new genetics lives up to its promise of inventing a cure or an effective treatment for HD in my lifetime, the activism of affected families, in collaboration with the scientists, has helped to change the story in our lives and also in writing. The challenge is not only to change "fate" but also to claim the act of mapping ourselves.

WORKS CITED

Huntington, George. "On Chorea." *Medical and Surgical Reporter* 26 (1872): 317–21.

Kleinman, Arthur. *The Illness Narratives: Suffering, Healing, and the Human Condition.* New York: Basic Books, 1988.

Muncey, Elizabeth B., and Charles B. Davenport. "Huntington's Chorea in Relation to Heredity and Eugenics." *American Journal of Insanity* 73 (1916): 195–222.

Rafter, Nicole Hahn. *White Trash: The Eugenic Family Studies, 1877–1919.* Boston: Northeastern University Press, 1988.

Wexler, Alice. "Chorea and Community in a Nineteenth-Century Town." *Bulletin of the History of Medicine* 76, no. 3 (2002): 495–527.

——. *Mapping Fate: A Memoir of Family, Risk, and Genetic Research.* Berkeley: University of California Press, 1985.

CHAPTER 9

Moral Non-fiction: Life Writing and Children's Disability

Arthur W. Frank

Suffering has always animated life writing. During the nineteenth century, persons who had no other claim to public recognition wrote narratives of personal suffering—particularly captivity, slavery, war, and poverty—creating a publication niche and considerable readership.[1] Today, illness and disability have displaced the nineteenth-century topics in popularity. Commercially published life writing about illness is the tip of an iceberg that includes personal and institutional Web sites, "journaling" groups, and stories elicited in research interviews and life histories.

In previous centuries, illness and disability entered people's stories contingently, as aspects of lives being described for more general purposes. Now these experiences become the occasions for life writing. The reception of these writings depends on (and subsequently reinforces) the cultural recognition that illness and disability provide for—even require—the reevaluation of lives. *How to respond* to illness and disability—what is done with the body, what happens in relationships, and how existential and spiritual attitudes change—is presented as a sequence of choices. The writer's identity becomes crucially implicated in how she or he makes these choices: a person's responses are a measure of his or her character.

1. Fabian provides a historical review of nineteenth-century narratives of personal suffering.

In this essay I describe life writing about illness and disability as moral non-fiction.[2] I derive this term from John Gardner's 1978 book— or manifesto—*On Moral Fiction*, which is discussed herein. I argue that at a time when canonical, institutionalized standards of public and private morality have broken down, moral non-fiction offers a form and forum for personal reflection on questions of value.[3] Illness and disability test the writer, who then tests which values are to be acted upon, when, in what ways.

My objective is not to formalize the moral reflection offered in life writing, since life writing is already, in one of its dimensions, a reaction against previous formalizations of moral thought. Rather I present, first, one version of why moral non-fiction about illness and disability is *necessary* today; second, how our present moral climate makes such writing *difficult*, but all the more important for that difficulty; third, how such life writing *works*, illustrated with a particular text; and finally, what sort of morality we can hope to find in moral non-fiction, and *what it can do* for us. By "us" I mean people who need guidance on the perennial question of how we are to live: what ways of living are better than others, and how we become the sort of people we want to be. These questions are the core of what I mean by *moral*.

Life Writing as Remoralization

Having written my own illness narrative (*At the Will of the Body*) and been involved in several life writing projects since, I have taken a variety of perspectives toward life writing about illness.[4] As an

2. Two notes on my usage of "moral non-fiction." First, I avoid the term "pathography" to describe life writing about illness and disability. With all respect to colleagues who find this term useful, I reject it as an attempt to medicalize writing that is often undertaken in reaction against the way the writer feels identified by medicine. No ill or disabled person ever described himself or herself as sitting down to write a "pathography," so what are the politics of assimilating their writing to that term? The neologism presents this writing as available to a professional, specifically medical, gaze. The objective of most of those who write about their illnesses and disabilities is the opposite: to represent professionals, specifically physicians, through the gaze of those they treat. For additional objections, see Frank, *Wounded Storyteller* 190, n. 34. Second, although Gardner's essay is concerned with fiction, his importance to this chapter lies in his social-philosophical critique of contemporary moral awareness, not his literary criticism. This critique is as applicable to the conditions in which nonfiction is written and read as it is to fiction.

3. Major sociological works on public and private moralities include Bellah et al., Smart, and Wolfe.

4. Most notable among these projects was my editorship from 1994 to 1996 of the "Case Stories" series in the journal *Second Opinion*, which was published by the Park Ridge Center, Chicago. I now serve as an editorial adviser to *Illness: A Journal of Per-*

advocate for personal narratives of illness, I have told physicians and other clinicians that they should attend to this writing as a way to understand the depth of what their patients are living through and to see what their own behavior looks like to their patients. I have encouraged ill people to read and to write personal accounts of illness for reasons that funnel back to the argument most frequently identified with Victor Frankl's influential reflections on Holocaust survival: suffering becomes more bearable when it has some meaning.

My advocacy is grounded in my understanding of personal narratives of illness as acts of *remoralization*. I derive this term from Arthur Kleinman's usage of *demoralization* in his classic study *The Illness Narratives*. Kleinman advanced a new idea: chronic illness wears people down not only by its physical effects of pain and debility but also by the social treatment that patients receive. This message was hardly news to ill people, but Kleinman's eloquent, scholarly advocacy advanced the legitimacy of medical demoralization as a topic for study. He writes, "The contribution of professional orthodoxy to inadvertently heighten the passivity and demoralization of patients and their families is all too common in the treatment of the chronically ill" (128). Demoralization begins in the professional views that the patient has nothing to contribute to clinical judgment (129), and that clinical judgment is all that needs to be known about patients.

Against these reductive medical views, Kleinman argued for a socially contextualized view of chronicity as a condition created and sustained in relationships. Let me quote at length, because this essay is a continuing development of the critique that Kleinman initiated:

> Chronicity is not simply the result of pathology acting in an isolated person. It is the outcome of lives lived under constraining circumstances with particular relationships to other people. Chronicity is created in part out of negative expectations that come to be shared in face-to-face interactions—expectations that fetter our dreams and sting and choke our sense of self. Patients learn to act as chronic cases; family members and care givers learn to treat patients in keeping with this view. We collude in building walls and tearing down bridges. We place complex individuals in simple, unidimensional roles (the disabled, the life threatened) as if this were all they are and can be. We turn our backs on poisonous relationships. We become part of demoralizing situations, and add unhelpfully to feelings of threat and fear. (180)

sonal Experience. I have supervised graduate theses and dissertations on Web-based illness narratives, consulted on a variety of university press manuscript submissions, and engaged in countless conversations with people who were writing about their illnesses.

This passage—applicable also to the critically ill and the disabled—initiates contemporary thinking about how socially constructed and legitimated master narratives of identity can demoralize people, and how people tell counterstories to resist the assimilation of their selves to such narratives. But ideas of master narratives and counterstories get me ahead of my story.

Illness and disability call upon people to become morally engaged because they have everything to lose, but also to gain. Illness is inherently a moral experience, and life writing about illness is inherently moral, as it seeks to sort out what was lost, gained, and preserved. My briefest statement of when a decision is moral is that the actor understands how she or he acts in some situation as constituting a durable statement of who that person is—our actions affect our own and others' sense of our worth as persons. Charles Taylor writes that with Romanticism, people developed the idea that each life has a unique point, and it becomes possible to miss the point of your life. A moral decision is any action that a person understands as affecting her or his progress toward finding or achieving the unique point—or points—of her or his life. I have sought to understand personal writing about illness not as having an instrumental health benefit for the writer-as-patient,[5] but as a means by which the writer seeks to remoralize his or her life. Illness is understood, in Taylor's terms, as an occasion for seeking the point of one's life, and often for claiming a shift in what the point is understood to be.

For some, the moral occasion of illness goes beyond their immediate relationships. Illness is an occasion to offer testimony about a suffering that society too often ignores, compartmentalizes, and diminishes. The writer of the illness narrative is primarily a witness, whose testimony speaks not only for himself or herself but also for a larger community of those who suffer. Being a witness is moral work.

I now catch up with the ideas, mentioned earlier, of master narratives and counterstories. While I was reading and writing about personal narratives of illness (in the early to mid-1990s), a variety of academic disciplines were taking some form of narrative turn, producing a literature that exceeds what any scholar could possibly assimilate. That literature has been most meaningful to me when it discusses how identity is constructed in narratives. The plural of "narratives" is important, and it is more adequate to say: how the overlapping, mutually implicated, complementary, and sometimes contradictory identities of a single person are constructed in narratives that have multiple origins and purposes and that vary in their degree

5. As an example of such work, which has its own very real utility, see Pennybaker.

of both internalization and external force. A life is the stories that make up the life, but people do not make up these stories for themselves. People build their own stories on the narrative scaffolding that their local worlds make available, and these scaffoldings constrain the kind of story that can be told, even as they enable the possibility of storytelling.[6] To put the issue in political terms, people are subject to stories others tell about them.

The feminist bioethicist Hilde Lindemann Nelson provides a useful summary of this research from her own disciplinary perspective of philosophy. Nelson describes how some persons are systematically damaged by the stories that categorize and denigrate the identities to which these people are relegated: "A person's identity is damaged when a powerful social group views the members of her own, less powerful group as unworthy of full moral respect" (xii). Kleinman had described such damage as the demoralization of ill people who are assimilated to reductive categories such as "the disabled" and "the life threatened." Nelson's contribution is to detail the narrative work of resistance that such "damaged" people do to restore themselves to full moral respect; she calls this work the telling of counterstories: "Counterstories, then, are tools designed to repair the damage inflicted on identities by abusive power systems. They are purposive acts of moral definition, developed on one's own behalf or on behalf of others. They set out to resist, to varying degrees, the stories that identify certain groups of people as targets for ill treatment. Their aim is to reidentify such people as competent members of the moral community and in doing so to enable their moral agency" (xiii).

Counterstories are perhaps the most significant form of what I have been calling remoralization work. To summarize: illness becomes a moral occasion when the ill person engages in some work, including writing, that remoralizes his or her identity. What is moral is also political: because demoralization is a political project to delegitimate the values, perspectives, and identities of some persons, remoralization affects the distribution of social resources conventionally known as power. Put more bluntly, life writing about illness and disability upsets the conventional identities assigned to these groups. The claims staked out in two titles are exemplary: *A Whole New Life*, Reynolds Price's account of his experiences with cancer, and *Nothing about Us without Us*, James Charlton's autobiographically informed study of the disability rights movement. Price writes about personal, spiritual transformation through illness; the centerpiece of his book is a mystical

---

6. For a sociological perspective on the resources that storytellers draw upon, see Holstein and Gubrium.

vision of Christ that gives Price strength to continue living when his suffering seems overpowering. Charlton writes about the need for changes in laws, policies, and attitudes; he protests "conditions that cry out for attention and are, in themselves, a fundamental critique of the existing world order" (5). These personal and political forms of writing seem two sides of the same coin.

Charlton calls the disability rights movement "an epistemological break with old thinking about disability" (5); the same might be said of all life writing about illness. Life writing breaks with the epistemology of the ill or disabled person as the object of knowledge—one who is observed and recorded by others—and asserts such persons' claim to be knowing subjects. For the ill and disabled to speak for themselves is already a counterstory to the traditional medical account and its epistemology.

But telling a counterstory that makes a moral claim is one thing; making a *good* moral claim is another. The title of Tod Chambers's 2001 review of Nelson catches the problem neatly: "And the Counterstories Will Set You Free (Well, at Least the Good Ones Will)." Thus, in the final section of this essay I turn to the problem of criticism of life writing about illness and disability: What is a good story to tell about oneself? But I consider first the general problem of moral writing at the present time, and then how illness and disability narratives do their moral work.

Moral Nervousness and Moral Freedom

People, in both academic audiences and illness groups, generally approve of my descriptions of illness experience and agree with my values; but introducing the word *moral* generates a nervousness that needs to be examined, because this nervousness suggests what is at stake in life writing about illness and disability. Nervousness focuses on the idea that seems inherent to any notion of morality: some ways of living are to be preferred to other ways. This reluctance to make comparative judgments between ways of living was described and refuted a quarter century ago by Gardner. He was advocating a certain critical standard for fiction, but what he wrote is generally applicable to understanding why people resist identifying life writing about illness as *moral* nonfiction.

Gardner wrote in *On Moral Fiction*: "Sophisticated modern free society tends to be embarrassed by the whole idea of morality and by all its antique, Platonic- or scholastic-sounding manifestations—Beauty, Goodness, Truth" (19). The sociologist Alan Wolfe, interviewing diverse Americans across the country, found that "the language of virtue is not on the tip of most Americans' tongue" (19). Whether people are embarrassed or not, they don't think that way: " 'Virtue' and 'vice' are simply not part of their everyday vocabulary" (19), Wolfe concludes. Wolfe does not conclude, however, that Americans are less moral in their actions than those who use a vocabulary of virtue and vice. "There can also be something dignified about the ways in which people consider the conditions of themselves and their society," he writes. "If they cannot offer the examined life, they can offer the experienced life. Morality for them is not likely to be based on abstractions but on consequences" (17). Life writing offers "the experienced life," emphasizing not abstractions but consequences.

Wolfe summarizes Americans' morality as what he calls "moral freedom," and this idea seems crucial to the ethics of life writing: "Moral freedom means that individuals should determine for themselves what it means to lead a good and virtuous life. Contemporary Americans find answers to the perennial questions asked by theologians and moral philosophers, not by conforming to strictures handed down by God or nature, but by considering who they are, what others require, and what consequences follow from acting one way rather than another" (195). Moral freedom thus seems to require occasions—and media—in which people can consider who they are, what others require, and what consequences follow from one action rather than another.

Gardner understands fiction as one such medium. He depicts fiction as moral experiment: "We recognize art by its careful, thoroughly honest search for and analysis of values. . . . [I]t explores, openmindedly, to learn what it should teach. It clarifies, like an experiment in a chemistry lab, and confirms. . . . [M]oral art tests values and rouses trustworthy feeling about the better and the worse in human action" (19). Moral non-fiction fits the same description. Moral fiction and non-fiction seem necessary and natural media for people who value not the philosophically "examined life" but rather the "experienced life," in Wolfe's terms quoted earlier. Of particular importance is Gardner's phrase that such writing explores "to learn what it should teach." The story is the discovery of what is "better and worse," at least in the life of the writer, and that qualification takes us back to moral nervousness: the nervousness of claiming one way of living as better and another as worse.

I have presented Gardner and Wolfe as if their ideas were compatible; that compatibility goes only so far. Sometimes Gardner writes as if he would readily accept Wolfe's moral pragmatism: "Morality, then, describes actions or preparations for action. . . . [M]orality is infinitely complex, too complex to be *knowable* and far too complex to be reduced to any code, which is why it is suitable for fiction, which deals in understanding, not knowledge," as experiential nonfiction, life writing, does also. "This does not mean that morality is out of our reach but only that it is beyond the strictly analytical process that leads to knowing" (135). Yet Gardner is not advocating what the research of Robert Bellah and his colleagues sometimes found in their interview studies in the 1980s: a do-it-yourself moral invention. Perhaps the most cited passage in *Habits of the Heart* describes a nurse whom the authors call Sheila Larson, who is quoted as saying: "I believe in God. I'm not a religious fanatic. I can't remember the last time I went to church. My faith has carried me a long way. It's Sheilaism. Just my own little voice" (221).

If moral freedom means "my own little voice," Gardner wants no part of it. "Either there are real and inherent values, 'eternal verities,' as Faulkner once said, which are prior to our individual existence, or there are not," Gardner writes. If not, the consequences are disastrous: "We're free to make them up, like Bluebeard, who reached, it seems, the existential decision that it's good to kill wives" (24). Bluebeard is Gardner's trope for the dangers of unquestionably following "my own little voice."

I find no contradiction between Gardner's assertion that morality is too complex to be reduced to any code and his claim that there are— there have to be—eternal verities. To claim that eternal verities are real is not to say that humans have a transparent knowledge of what these are or how they should be applied in any situation that life presents. The knowledge and application of values, inherent as those values themselves may be, takes us back to the complexity of morality and the need for occasions that *test* values—Gardner's metaphor of a chemistry experiment, quoted earlier—to find out if they "rouse trustworthy feelings about the better and the worse" (19). As I read Wolfe's interviews, I hear his respondents using the interview situation to test whether their feelings about their values are trustworthy. Charles Taylor's arguments are the most recent exemplars of the idea that moral life is founded in dialogue, and the closest humans can get to moral certainty is the dialogical affirmation of others.

Gardner holds up moral fiction, and I hold up moral non-fiction, as occasions for testing whether one's own little voice expresses what's better and worse. Writing offers one's own voice to others, for their affirmation and criticism. One way of describing how Bluebeard goes wrong is that he removed his own little voice from dialogue with other voices. There is no indication that Sheila Larson makes that mistake. If she keeps her "own little voice" open to the voices of others, then her responsible exercise of moral freedom may differ from Bluebeard's irresponsible moral freedom.

In an age of moral freedom, life writing allows writer and reader an opportunity to measure their experience of life against others' experiences. I follow Gardner's claim that such writing "clarifies life, establishes models for human action, casts nets toward the future, carefully judges our right and wrong directions, celebrates and mourns. It does not rant. It does not sneer or giggle in the face of death, it invents prayers and weapons. It designs visions worth trying to make fact" (100). Gardner advocates writers' claiming—as I've suggested that Price and Charlton claim—"that some things are healthy for individuals and society and some things are not" (101). A writer who makes this claim is willing to generalize from his or her own experience to the lives of others, even to society as a whole. Yet this claim is, as Gardner says, never forced on anyone. The writer "merely makes his case, the strongest case possible" (101).

Nervousness about writers claiming that what's healthy for individuals and society—and, by implication, what's less than healthy or downright wrong—is well founded. Gardner readily acknowledges that much moral assertion often "turns out to be some parochial group's manners and habitual prejudices elevated to the status of ethical imperatives, axioms for which bigotry and hate, not love, is the premise" (74). Many Sheila Larsons, who claim to believe in God, value their faith, and yet do not go to church, might cite personal and community histories of such moral thuggery. For Gardner, however, to draw a dichotomy between universal ethical ideals and following one's own little voice misses how moral life works: "To say that no one can spell out in detail the exact rules of ideal child-rearing is not to say that the ideal does not exist for our intuition or that it is not sometimes approached by good parents. . . . [It] is not to say that the Good is a matter of opinion" (136–37). The bridge between universal ethics and one's own little voice is dialogue. Moral writing is a medium in which people can express their intuitions about the ideal and their practices for attempting to reach it. The values they report are not matters of opinion, but neither do they force any exact rules on anyone else. That balance is moral freedom.

How Moral Non-fiction Works

Like all genres, life writing about illness and disability includes multiple subgenres. I want to consider the subgenre of fully abled parents writing about their seriously disabled children. Two texts provide a general context: Michael Bérubé's *Life as We Know It*, in which Bérubé, a literary scholar, writes about the early childhood of his son Jamie, who lives with Down syndrome, and the philosopher Eva Kittay's essay "Not *My* Way, Sesha, *Your* Way, Slowly," about Kittay's daughter, who has what she calls "profound intellectual disabilities" with attendant physical problems. I concentrate on Sam Crane's book *Aidan's Way*, about his son Aidan. Like Bérubé and Kittay, Crane is an academic, a professor of Asian studies specializing in Chinese politics.

Aidan was born without a corpus callosum connecting the left and right hemispheres of his brain. He suffers major seizures as well as constant minor ones. He is blind, requires feeding through a tube, is without speech, and is functionally quadriplegic. Yet this description, following cultural conventions of appropriate introductory information (and reflecting the medicalization of those conventions), contradicts and betrays Crane's intention in writing about Aidan, which is to rescue him from being reduced to his disabilities. Crane writes of the medical profession's "quick categorization" of "these sorts of kids": "They were too quick to embrace an easy, formulaic answer . . . too busy to look beyond facile stereotypes" (132). Crane and his wife, Maureen, are relieved when they finally meet a specialist who is disabled: "With his cerebral palsy placing him among 'these sorts' of people, [Dr. Rudi] more readily looked on Aidan as an individual" (133). That's Crane's message in brief: look on Aidan as an individual, and be willing to learn from him.

Aidan's Way, like most writing in this subgenre, is animated by the tension between institutional reductions of the child to his or her disabilities (hospitals and schools are the usual suspects, followed by insurance companies) and the celebration of the child as a life. The bioethicist Thomas Murray wrote a book on parenthood and moral obligation, gracefully titled *The Worth of a Child*. That title expresses the theme and problematic of this subgenre: How does a parent assert terms for valuing a child whom many others in society (including institutions on which the child depends) devalue? Bérubé, Kittay, and Crane all seek to affirm the worth of their children. Each does so by emphasizing the dialogical relationship between parent and child: how their lives are better for having been shaped by their children. What Crane writes of his second (developmentally normal) child, Margaret, that "her baby-ness was informing my adulthood" (139), could be an epigraph for the subgenre. When such a statement is made about a developmentally normal child, it creates little narrative tension. Tension arises, and animates narrative, when the adult discovers value in being shaped by the disabled child's permanent baby-ness.

An additional tension is between the epistemological break described by Charlton—those who were spoken for now speak for themselves—and the practical necessity of a parent's speaking for a child who cannot speak for himself or herself. Among Jamie, Sesha, and Aidan, only Jamie may someday be able to narrate his own experience in language. Bérubé writes that after Jamie's first two weeks in pediatric intensive care, "he started becoming a narrative" (40). Jamie's problem, which requires his father to represent him, is how his narrative will be told: in whose language, reflecting whose interests. Bérubé describes his infant son as "a thoroughly medicalized child. . . . [T]o talk about him was also to talk about his procedures and prospects in medical terms" (41). But because medicine has no treatment to cure Jamie—to render him developmentally normal—he is then constructed as a cost, a burden, and, at worst, a mistake. Bérubé writes that increasing pressures to abort fetuses who test positive for Down Syndrome creates a problem "of defending the individual's right to do a bad thing" (49), that is, to carry these fetuses to full term. Crane reports hearing, through one of Aidan's aides, that an insurance company representative had said, about Aidan, "It's all their fault, the parents, for keeping these kinds of kids alive" (243). Thus parental narratives are acts of justification: the parent-writers justify their children's right to exist.

Justification requires making lives like those of Jamie, Sesha, and Aidan *narratable*, to use Bérubé's word for what he is trying to do for Jamie. This subgenre presents narratives about the limits of what is narratable: the writing is inherently reflexive, questioning what sort of story it is, and even its own claim to be a story. This reflexivity is moral work, since what's at stake is personhood and its entitlements. If Jamie's life is not narratable, then Jamie becomes one of "these kinds of kids," and his entitlements—to birth, to care and services, to respect as a person—are in jeopardy. Bérubé, Kittay, and Crane all write with an acute awareness of this jeopardy: the pressures to institutionalize their children, and the brutal history of such institutionalization.

The parents' narrative problem was described early in the last century by the Russian critic and philosopher Mikhail Bakhtin as the moral imperative of the author never to "finalize" a character, that is, to speak the last word about that character, as diagnostic and other medical practices finalize a patient. As Crane and his wife realize the extent of Aidan's disabilities, Maureen breaks down, crying to Aidan's aide, Linda, "They'll rush to judge him, reduce him to some inferior status. . . . That's what they'll do, won't they?" (40). "Yes," the aide replies. "That is what they will do" (40).

The opposite of finalizing a character is dialogue, and if this essay has room for only one quotation from Bakhtin about dialogue, perhaps this is most relevant to the narratability of the ill and disabled: "In Dostoevsky's works there is literally not a single significant word about a character that the character could not have said about himself (from the standpoint of content, not tone)" (278). That's the bind for writers like Bérubé, Kittay, and Crane. They object to what others say about their children. But as parents and as writers, they necessarily say things about their children that their children could not say about themselves, in content or tone. They resolve this dilemma, and keep a dialogue open, by refusing to say any last word about their children. The child's future—his or her horizon of possibilities—is kept open, though this requires nothing less than redrawing the horizons of human possibility itself. Thus these writings become teachings in the morality of respect: not principles of respect, as in Kantian respect for persons, but *practices* of respect, which the writing not only describes but also *reflexively exemplifies.*

Crane's writing seeks a particular balance. Aidan's most narratable stories in terms of conventional expectations of narrative are his medical crises: his seizures and resuscitations, his recurrent pneumonias, and an attack of kidney stones. These are easy narrations with dramatic precipitating crises—Aidan has some obvious distress, and at the extreme stops breathing—then there is a journey into an alien medical territory, a period of misdiagnosis with risk of death, finding a specialist who takes Aidan's problem seriously and does the necessary investigation, and finally some resolution to the crisis. Those episodes are what the world counts as narratives: they have beginnings, middles, and ends, good people and bad people, frustration, discovery, and finally the intervention that resolves the initial crisis. These narratives are what the medical anthropologist Cheryl Mattingly calls "event centered" (8). Crane's problem is that event-centered narrations turn Aidan into a medical event; he becomes an object of others' attention, not a subject affecting others.

Mattingly suggests that there are also "experience-centered" narratives; unlike event-centered narratives, which report events that have happened, experience-centered narratives create experiences (8). Mattingly explains "how narratives shape action":

> Narratives are not just about experiences. Experiences are, in a sense, about narratives. That is, narratives are not primarily after-the-fact imitations of the experiences they recount. Rather, the intimate connection between story and experience results from the structure of action itself. Many kinds of social actions (including many therapeutic interactions) are organized and shaped by actors so that they take on narrative form. Thus narrative and experience are bound in a homologous relationship, not merely a referential one. (19)

This "homologous relationship" can be seen working in the following passage, in which Crane begins a long description of his daily ritual of bathing Aidan:

> Every morning, before taking him into the social world of school, I wash Aidan. We do this while he is still in bed, lying straight on his back. Starting with his face, I slip my left hand under his head to steady it and speak to him, alerting him to the coming shock of dampness on his brow. Even with my spoken introduction, the first swipes of the warm washcloth invariably startle him. He widens his eyes in reaction to the wet assault. I carefully rub under and behind his ears, working toward his eyes to cleanse away the sleep from their inner corners. Soap comes next, soap on cheeks and forehead and chin, soap to dissolve the dirt from his smooth skin. (167)

This description continues for another two pages, in the detail required to slow the reader down to Crane's pace as he performs this ritual—Aidan's pace. "He inspires silence in me" (253), Crane writes. For Crane's description of washing Aidan to have its practical moral effect, it has to inspire silence in the reader. In Mattingly's terms, the narrative of washing has to create the experience of engaging Aidan. Crane has to narrate washing to make his commitment to caring for Aidan sensible to himself—he has to give his care narrative structure—and he has to narrate care to give it a public claim.

"Since he has no conventional voice of his own," Crane writes about Aidan, echoing similar statements by Bérubé and Kittay, "we [his parents] find ourselves speaking for him, narrating his life to the world. We do this every day in the immediate ambit of his activities" (253). And Crane does it in his life writing. "For myself," he continues, "I have found that I can write his life as well as speak it. And this has enlarged his imprint on the world" (253). Thus we move from the homologous relationship of narrative and experience as it informs an individual life to the issue of individual lives informing society.

When Crane narrates bathing Aidan, he not only gives meaning to his daily action, transforming a chore that could, in some schemes of value, become burdensome and meaningless into a time of intimacy, tactile dialogue, and affirmation of life. But also, in washing Aidan each day, Crane renews the world; he does not claim this explicitly—he need not. The expanded force of his narrative is to claim that a form of experience is fully narratable: washing Aidan becomes as important as anything else Crane does, and his story of this washing is as important as his stories about his work as a political theorist, commenting and occasionally intervening in Asian politics. Those political stories are more conventionally narratable: political interventions are what

Mattingly calls event-centered. The moral excellence of Crane's book is that his prose is far more lyrical as he describes washing Aidan than when he describes taking on the prime minister of Singapore.

To give the work of washing Aidan an equal or greater value than encountering a prime minister is to create the possibility of a valued experience for other parents who suddenly find themselves caring for children like Aidan, and who, like Crane, wonder what kind of experience—what kind of life—this can be. Crane describes a moment soon after Aidan was born when he forgot to give him his seizure medication; his wife said nothing but "shot me a hard glance" (55). He snaps. "The sunshine was suddenly ineffectual, the atmosphere darkened. In a quick and violent motion I hurled across the room the small ceramic bowl I had been holding. It darted like a Frisbee, low and hard, into the dining room, and shattered loudly against the wall. The cat scrambled upstairs; the dog hopped to her feet. My face flushed and my hands trembled. A million thoughts swirled in my head simultaneously, merging into a blurred mass of hostility" (55–56). The scene recalls Bakhtin's description of moments of the fantastic in literature: "We emphasize that the fantastic here serves not for the positive *embodiment* of truth, but as a mode for searching after truth, provoking it, and most important, *testing* it" (114). Crane's anger takes on the fantastic quality of rage as madness, in which the sun darkens and time seems suspended in the flight of the bowl he throws. What is tested is truth—the moral truth of his relationship to Aidan, and thus his relationship to all that is unpredictable and vulnerable in life, including loss. But what counts as truth is not an abstract proposition; it is the truth of Crane's own character. In the particular genre that Bakhtin is discussing in the passage quoted earlier, the *menippea*, Bakhtin emphasizes that the character represents an idea, and "the issue is precisely the testing of an *idea*, or a *truth*, and not the testing of a particular human character" (114). In moral life writing, idea and character cannot be disentangled. The truth of the value of washing Aidan is the narrator's capacity, which becomes the reader's capacity, to realize the moral significance of washing, and how washing is narratable.

Ultimately moral non-fiction, for all its autobiographical particularity, claims to expand the writer into Everyperson. Crane's washing of Aidan is more than a metonym for his care of his son; it is also a metaphor for a mode of attending to the world to which Crane is calling us. That mode of attending is a calling, in the religious sense. *Aidan's Way* is moral non-fiction because Crane's own developmental narrative—from anger to compassionate service—expresses a *better* way to live. Crane learns this better way from Aidan, but not directly;

here again is the homologous relationship between narrative and experience. Crane's capacity to recognize what Aidan has to teach him is mediated by his reading of classic works of Asian spirituality: the *I Ching* and the Taoist writings of Chuang Tzu and Lao Tzu. Crane's title seems to echo the "way" in the title of Lao Tzu's *Tao Te Ching*. One of the earliest English translations of this title, now conventionally left untranslated, was *The Book of The Way and Its Power*. In The Way, Crane learns Aidan's way, and no less: Aidan sets his father on The Way.

What is at stake in the value of bathing Aidan is more than one parent's peace of mind. It's nice that Crane himself has found tranquillity where once there was anger, and there's certainly a moral point in that transition, but Crane and his fellow parent-writers stake a more expansive claim. Near the end of his book, Crane tells the story of getting a letter from his insurance company (all three writers are blessed with generally excellent insurance, and acknowledge that benefit as making their circumstances atypical), denying reimbursement for the special liquid food that Aidan needs to receive through his feeding tube. This tube was installed permanently because bits of food were getting into his lungs, causing recurrent life-threatening pneumonia. Crane beats off this challenge, reflecting bitterly on how the medical credentials of the person who signed the letter of denial impugned the ethics of medicine. He then reflects on the social scheme of values that generated the denial, and how these threaten not only Aidan but also our concept of humanity.

The moral *and* policy issue at stake in parental narratives of children's disability is what Crane calls "our [socially and culturally pervasive] calculations of an individual's value ... the possibilities of personhood" (249). There is a large philosophical literature on moral personhood,[7] much of it oriented to literary texts, but I remain focused on Crane and how his genre of life writing makes moral claims.

"His value comes," Crane writes of Aidan, "precisely from the challenge he poses to the usual definitions of 'value'" (249). He continues later, "With Aidan, it's never about utility or productivity, it's about humanity" (249–50). He does not elaborate this point theoretically; he shows how it happens. The contrasting values of productivity and humanity have their flash point at school. One level of conflict is budgetary: state laws mandate certain services for Aidan, and these legally fixed expenses then cut into school budgets that are constrained by other laws limiting increases in taxation. Parents of developmentally normal children have some justification for resenting the expenses of special needs children. But for Crane these considerations miss the

7. See Eldridge.

point on two levels. First, they presume scarcity, and he engages in successful political campaigning to change the tax increase limits. More important, arguments about budgets miss the point of what schools need to teach.

Bérubé argues eloquently that when special needs children are removed from classrooms, the "normal" children (the scare quotes indicating the social construction of normality) are taught the legitimacy of off-loading responsibilities of care: "One thing they'll learn is an implicit lesson I learned as a child: *The 'disabled' are always other people. You don't have to worry about them. Somebody else is doing that*" (205). Bérubé calls this "growing up ignorant" (205). Its consequence is to reify distinctions between "normal" and "abnormal" which then become distinctions of worth, or entitlement to personhood. The consequences go beyond disability issues. The children are being taught a lesson about the limitations of their moral responsibility; there's a whole world of suffering that the children are taught they don't have to worry about.

What Bérubé argues at considerable theoretical length, Crane argues with stories: simple anecdotes of Aidan's classmates learning, first, not to be afraid of his seizures and other fearsome behavior. The children then learn how to interpret the world to Aidan though his sense of touch; in making the world available to Aidan, they learn their own values. These stories might, in another context, be sentimental or cute. Perhaps Crane has to put them at the end of his narrative because by then the reader has learned what the stakes are: how people who have grown up ignorant, as Bérubé puts it, act and fail to act. We know how much it counts for these children to cultivate a moral sense that includes Aidan.

Two final points can be made about *Aidan's Way* and about the genre of life writing it represents. The first is that while such writing is non-fiction, it seems well described by Mattingly's term "anti-mimetic," by which she means that such narratives derive their power "by transforming and distorting life as lived" (25). I am not suggesting that Crane distorts his report of his life. What counts as "his life" is already shaped by a narrative, before he produces the written narrative representing this life. As Mattingly describes this loop: "Experience requires the transformation and distortion that narrative imposes in order to be meaningful" (25). Crane's depiction of his daily bathing of Aidan is, again, a clear example: what he experiences as he bathes his son is already transformed by being experienced as narratable. If Crane's early anger was an untransformed response, his later calmness is "distorted" by the narrative that he lives, reads (in the Chinese wisdom literature), and writes, but not in any causal order; each aspect of experience conditions the whole.

The second point concerns how such a story ends. Partway through the book I found myself wondering if Aidan would die; his life expectancy is limited, according to medical judgment. Death is, certainly, the ultimate closure, and Aidan's death would offer closure to a discomforting story. The final moral lesson of the book is to question what sort of closure the reader desires, in narrative and in life. Tod Chambers and Kathryn Montgomery, in their analysis of plot in the narration of bioethics cases, contrast aesthetic closure with the medical "desire to bring order" (83) and to have the case close in a way that, to return to Bakhtin's term, finalizes the patient and the events of treatment. They also describe aesthetic closure, quoting Barbara Herrnstein Smith's lovely phrase, as "the expectation of nothing" (83).

Aidan is left unfinalized, and thus able to *be*, when his parents, his classmates, and the readers of his story reach this expectation of nothing, which becomes *no-thing* in the Zen language that Crane uses to inform his experience. To expect no-thing is to expect every-thing, and to be equally open to all possibilities. That is the silence to which Aidan's way leads Crane, and to which Crane leads his readers. Medical case conferences, Chambers and Montgomery remind us, seek solutions. Aidan's way leads to no solution, and that realization that no-solution is a way to live solves everything.

Moral Perfectionism and the Good Story

The morality that Gardner finds practiced in moral fiction, and that I have tried to locate in the practice of Crane's moral non-fiction, has been described by philosophers as moral perfectionism, by which they mean not an obsessive demand to achieve some standard of perfection, but morality as an ongoing story of possibilities, realized and as yet unrealized, with perfection always beyond the horizon. Moral perfectionism is the complement—not the stand-alone alternative—to legislative morality, which is the morality of rules and codes, justified by expertly deduced principles. The core of moral perfectionism is the belief that "there is a need for something *prior* to principles or a constitution, without which the best principles and the best constitution would be worthless" (Putnam 36).[8] The problem with moral perfec-

8. Putnam is describing the philosopher Emmanuel Levinas. The idea of moral perfectionism is from Stanley Cavell, who describes perfectionism as "a competing theory of the moral life that spans the course of Western thought, and concerns what used to be called the state of one's soul, a dimension that places tremendous burdens on personal relationships and [on] the transforming of oneself and of one's society" (quoted in Putnam 58, n. 6).

tionism is the rationale for legislative morality: the "my own little voice" problem discussed earlier in this essay.

The advocates of legislative morality argue that stories are seductive: anybody can make a course of action sound good in the right story. Gardner's Bluebeard trope suggests this problem. Gardner could easily imagine Bluebeard telling his own "counterstory" to the oppressive morality of conventional marriage.[9] Gardner thus calls for criticism to provide the dialogue in which the moral worth of the story is contested. Criticism requires the capability to sustain an unfinalized dialogue in which morality is perpetually troublesome, and the critic's own moral maturity and emotional honesty are always subject to improvement.[10]

Moral perfectionism is inherently dialogical, and as such, necessarily unfinalized; the "perfect" is a process, not a fixed goal. This process is a struggle. "The nature of a free society," Taylor writes, "is that it will always be the locus of a struggle between the higher and lower forms of freedom" (78). To which I would add that the struggle is also over which forms of freedom are "higher and lower." Crane's argument is that Aidan's claim on social resources is a higher form of freedom. Insurance companies and school boards deprecate keeping "these sorts of kids" alive—and in school—as a lower form of freedom, in the sense that other social priorities trump that freedom.

Crane recognizes that insurance companies and school boards have real problems: providing health care and education to the most people in the most efficient manner. What he contests is their standard of efficiency. His argument against that standard of efficiency is his story of Aidan's life: the effect of that life on others, and Crane's personal witness to how Aidan has changed him. The critic—who is any reader—has to take a stand, which means living his or her life with certain sympathies and priorities.

This argument-in-story never aspires to be what philosophers would call a knock-down argument; the point is not to knock anyone down but to keep everyone open to different stories, different images of life's possibility, and different affirmations. Each of us has to make decisions between different stories that make different claims on us, and each of these claims may be honorable. We do not act on principles that

9. Gardner's early novel *Grendel* employs the trope of retelling the epic *Beowulf* from the perspective of the monster, who, in the original, embodies evil; the monster may still be evil, but what is "evil" now depends on which cave you crawled out of. Literary counterstories do not, however, imply moral relativism. Rather, the dialogue of story and counterstory requires the reader to develop an increasingly nuanced sense of what evil is, and nuance is at the core of moral perfectionism.

10. See Gardner, *Moral Fiction* 146.

hold for all times. We act as best we can at a particular time, guided by certain stories that speak to that time, and other people's dialogical affirmation that we have chosen the right stories.

Unfinalized dialogue is exemplified by Crane's activism in leading a local voting campaign to waive limits on property tax increases so that the school board could have more money to meet the needs of all students. The vote increased taxes that year, but nothing was finalized: another year, another vote, and so, in Taylor's phrase (78), the struggle continues. How people voted depended on which stories they found compelling. Their votes were acts of practical criticism, since they responded to the same question that Gardner quotes I. A. Richards asking about judging artworks: "Why prefer this picture to that" (*Moral Fiction* 130). Gardner then makes a crucial dialogical observation about Richards's question: "A moment's thought shows that the usefulness of these questions is precisely that the critic . . . can never answer them in the same way twice" (130). As soon as I have heard one story, I hear another, and my sense of the first changes. For moral perfectionism, that constant change is no problem; on the contrary, the openness to change is the beginning of moral maturity.

Legislative morality wants moral perfectionism to legislate standards for the good story, pointing out—correctly—that not all stories are equally good. Moral perfectionism agrees that not all stories are equal but wants unfinalized dialogue: a continuing contest of alternative images of how we should live, each competing for moral affirmation. Moral perfectionism accepts that any vision of the good will change: Aidan's physical condition is going to change, his sister will get older and will have different needs, the family will require different adaptations, which may involve different moral images of what is good. That is not a problem; it's life.

Moral perfectionism, including what I have called moral freedom, is inherently a dialogue of stories—moral nonfictions—that reinforce and contest one another's images of the good. There are, as Gardner says, quoting Faulkner, eternal verities, but as people make moment-by-moment decisions between competing claims on their lives and resources, it is no easy task prioritizing each claim according to these verities. The best any of us can do is to tell one another our stories of how we have made choices and set priorities. By remaining open to other people's responses to our moral maturity and emotional honesty—their practical criticism of making our stories part of their lives or rejecting those stories and telling different ones—we engage in the unfinalized dialogue of seeking the good.

WORKS CITED

Bakhtin, Mikhail. *Problems of Dostoevsky's Poetics*. Trans. Caryl Emerson. Minneapolis: University of Minnesota Press, 1984.

Bellah, Robert N., Richard Marsden, William Sullivan, Ann Swindler, and Steven Tupton. *Habits of the Heart*. Berkeley: University of California Press, 1996.

Bérubé, Michael. *Life as We Know It: A Father, a Family, and an Exceptional Child*. New York: Pantheon, 1996.

Chambers, Tod. "And the Counterstories Will Set You Free (Well, at Least the Good Ones Will)." *Medical Humanities Review* 15, no. 2 (2001): 98–101.

Chambers, Tod, and Kathryn Montgomery. "Plot: Framing Contingency and Choice in Bioethics." In *Stories Matter: The Role of Narrative in Medical Ethics*. Ed. Rita Charon and Martha Montello. New York: Routledge, 2002. 77–84.

Charlton, James I. *Nothing about Us without Us: Disability, Oppression, and Empowerment*. Berkeley: University of California Press, 1998.

Crane, Sam. *Aidan's Way: The Story of a Boy's Life and a Father's Journey*. Naperville, Ill.: Sourcebooks, 2003.

Eldridge, Richard. *On Moral Personhood: Philosophy, Literature, Criticism, and Self-Understanding*. Chicago: University of Chicago Press, 1989.

Fabian, Ann. *The Unvarnished Truth: Personal Narratives in Nineteenth-Century America*. Berkeley: University of California Press, 2000.

Frank, Arthur W. *At the Will of the Body: Reflections on Illness*. 1991. Boston: Houghton Mifflin, 2002.

——. "Illness as Moral Occasion: Restoring Agency to Ill People." *Health* 1, no. 2 (1997): 131–48.

——. *The Wounded Storyteller: Body, Illness, and Ethics*. Chicago: University of Chicago Press, 1995.

Frankl, Victor E. *Man's Search for Meaning*. New York: Washington Square Press, 1959.

Gardner, John. *Grendel*. New York: Alfred Knopf, 1971.

——. *On Moral Fiction*. New York: Basic Books, 1978.

Holstein, James A., and Jaber F. Gubrium. *The Self We Live By: Narrative Identity in a Postmodern World*. New York: Oxford University Press, 2000.

Kittay, Eva Feder. " 'Not My Way, Sesha, Your Way, Slowly': 'Maternal Thinking' in the Raising of a Child with Profound Intellectual Disabilities." In *Mother Troubles: Rethinking Contemporary Maternal Dilemmas*. Ed. Julia E. Hanigsberg and Sara Ruddick. Boston: Beacon Press, 1999. 3–27.

Kleinman, Arthur. *The Illness Narratives: Suffering, Healing, and the Human Condition*. New York: Basic Books, 1988.

Mattingly, Cheryl. *Healing Dramas and Clinical Plots: The Narrative Structure of Experience*. Cambridge: Cambridge University Press, 1998.

Murray, Thomas H. *The Worth of a Child*. Berkeley: University of California Press, 1996.

Nelson, Hilde Lindemann. *Damaged Identities, Narrative Repair*. Ithaca: Cornell University Press, 2001.

Pennybaker, James W. "Telling Stories: The Health Benefits of Narrative." *Literature and Medicine* 19, no. 1 (2000): 3–18.

Price, Reynolds. *A Whole New Life: An Illness and a Healing*. New York: Atheneum, 1994.

Putnam, Hilary. "Levinas and Judaism." In *The Cambridge Companion to Levinas*. Ed. Simon Critchley and Robert Bernasconi. Cambridge: Cambridge University Press, 2002. 33–62.

Smart, Barry. *Facing Modernity: Ambivalence, Reflexivity, and Morality*. London: Sage, 1999.

Taylor, Charles. *The Malaise of Modernity*. Concord, Ontario: Anansi, 1991.

Wolfe, Alan. *Moral Freedom: The Search for Virtue in a World of Choice*. New York: Norton, 2001.

CHAPTER 10

When Life Writing Becomes Death Writing: Disability and the Ethics of Parental Euthanography

G. Thomas Couser

With the passage of its Death with Dignity statute in 1994 (which survived an attempt to repeal it by referendum in 1997 and an effort by U. S. attorney general John Ashcroft to overrule it in 2002), Oregon became the first state in the United States to legalize physician-assisted suicide, a form of voluntary active euthanasia. Subsequently, other states, including Hawai'i, have proposed similar legislation. In the United States, the public debate over the ethics of euthanasia, especially physician-assisted suicide (PAS),[1] has been carried out in a variety of venues, such as courts, legislatures, and the mass media. Of these venues, perhaps the least attended to has been life writing. Granted, there are few personal narratives of euthanasia in print, and that may not seem surprising: one might wonder who would want to read one, let alone write one. Yet the number of narratives continues to grow, and the neglect of personal accounts of euthanasia by students of life writing represents an odd omission in a field that has been very attentive to representations of trauma.[2]

---

1. Ironically, among some disabled people, PAS is understood as an acronym for personal assistant services.

2. In the United States, published book-length accounts of assisted suicide are not new. For example, in 1957, the journalist Lael Tucker Wertenbaker published an account of her husband's suicide, *Death of a Man*, and in 1976 the Quaker writer Jessamyn West (best known for *The Friendly Persuasion*) published an account of her younger sister's suicide, *The Woman Said Yes*. Additional accounts have been

Narratives of euthanasia warrant close attention today because they may constitute, as Herbert Hendin has claimed, "the ultimate marketing technique to promote the normalization of assisted suicide and euthanasia" (49). Most such narratives concern people of advanced years, with terminal illnesses that cause them unremitting and presumably unmitigable pain. Readers will find themselves in sympathy with the plight of the ill persons, and those readers not unalterably opposed to suicide on religious or moral grounds may accept their suicides as rational and ethical acts. More problematic, and hence perhaps more revealing, are accounts that deal with similar crises in the lives of much younger persons. Such accounts are useful not just for what they encompass but also for what they elide as considerations in the choice of death. In particular, they illuminate the role played by disability in the discourse of euthanasia. Finally, they expose the dangers of parental surrogacy in both the ethics of euthanasia and the ethics of life writing.

■

What I call euthanography—narratives in which euthanasia (in any form) is considered (but not necessarily committed)—is a distinct subset of the specialized (but expanding) subgenre of narratives by suicide "survivors" (where the term applies not to someone who attempts suicide and "fails" but rather to someone who is bereaved by the suicide of a loved one). Richard K. Sanderson notes that survivors of unassisted suicide "may blame themselves for the death, and they may imagine, often correctly, that they are being blamed by others. Though their grief may be especially intense and prolonged, the shame attached to suicide frequently deprives them of the social support normally available to the bereaved" (33). Survivor-narrators of assisted suicide are in a significantly different, but equally delicate, position. They are likely to be less devastated, since the suicides they survive do not surprise them and do not seem directed at them. While some survivor-narrators—especially children of suicidal parents—may feel that they were manipulated into their assistance, they lack the obvious claim to victimhood of other suicide survivors.

published by Betty Rollin (*Last Wish*, 1985); Derek Humphry, a co-founder of the Hemlock Society (*Jean's Way*, 1978); and Judy Brown (*The Choice*, 1995). Although they evince awareness of both the transgressiveness of assisted suicide and the trickiness of going public with it, these accounts are not impelled by commitment to a cause. The narrators' motives are personal rather than political—to honor the decision of the deceased and to justify their own involvement in the suicide. In contrast, more recent accounts are distinguished by their awareness of being ethically and politically controversial. This reflects the increasingly urgent public debate over the ethics of euthanasia.

Their situation may be somewhat less difficult emotionally than that of survivors of unassisted suicide, but it is more complicated both ethically and rhetorically. As Sanderson points out, suicide is almost always a relational act in that it occurs, and acquires meaning, in a social, primarily familial context:

> Suicide, according to most clinicians, is more than a deliberate act of lethal self-destruction: It is also a *communication*, an interpersonal or "dyadic" act, a self-dramatization performed before an audience consisting of the suicide and of *other* persons, usually members of the suicide's family. . . . [T]he most noteworthy feature of narratives by suicide survivors is that they are responses not simply to an experience but to a relational act, to a communication. (35)

Assisted suicide is not only relational but co-intentional. Considered as communication—an act of self-definition as well as of self-destruction—the suicide is collaboratively composed; the assistant is not so much the recipient of this communication as its co-author and co-performer. Whereas survivors of solo suicide typically distance themselves from the act, condemning it even as they struggle to interpret it, survivors of assisted suicide must defend the act. Thus, their role as life writers is effectively determined by their complicity in the death they narrate.

Narratives of assisted suicide, then, tend toward apologia in a different way from narratives of unassisted suicide. Whereas the survivor of unassisted suicide may simultaneously try to understand the act *and* to characterize it as irrational and wrong, the survivor of assisted suicide strives to rationalize the act in two senses at once: to make it seem both reasonable and right. (To do otherwise is to admit having acquiesced in an unnecessary death, which would compromise its status as euthanasia.) At the same time, if the act seems to have been initiated or singlehandedly authored by the survivor, the deceased will be seen as a victim.[3] Like the survivor of unassisted suicide, the suicide assistant must avoid at any cost seeming to have initiated or orchestrated the act; but unlike the survivors of solo suicide, suicide assistants are necessarily implicated and complicit in the act. To be rhetorically compelling and ethically satisfying, euthanography must present the suicide—without obviously self-serving "spin"—as rational, autonomous, and uncoerced. Thus, issues of autonomy and authority are crucial in euthanography; even those who approve of

---

3. In such cases it constitutes what Margaret Pabst Battin calls "manipulated suicide."

"rational suicide" should be concerned that such acts are freely chosen and fairly represented.

Narratives of euthanasia by those who acquiesce or assist in it come as close, perhaps, as any life writing can to realizing the trope of biography as a kind of "taking" of another's life, because they so literally recapitulate and rationalize the process by which death is chosen and brought about.[4] Such narratives aspire to present the ending of their subjects' lives as euthanasia in the literal sense, that is, good (desired or desirable) death; the assistant's understandable and well-intentioned impulse is to close off doubt and second-guessing. Indeed, this is virtually a generic requirement; it is difficult to imagine an assistant—especially a parent—suggesting that the death in question was a mistake.

And yet, as Hendin has noted, "even in cases advocates believe best illustrate the desirability of legalizing assisted suicide, there is ample room to question whether the death expressed the patient's wishes and met his or her needs. To dramatize these model cases, advocates present them in some detail—and this creates the opportunity to see the discrepancy between the theory and the practice of assisted suicide and euthanasia" (49–50). These accounts, then, are susceptible to oppositional reading, which suggests that the deaths depicted are not necessarily good deaths, despite having been chosen in good faith and after apparently rational consideration.[5] Reading between the lines does not so much tease out emotional ambivalence about the decision, which is all too manifest, as uncover aspects of the cases that may have played a significant role in scripting the death without having been explicitly considered. That is, close reading can sometimes discover ways in which the outcomes are even more overdetermined—and thus less autonomous—than they initially appear. Indeed, if, as Carolyn Ells has argued, "autonomy is attributable only to socially situated selves" (611), then the idea of self-determined death becomes inherently problematic.

Euthanography may be unpleasant to read in the best of circumstances—that is, when the reader is convinced that the death in ques-

---

4. The locus classicus of this trope is a letter from Henry Adams to Henry James, in which Adams likened biography to literary homicide. The thrust of his letter was to characterize his autobiography as a preemptive taking of his own life as protection against unauthorized biography (512).

5. In *Seduced by Death*, Hendin critiques several such accounts, including that of the physician Timothy Quill—not, as I initially suspected, a pen name—who assisted a patient's suicide and then wrote about it, first in the *New England Journal of Medicine* and later in a book, *Death and Dignity*, and that of Andrew Solomon, whose account of assisting his mother's suicide appeared in the *New Yorker*.

tion is a good one. Reading against the grain may be particularly uncomfortable, because dissenting reading is tantamount to second-guessing an elaborate defense of a painful choice. Since readers operate at a remove from the world in which a real person chose to die, however, readers are not in a position to take issue with the actual decision making; the process by which these life-or-death decisions were reached and carried out is accessible to readers only through the narrative's mediation. As readers, we know only what we are told, and we can respond only to the representation of these events—a second-order phenomenon at best.

Yet that very mediation, which insulates assistants from direct observation, also invites and warrants appraisal, since it involves the literal publication of their acts. (That is, the act of representation by the assistants waives any claim to privacy that would otherwise protect them from scrutiny.) As readers, then, we may reach different conclusions from those of the individuals represented; indeed, narratives of euthanasia, not surprisingly, may arouse strong—and conflicting—emotions in readers. Critics are justified in articulating those differences; to do so is to respond to the texts' implicit invitation to engage in the debate over euthanasia and PAS. There is, then, a subtle but significant distinction between second-guessing the actual decisions and evaluating their retrospective public representation. If a narrative offers us an account in which some crucial step is omitted in the procedure of exercising the right to die, then we can say that the text fails rhetorically. (In real life, the step may have been taken; narratives are necessarily incomplete.) It should be remembered, then, that my discussion concerns textual figures, not their historical counterparts. It may seem presumptuous to take issue with published accounts of such agonized decisions, but it is not invasive, and whatever presumption is entailed may be justified by the importance of the stakes for other lives, whose ends are yet to be determined. Painful as it is to read and respond to, euthanography is an extreme instance of contemporary memoir as quality-of-life writing—that is, narrative that rehearses difficult bioethical questions and that underlines the potential life-giving and life-taking power of parental life writing.

■

Two narratives published around the same time present similar scenarios with very different outcomes. The first, *Saying Goodbye to Daniel: When Death Is the Best Choice* (1995), is Juliet Cassuto Rothman's account of her son's decision to discontinue life-sustaining medical treatment after a diving accident that paralyzed him at the age of twenty-one. Rothman's book recounts the decision of a young man, with his mother's support, to end his life rather than to live with what he considered unbearable or futile suffering. The second offers a counterpoint to the first: *Rescuing Jeffrey* (2000) is Richard Galli's account of the ten days following a diving mishap that left his teenaged son with quadriplegia. In the immediate aftermath of this devastating event, his parents determined that Jeffrey, who was not yet eighteen, should die, and they planned to have his physicians "pull the plug"—without informing Jeffrey or giving him a choice—as soon as they were assured that the hospital's ethics committee would not object or interfere. According to his father's brief account, however, within ten days of the accident (about the time they got the go-ahead from the hospital), his parents changed their minds.

The accounts of Julia Rothman and Richard Galli deviate from the exemplary scenario of euthanasia in three ways. (Because both Daniel and Jeffrey required life support, their situations did not involve physician-assisted suicide.) First, they have to do with young protagonists, men in their late teens or twenties. Their predicaments are particularly poignant because, as the cliché goes, these young men should have had their whole life ahead of them. Second, both narratives have to do with severe disability rather than terminal illness (cancer and amyotrophic lateral sclerosis, ALS, being the paradigmatic illnesses in euthanasia narratives). Third, they are accounts in which parents oversee or make the crucial decision, a significant deviation from the usual generational perspective, which is that of a surviving spouse (Wertenbaker, Humphry), sibling (West), or child (Rollin, Brown). For these reasons, they cast in high relief some of the ethical issues inherent in euthanasia and life writing in extremis.

Rothman's and Galli's narratives are especially revealing if read against each other because, while the nature and the circumstances of the young men's injuries are very similar, the outcomes are diametrically opposed. Daniel Rothman and Jeffrey Galli were both injured in diving accidents. In the summer of 1992, Daniel Rothman, a Delaware resident, had completed his junior year at the University of Rochester, where he was a dean's list premedical student; he was working and living with fraternity brothers in Rochester when he incurred his injury. After being treated for a month at a local hospital, he was flown by private jet to Swedish Hospital near Denver to be stabilized in preparation for transfer to nearby Craig Hospital for rehabilitation. A rising high school junior, Jeffrey Galli was injured, as his father sardonically notes, on Independence Day 1998, during a party at the house of family friends in his Rhode Island hometown. His parents rescued him from the bottom of the swimming pool, and he was rushed to a local hospital. Both men were diagnosed with injuries in the upper cervical area of the spinal column. Initially Daniel Rothman's injury was thought to be at the C4 level—he was able to breathe and talk—but he later lost function and was rediagnosed as having a C1 injury, the uppermost level. Jeffrey Galli's injury was located at the C1-C2 juncture—also a very high spinal cord injury.

The difference between the levels of their injuries, though seemingly minimal, was not trivial. Daniel's injury and its complications proved more extensive than Jeffrey's; at least, Daniel's condition was considerably harder to stabilize. While both were dependent on ventilators to breathe, Daniel suffered losses of ventilator pressure (a terrifying but apparently quite common occurrence), fevers, blood clots, terrible headaches, adult respiratory distress syndrome (ARDS, a result of a decrease in the elasticity of lung tissue), and a number of cardiac arrests. At the time of his decision to die, the prognosis was that he would improve little if at all and might live only a few years. Hope of returning to college in the near future, much less attending medical school, which had seemed feasible when he was first injured, now seemed unrealistic. Jeffrey Galli also took a long time to stabilize, but he suffered fewer crises, and he was able to resume high school classes six months after his accident.

For all their seeming engagement (by virtue of their topics) with the public debate over euthanasia, neither Rothman's nor Galli's book presents its life-or-death decision primarily in the terms of that debate. Neither one explicitly weighs the larger issues, much less generalizes its lessons; both seek to distance themselves from "causes" (which may be evidence of awareness of their controversiality). Richard Galli makes this disclaimer in his prologue: "Because the story is told primarily from my private thoughts and memories, it is nothing more than a glimpse of one father coping with the ruination of one son. The story is neither universal nor emblematic. It is not political and it may not be instructional. It is just a story" (1–2). He reiterates this claim toward the end: "This tragedy had been delivered to us by chance, not politics. The accident had no agenda. For Toby and me, Jeff was the only agenda. Jeffrey was not a flag bearer for any point of view. He represented no constituency: not handicap rights, not social or medical policy, not religion. I refused to position Jeffrey into someone else's context" (165). Even when he presents his case for removing life support to the hospital ethics committee, Galli does not directly address the substance of the decision—whether Jeffrey should live or die. Rather than arguing for Jeffrey's death, Galli asserts parental prerogative and qualification to make the decision, knowing that the board will permit parents to exercise life-or-death power only if it regards them as responsible and caring. Thus, the presentation is ultimately more about "ethos" and procedural ethics (who gets to decide Jeffrey's fate and why) than about substantive ethics (what his fate should be).

But despite disclaimers, both books must be regarded as in some sense political. If, as feminists argue, the personal is political, and if, as postmodern theorists insist, the denial of ideology is itself an ideological position, then both books are in some degree both political *and* ideological, whether overtly or not. And I would argue that while neither book adequately defends its outcome, they and narratives like them are for that very reason highly pertinent to the ongoing debate about euthanasia. If the authors themselves do not, and perhaps cannot, fully account for their narratives' strikingly different outcomes, we may mine the texts for the "absent but implicit," the factors not explicitly factored in, features that may have affected the decisions and that may affect other such choices without being consciously considered. For it is the nature of such narratives to evince issues that elude examination by their authors. And whatever the relative degrees of Jeffrey's and Daniel's injuries, it would be naïve to assume that the radical disparity between their fates, literally between life and death, was entirely a function of their physiological conditions.

The conventional discourse of "rights"—including the right to die—locates autonomy in an atomistic individual, minimizing or denying the relational, and occluding the context in which life decisions are in fact made. Narratives of euthanasia can be instructive precisely because they afford an opportunity to examine the act in context rather than to contemplate it in the abstract. One concern that may play an unacknowledged role in the decisions regarding Daniel and Jeffrey (and in similar scenarios) is the matter of parents' expectations for their offspring. In this regard the scenarios exhibit significant differences. At twenty-one, the youngest (and only male) of three children, Daniel had left home for college; had he survived, his disability would have returned him to his parents' care (if it allowed him to live at home, which was far from certain). In contrast, at seventeen, the elder of two siblings, Jeffrey was still very much in his parents' care; having him at home would be a restoration, not a reversal, of previous living arrangements.

Both sets of parents seem to have had high expectations for their sons in terms of achievement, but the four-year difference in age may be significant: the Rothmans may have had more invested in a specific life course for Daniel, a college junior, than the Gallis did for Jeffrey, a high school junior. At the time of his accident, Jeffrey Galli was less far along in shaping his life choices than Daniel Rothman, who was on course to his father's profession, medicine.[6] Perhaps more important, Jeffrey had been performing poorly in high school in the years immediately preceding his accident. After a period of withdrawal and dysfunction, he had been treated for depression, and his attitude and performance had begun to improve. Indeed, one of the ironies of his accident, by his father's account, is that his presence at the July Fourth pool party at which he nearly drowned was a sign of his recovery; at this point the Gallis were grateful merely for the revival of his interest in other people.

Jeffrey's accident was an ironic reversal of a projected life trajectory but not as severe a disruption as Daniel Rothman's. Although both young men considered themselves responsible for their own injuries, it may be significant that Jeffrey's first response when seeing his parents was to ask what happened, whereas Daniel's first reported remark to his father after his accident was, "I messed up, Dad. . . . I really messed up" (Rothman 13). The implication is that he feels responsible not just for screwing up his life but also for disappointing his father. In any case, a full consideration of a son's decision whether to live or die might take into account the implications of his disability with regard to his past and his projected future within the developing family narrative. For all the justified concern with autonomy in the crucial decision, disability is something that happens to families, not just to individuals; its consequences and costs are shared, not borne solely by the disabled person.

One concern about the competence of people who suffer catastrophic injuries like those of Daniel and Jeffrey is that acute depression, which is common in such circumstances, may cloud their judgment. A clinically depressed patient would clearly not be considered competent; a more difficult question is whether "a depressed state of mind that is serious but does not render a patient incompetent" should militate against a decision to die.[7] Is a quadriplegic's wish to die a function of an irrational state of mind, or is it a rational response to an insupportable condition, a realistic assessment of the likely quality of his or her life? (This is to ignore for the moment the crucial issue of how much that quality of life is determined by physiological deficit and

6. That disability does not necessarily rule out a medical practice is illustrated by the career of the psychiatrist Arnold Beisser, but Beisser contracted polio after he graduated from medical school. (See his autobiographical book *Flying without Wings*.) A disability as severe as Daniel's would rule out pursuit of a medical degree, yet it could be argued that some experience of disability might be a desirable attribute in certain fields of medicine.

7. Beauchamp and Childress 148.

how much by social and cultural conditions.) This is an especially problematic question because those in a position to evaluate such wishes are rarely disabled themselves and may view severe disability as a fate worse than death. In fact, however, most people who live with severe disability (especially those disabled from birth) rate the quality of their lives higher than do those in the general population. This helps to explain why, as Hendin writes, "no group is more justifiably concerned about legalization [of PAS] than people with disabilities.... [I]f assisted suicide and euthanasia are given legal sanction, disabled persons are, in disproportionate numbers, likely to be seen as appropriate candidates" (212).

It may seem counterintuitive that Jeffrey, the depressive son, lives while Daniel dies. But perhaps Jeffrey's survival was influenced in part by his parents' familiarity with depression, their understanding of the way in which it can skew judgment of one's circumstances. In any case, one family had recognized and addressed depression as a treatable medical condition; the other had not. Whatever their actual circumstances—and readers are not in a position to diagnose either young man (or his parents, for that matter) as depressed—it is noteworthy that both narratives minimize consideration of the young men's states of mind. Behaviors that seem symptomatic of depression—withdrawal, refusal of visitors, and the like—might raise some questions as to competence, but in neither narrative is this much explored. No one would deny, I think, that the objective circumstances of both young men are grim. But the narratives' failure to consider that depression (on anyone's part) may play a decisive role is worrisome. (In the Gallis' case, of course, Jeffrey's competence is not at issue, since he is not making the decision; but his state of mind is relevant in that parents might be more inclined to end the life of a son who displayed little will to live.) Although depression does not play an explicit role in either case, the Galli family might be described as having been inoculated, if not immunized, against it in the sense that they had reckoned with it already.

Hendin warns that "in their depression, their ambivalence about dying, and their need to test the affection of others, medically ill patients who request assisted suicide are not different from patients who become suicidal for other reasons.... Most are looking for a response that indicates that their fears will be addressed, that their pain will be relieved, and that they will not be abandoned" (159). It should be obvious, though it is easily overlooked, that it is not only individuals suddenly stricken by disease or disability but also their families who may experience shock, depression, or despair immediately after catastrophic illness or injury. Also relevant is the family's acquisition of the "courtesy stigma" that extends to those closest to individuals whose identities are "spoiled" by disability.[8]

Hendin suggests that the outcome in crises like these is often determined by those closest to the patient, in particular by whether they respond to the undercurrent of ambivalence in the expression of a wish to die or only to its overt content (185). So the mental state of the immediate family and prospective caregivers also has to be considered. All parties need a period in which to adjust their sense of the future to new realities. What Hendin says about terminal illness is also applicable to severe disability, which may seem to offer no relief short of death: "Watching someone die can be intolerably painful for those who care for the patient. Their wish to have it over with can become a form of pressure on the patient that must be distinguished from the patient's own wants" (57). That wish, of course, need not be expressed—or even conscious—to be communicated effectively to the diseased or disabled person.

Another factor may have been decisive, though it may seem adventitious and insignificant: Jeffrey Galli was injured and hospitalized close to home, while Daniel Rothman was injured and hospitalized far from home. Although friends seem to have rallied around both families initially, support was more intense, immediate (in both senses), and sustained in the Gallis' case. Once Daniel Rothman was hospitalized near Denver, it was difficult for friends and family to visit with any regularity, frequency, or duration. In contrast, Richard Galli speaks of the constant, at times claustrophobic, presence of close friends and family in the ICU waiting room and the logistical and emotional support of others outside his immediate circle of friends and acquaintances—what he calls "the wave." As Daniel's stay in Swedish Hospital stretched on from summer into fall, his mother canceled her classes and dropped other professional obligations to be with him while her husband maintained his medical practice. She was thus isolated from the direct support of family and friends in a way that the Gallis were not; she became, in effect, Daniel's sole companion, interpreter, advocate, and lifeline. (Unable to speak aloud, he communicated by mouthing words.)

The importance to the injured person of having family present and to the nearest relative of having other support nearby is evident when Juliet Rothman returns home to Delaware for a few days to settle

8. Goffman 30. One way of reading Kafka's "The Metamorphosis" is as an account of a family's response to their contamination by such a stigma.

affairs. At this point she is considering commuting from Denver to her job, but when she returns to Daniel's bedside, she finds that his condition has taken a dangerous downturn in her absence, and she resolves to be with him for the duration. Although she does not complain, the effect of this arrangement is to raise the price she pays for his confinement in the hospital: his confinement effectively sequesters her as well. The more she mothers him, the less time she has for herself; it seems that she can have a son or have a life. (She selflessly gives up her work and home life for the time being.) The Gallis were somewhat insulated from this dilemma; after nearly living in the ICU waiting room for the first few days, they were able to commute from their home nearby, and were able to resume more normal patterns of life sooner.

Feminist ethics provides a helpful perspective on the ethics of care that impels Rothman much of the time. Some feminists have worried that Carol Gilligan's association of an ethics of care with women may valorize characteristics that are by-products of oppression: exalting an ethics of care risks reinforcing women's roles as the primary nurturers and carers in patriarchal systems. (Consider the relative prestige and remuneration of the "caring" and the uncaring professions.) Such analysis illuminates Juliet Rothman's position: as much as we may admire the sacrifices she makes out of an ethics of care—of her time, professional gratification, and income—we may see her position as unsustainable and finally unjust. As long as the burden of being Daniel's primary caregiver is exclusively hers, she is called upon to give up too much, and this may redound to his disadvantage. Understandably, none of this is stated in the narrative, but readers may detect considerations that may escape the notice of narrators.

Another pertinent difference is that while both sets of parents dutifully "do their homework"—that is, they research spinal cord injury and rehabilitation—only Richard Galli seems to have sought out personal accounts of surviving spinal cord injury in response to his son's injury. At one point Galli admits that he would have done more research before buying a toaster than he had done before determining to "kill" (his word) his son (76), and he is perplexed and shocked by this impulse. He then undertakes further research, reading several narratives, including those of the actor Christopher Reeve and the college hockey player Travis Roy. He gives these stories no credit for the positive outcome in his son's case; on the contrary, when he argues for Jeffrey's death in front of the ethics committee, he rejects them as irrelevant on the grounds that both Reeve and Roy are celebrities with resources that Jeffrey entirely lacked. This is a fair point: disabled celebrities may be unrealistic and inappropriate models for people like

Jeffrey. Nevertheless, one wonders whether reading their accounts may have helped Galli to visualize life after spinal cord injury, to imagine how life as and with a quadriplegic might be manageable and meaningful.

The issue of the imaginability of living with disability is crucial. A rarely discussed but undeniable, perhaps decisive, factor in quality-of-life determinations is the preexisting attitude toward disability on the part of patients and their families. Different individuals may have very different responses to the same level of impairment; indeed, one of the things that reading narratives such as these reveals is the wide variation in tolerance of permanent severe disability. Robert Murphy's *Body Silent*, Archie Hanlan's *Autobiography of Dying*, Albert B. Robillard's *Meaning of a Disability*, and Mitch Albom's best-selling *Tuesdays with Morrie* are all narratives in which men—not incidentally all professors of the social sciences—face deterioration and certain death from progressive paralysis (a spinal tumor in Murphy's case, ALS in the cases of Hanlan, Robillard, and Morrie Schwartz). They do so with remarkable equanimity, even curiosity, about the way in which their bodily transformation entails stigmatization and ostracism. To my knowledge, none of them committed suicide; at least, none of them reports contemplating, much less planning, suicide. All are saddened and disturbed by their deterioration, but all endure a high degree of paralysis without feeling the need to arrange their deaths. This has a good deal to do with their age and maturity, of course; they have resources—intellectual and emotional—to fall back on (indeed, to share) that are not available to men in their teens and twenties. For older men, masculinity and potency are less at stake in disability. And for these men, generating their narratives is itself an enactment of their continued sense of authority.

Although there is, as we have seen, a significant difference between their ages, the relative youth of Daniel and Jeffrey makes them both vulnerable to choosing to die or to having death chosen for them. Both sets of parents invoke their sons' physicality to justify their sons' deaths, as though they might decide differently about less robust young men. Perhaps they might. But to choose death at this point is to assume that such sons could never—would never—outgrow this characteristic, whereas the importance of mobility and athletic skill tends to recede with age for most men. Further, acquaintance with disability—or, lacking firsthand acquaintance, the ability to view it in a certain light—may literally be life-saving; de-stigmatizing disability may make the seemingly unendurable endurable. Richard Galli touches on the issue of the preexisting attitude toward disability in this passage:

> "I have never been in a situation where there was no out," I told [my wife]. . . .
>
> But now this situation had only two possible outcomes: Jeff would die or he would live trapped in his quadriplegia. I couldn't imagine that, couldn't visualize it. . . .
>
> I suffered from a failure of the imagination. Paralysis was repugnant to my imagination. (171)

A related passages is found in *Daniel*, when Daniel's physician in Rochester announces that he can't "imagine how he could want to live" in that condition, and Juliet Rothman responds that what matters is whether Daniel can (64).

It also matters whether the people around him can. Richard Galli's inability to imagine his son as a quadriplegic needing help with toileting (his cognitive impairment, one might say) is not surprising or blameworthy; prior to Jeffrey's accident, he had no need to imagine such a situation. Presumably Jeffrey also struggled to envision living with disability. The narrative affords us little insight into his thought processes—and we need to remember the difficulty of communicating with him during the ten days covered by the book—but it is a good sign when he asks his father whether, once he is able to resume his education, he "will have to go to a school for cripples" (159). In this brief comment, he reveals both a prejudice against disability and an incipient ability to imagine living as a disabled person. (It is important that the answer to his question—no, he could rejoin his classmates in his old school—is a function of public policy and not his degree of impairment.)

Although euthanasia is typically invoked in cases of terminal disease, a difference between disease and disability is pertinent here: whereas "diseases 'follow a *course*' and therefore prove familiar and domesticated by virtue of a belief in their determinate status (i.e., the ability to confidently narrate their future), disability might be characterized as that which exceeds a culture's predictive capacities and effective interventions."[9] Thus, part of the challenge of living with disability is precisely that it seems—sometimes, paradoxically, because of its "stability" (stasis)—unpredictable, unnarratable, that is, inassimilable within the usual narrative formulas. This fundamental resistance of disability to domestication—conceptual and literal—may illuminate the phenomenon of the "cure or kill" response to disability, according to which the disabled are tolerated only if, and as long as, their condition is deemed rectifiable; when cure or improvement proves impossible, sympathy often turns to hostility and aggression. Family members may be capable of supporting people in very poor

9. Mitchell and Snyder 3.

condition, so long as there is hope of improvement. Once that hope is lost, however, hostility—initially evoked by the damage disability inflicts on a loved relation—may be deflected onto the person "afflicted" by it. This is manifest in Richard Galli's response to his son's impairment, a powerful expression of the rationale—or (psycho)logic—of euthanasia: "For myself, I wanted to destroy his paralysis, to get it out of my world, to fix it, to conquer it. I was greedy to loosen its grip on Jeff, on me, and on the whole privileged world in which we lived before paralysis intruded. Jeffrey's death would be a victory over his paralysis" (36). When disability defies rehabilitation, the impulse to eradicate it may be deflected onto its "victim."

This cultural phenomenon—not just a "cultural text" but the lack of alternatives to that text—is implicated in narratives of euthanasia in two ways. First, the lack of familiar plausible (i.e., non-celebrity) scripts of surviving, much less thriving, after catastrophic impairment tends to reinforce and perpetuate the inability to imagine it in new cases. Even when such accounts exist, to expect parents to read and assimilate them in the immediate aftermath of accidents such as those suffered by Daniel Rothman and Jeffrey Galli may be unrealistic; parents in such crises have more immediate concerns. But as such accounts proliferate and become better known (without necessarily being read), the easier it is to imagine each new case. If, because such disabled lives have been written, there is known to be life after severe disability, such "lives" may reproduce themselves. Life writing in such cases may less frequently become death writing.

In this regard, of course, *Rescuing Jeffrey* may seem disappointing in its brevity. The narrative covers only the first ten days after the accident; resolution is provided at that point by the shift from the intention to kill Jeffrey to the decision to let him survive. As the narrative proper ends, he is still in the ICU, his condition more or less stable. A one-page postscript summarizes the next twelve months, during which Jeffrey underwent rehabilitation, returned home, and resumed classes at his high school in January 1999. The book jacket updates this sketchy narrative slightly: "Jeffrey Galli will graduate from high school in spring 2000, and he plans to go to college." Additionally, the book's "Contact Information" advises readers that they may visit his Web site and contact him by E-mail. In the fall of 2001 his Web site revealed that he had begun to attend the University of Rhode Island. So, despite its brevity, the narrative resists definitive closure and invites readers to follow Jeffrey as he adapts to his new life.[10] The open-endedness of

10. Unfortunately, the Web site is composed entirely in the third person and seems to be, like the book, entirely his father's creation, but E-mail holds out the possibility of access to Jeffrey's point of view.

the book, whose story is deflected into cyberspace and extended beyond the book's covers, is itself an affirmation of the possibility of life after a serious spinal injury and an acknowledgment of its uncertainty.

In the extremity of their scenarios, these two narratives of euthanasia expose the dangers of writing anyone else's life—especially that of an immediate family member—for it is that very immediacy and familiarity that licenses and seems to justify the arrogation of narrative authority. It is inherent in parenthood, I suppose, to imagine and invest (emotionally as well as financially) in scenarios of children's futures and to seek to script those lives to conform to an imagined life course. Such nonverbal prospective "life writing" is unavoidable and usually benign; indeed, it may be essential to good parenting. Yet there are circumstances in which this impulse may become pathological. The circumstances of Jeffrey and Daniel would not seem to be such; they appear to be "best-case" scenarios of supportive parenting. But when events threaten to overwrite the anticipated scenarios with futures no parent likes to imagine for children, there may be a powerful temptation to preclude them from being realized.

Although intolerance of disability, not only in the "afflicted" but in relatives and caregivers as well, is hardly ever an explicit consideration in analyses of euthanasia, one cannot read narratives such as these without recognizing that it functions as a powerful conditioner, if not the determiner, of outcomes. No one should judge those who decide that there is no dignity except in arranging their own deaths while they are still in control of their bodies; but we should also attend to the examples of those—like Murphy, Hanlan, Robillard, and Schwartz—who find dignity and gratification in living with severe disability. Not to put too fine a point on it, prejudice against disability can literally be life-threatening.

■

Justifying another's suicide in narrative restages the problematic ethics of enabling it in the first place. Such narratives, rare though they are, may be particularly useful texts for thinking through some of the ethical dimensions of end-of-life decisions. Even when a life narrative is driven entirely by the desire to justify and legitimize a decision to end that life prematurely, the narrative may deconstruct itself, exposing flaws and gaps in its own implicit argument. The commitment of the decision-making process to writing, while intended to compel assent in the reader, lays the process open to ethical review and revision. Indeed, such narratives may suggest that, contra its advocates, it is euthanasia, not its criminalization, that constitutes a denial of death as a natural part of life—by attempting to bring it under human control.

What is striking about these two narratives—despite the survival of one protagonist—is that they reveal how quickly life writing can become thanatography in the face of severe disability. When someone becomes terminally ill or disabled, autobiography often gives way to memoir or biography: a narrator speaks about or for the vulnerable subject in the third person. (Interestingly, this happens even in *Rescuing Jeffrey*, whose subject survives; the narrative thus reasserts the very parental prerogative that Richard Galli seemed to have surrendered.) Perhaps the extreme version of surrogacy—speaking for another—is choosing death, and thus perpetual silence, for another person. Both Juliet Rothman and Richard Galli have this impulse, though neither finally acts on it. (Daniel chooses his own death; Jeffrey is allowed to live.) Indeed, postmortem narratives can sometimes be seen as attempts to "channel" the silenced voice of dead subjects. (In this regard, Juliet Rothman's second epilogue, "Echoes of Immortality," is particularly poignant; in it she makes posthumous contact with Daniel through dreams and numerological signs of his presence.) In the face of disability, then, life writing may morph from autobiography through biography into euthanography; in such instances, as in too many other contexts, writing *of* disability often amounts to writing *off* disability.

Richard Galli's book—again, despite its final, crucial turn toward life—nicely illustrates this impulse to eradicate disability. Here he projects himself into the situation of his son contemplating his future as he had imagined it before his accident: "He had the memory of that future even now, as he lay limp in his hospital bed. The memory of his future would last forever, but the future itself was gone. . . . Paralysis . . . ruins your future, but it leaves intact the memory of all your expectations" (49). Similarly, he invokes memories of Jeffrey's earlier adventures and concludes that these would always be his best memories; empathizing with his son's (imagined) sense of loss, the father projects regret and nostalgia ahead indefinitely into a literally hopeless future. This exercise of imaginative surrogacy reinforces Richard Galli's primary impulse to kill his son in order to spare him an anticlimactic life of nostalgia for his mobile, potent young body. That is, rather than allow his own sad prophecy to be fulfilled, Galli opts to deny his son any future at all. This seemingly empathetic anticipation of deep regret is a complex and seductive (and potentially fatal) act of surrogacy.

Such narratives also suggest, however, that reckoning with disability might recast the discourse of euthanasia. The argument for euthanasia typically pits the "right to die," justified by appeal to the principle of respect for autonomy, against the "duty to live," enforced by the traditionally paternalistic bias of medicine in favor of extending life at any cost. It is worth noting, however, that this picture of medicine may be increasingly anachronistic in an age of managed health care and far from universal health insurance. In Wesley J. Smith's view, with the advent of concepts such as "futile care," the balance has tipped away from the duty to live toward the duty to die, so that the burden may now be on those who wish to be treated; legalization of euthanasia tips the balance further toward the presumption of a duty to die.

In any case, as Carolyn Ells has argued, the experience of disability exposes the dangers inherent in a narrow definition of autonomy. Traditionally, the notion assumed an isolate atomistic individual: free, equal, and rational. Thus, she writes, the "considered moral judgments" of those endowed with autonomy needed only to be respected (608–9). (This notion is implicit in these narratives insofar as they take at face value their subjects' explicit wish to die, whether it is acted upon or not.) As bioethics has evolved—in part, in response to challenges from feminists—it has increasingly acknowledged as well "an obligation to promote autonomy" (609). In biomedical practice, however, the earlier concept of obligation prevails: autonomy is seen as a capacity of the atomistic individual to be respected, rather than as an attribute of the relational self to be nurtured in its context.

The experience of disability challenges this narrow conception of autonomy in a number of ways. For one thing, the very oppression entailed by disability may compromise autonomy by eroding self-trust and self-worth.[11] For another, as in the narratives discussed here, the acquisition of disability may be considered an inherent impediment to autonomy insofar as "losses can numb and shrink the self."[12] If autonomy—especially in such circumstances—is not something to be taken for granted as a component of personhood, but rather a state to be relationally achieved, the ethical complexity of our narratives becomes even greater.

∎

I hope I have suggested that the narratives discussed here reveal the dangers of a narrow construction of autonomy—how empty a gesture it may be to respect the autonomy of a person (perhaps especially a

11. See Mcleod and Sherwin.
12. Ells 610.

relatively young person) suddenly beset by a condition that drastically challenges selfhood, rewrites life narrative, and threatens to fore-shorten life itself. As Anne Donchin has observed, "the experience of trauma, so common among hospitalized patients, suggests that the self is affected, and perhaps partially constituted, by the changing circumstances to which it is exposed. For . . . it is the loss of connection experienced by trauma survivors that most imperils their autonomous selfhood" (239). When identity is fragile and in flux, when sudden disability or terminal illness demands the generation of new bases for a sense of self-worth, it may be worse than naïve to assume that even an express desire to die reliably represents autonomous will. Under such circumstances, meaningful respect for autonomy may mean allowing and enabling individuals to develop new centers and new equilibria. Accounts that inscribe futures where no future seemed plausible—and Richard Galli's book, extended by Jeffrey's Web site, turns out to be such an account, almost in spite of itself—perform an important service in part because they enact this process.

Further, they help to demonstrate the comprehensive sense of kinship that is crucial to the survival and flourishing of disabled people. Galli's narrative in particular, for reasons that should now be clear, suggests how he, his wife, his daughter, and, most important, Jeffrey benefited from the support offered by a diverse group of people—some related by blood, most by association. These individuals established themselves as kin in two separate but overlapping ways. First, they offered emotional and logistical support to the family in its crisis; second, but perhaps more significant, they "adopted" Jeffrey and invested in his future. They assumed what his parents privately did not: that he would and should have a life, even if permanently and seriously disabled. They thus affirmed "a more expansive sense of kinship across embodied difference that . . . is essential to the public presence of disability in contemporary postindustrial democracies."[13] Those who made up "the wave" assumed, as the Gallis said to Jeffrey, that he was still Jeffrey and that Jeffrey still belonged among them.

Narratives of disability can foster (or stunt) the growth of this sense of kinship—a public and communal rather than private and familial kinship—and can foster an ethics of caring (as distinct from curing). Some narratives, while protesting the contrary, will in effect draw a new line excluding a newly disabled family member from a preexisting kinship; others will retrace and reinforce an old border that includes the disabled family member; still others will draw a new boundary that expands kinship beyond the family. In acquiring a

13. Rapp and Grinsburg 534.

disabled member, a family may acknowledge (or deny) relations with others not hitherto known as "relations"—not only those who may step forward in support, but also those who may have been through a similar experience. Families and narratives that affirm this relation help to create and sustain an inclusive sense of citizenship.[14] If the subtext, the subliminal message, of medicine today is all too likely to be "cure, correct, or eliminate," the subtext of robust disability narratives is life without cure, but not without care.

WORKS CITED

Adams, Henry. *The Education of Henry Adams*. 1918. Ed. Ernest Samuels. Boston: Houghton Mifflin, 1973.

Albom, Mitch. *Tuesdays with Morrie: An Old Man, a Young Man, and Life's Greatest Lesson*. New York: Doubleday, 1997.

Battin, Margaret Pabst. "Manipulated Suicide." In *The Least Worst Death: Essays in Bioethics on the End of Life*. New York: Oxford University Press, 1994. 195–204.

Beauchamp, Tom L., and James F. Childress. *Principles of Biomedical Ethics*. 5th ed. New York: Oxford University Press, 2001.

Beisser, Arnold. *Flying without Wings: Personal Reflections on Loss, Disability, and Healing*. New York: Bantam, 1988.

Brown, Judy. *The Choice: Seasons of Loss and Renewal after a Father's Decision to Die*. Berkeley, Calif: Conari, 1995.

Donchin, Anne. "Autonomy and Interdependence: Quandaries in Decision Making." In *Relational Autonomy: Feminist Perspectives on Autonomy, Agency, and the Social Self*. Ed. Catriona MacKenzie and Natalie Stoljar. New York: Oxford University Press, 2000. 236–58.

Ells, Carolyn. "Lessons about Autonomy from the Experience of Disability." *Social Theory and Practice* 27, no. 4 (October 2001): 595–615.

Galli, Richard. *Rescuing Jeffrey*. Chapel Hill: Algonquin Books, 2000.

Gilligan, Carol. *In a Different Voice: Psychological Theory and Women's Development*. Cambridge: Harvard University Press, 1982.

Goffman, Erving. *Stigma: Notes on the Management of Spoiled Identity*. Englewood Cliffs, N.J.: Prentice-Hall, 1963.

Hanlan, Archie J. *Autobiography of Dying*. Ed. Muriel E. Nelson. Garden City, N.Y.: Doubleday, 1979.

Hendin, Herbert, M.D. *Seduced by Death: Doctors, Patients, and Assisted Suicide*. Rev. ed. New York: Norton, 1998.

Humphry, Derek. *Jean's Way*. New York: Quartet, 1978.

Kafka, Franz. "The Metamorphosis." In *The Metamorphosis and Other Stories*. Trans. Joachim Neugroschel. New York: Scribner's, 1993. 117–41.

Loving, Carol. *My Son, My Sorrow: The Tragic Tale of Dr. Kevorkian's Youngest Patient*. Far Hills, N.J.: New Horizon, 1998.

14. Ibid. 537.

Mackenzie, Catriona, and Natalie Stoljar, eds. *Relational Autonomy: Feminist Perspectives on Autonomy, Agency, and the Social Self.* New York: Oxford University Press, 2000.

McLeod, Carolyn, and Susan Sherwin. "Relational Autonomy, Self-Trust, and Health Care for Patients Who Are Oppressed." In *Relational Autonomy: Feminist Perspectives on Autonomy, Agency, and the Social Self.* Ed. Catriona Mackenzie and Natalie Stoljar. New York: Oxford University Press, 2000. 259–79.

Mitchell, David T., and Sharon L. Snyder. "Introduction: Disability Studies and the Double Bind of Representation." In *The Body and Physical Difference: Discourses of Disability.* Ed. David T. Mitchell and Sharon L. Snyder. Ann Arbor: University of Michigan Press, 1997. 1–31.

Murphy, Robert. *The Body Silent.* New York: Henry Holt, 1987.

Quill, Timothy. *Death and Dignity: Making Choices and Taking Charge.* New York: Norton, 1993.

Rapp, Rayna, and Faye Ginsburg. "Enabling Disability: Rewriting Kinship, Reimagining Citizenship." *Public Culture* 13, no. 3 (n.d.): 533–56.

Reeve, Christopher. *Still Me.* New York: Random House, 1998.

Robillard, Albert B. *Meaning of a Disability: The Lived Experience of Paralysis.* Philadelphia: Temple University Press, 1999.

Rollin, Betty. *Last Wish.* 1985. New York: Public Affairs, 1996.

Rothman, Juliet Cassuto. *Saying Goodbye to Daniel: When Death Is the Best Choice.* New York: Continuum, 1995.

Roy, Travis, with E. M. Swift. *Eleven Seconds: A Story of Tragedy, Courage, and Triumph.* New York: Warner, 1998.

Sanderson, Richard K. "Relational Deaths: Narratives of Suicide Survivorship." In *True Relations: Essays on Autobiography and the Postmodern.* Ed. G. Thomas Couser and Joseph Fichtelberg. Westport, Conn.: Greenwood, 1998. 33–50.

Smith, Wesley J. *The Culture of Death: The Assault on Medical Ethics in America.* San Francisco: Encounter, 2000.

Solomon, Andrew. "A Death of One's Own." *New Yorker,* May 22, 1995, 54–69.

Wertenbaker, Lael Tucker. *Death of a Man.* New York: Random House, 1957.

West, Jessamyn. *The Woman Said Yes: Encounters with Life and Death.* New York: Harcourt, 1976.

CHAPTER 11

Tales of Consent and Descent: Life Writing as a Fight against an Imposed Self-Image

Marianne Gullestad

This is a particularly alarming moment in European history, with right-wing populism gaining not only parliamentary representation in many countries but also considerable ideological influence all across the political spectrum. Despite different historical traditions and political cultures, the increasing color-coded discrimination against certain inhabitants is often surprisingly similar in many countries. In this essay I analyze what this discrimination does to young people.[1] It is based on an analysis of three of the contributions to the published volume *Black on White* (*Svart på hvitt*, 2001), containing fourteen individual life narratives by young people whom the editor, Hadia Tajik, describes as "multicultural and colored" (7). Their writings can be fruitfully regarded as a special case that highlights more general dilemmas of identification. I discuss their life writing as a countermeasure, as a disclosure of self that seeks to correct the negative stereotypes encountered in the public realm without revealing too much about their families. The writers struggle with the media's demand for intimate and dramatic incidents, with denigrating stereotypes—in everyday life, in the mass media, and in the parliament—and with the public silencing of their experience of this denigration.

My aim is to look at a profound value dilemma involved both in majority hegemony in Europe and in the way the young authors have

1. I thank John Eakin for his valuable comments.

attempted to circumvent the racist discrimination it imposes. When attempting to counteract discrimination, they appeal to descent, which presents itself as the "natural" foundation for a flexible and continuous image of the self. At the same time, the high value placed on descent is also central to right-wing populism. In contemporary ideologies, ideas about descent are intertwined in complex ways with ideas about culture and geography. Over the last few decades, European sociologists, philosophers, and political scientists have examined these ideologies and how they are used in the encounter with Third World immigrants to Europe after Word War II.[2] According to their findings, "culture" now replaces the notion of "race" in much political rhetoric. This, the researchers argue, makes the hierarchical element of traditional racism less prominent, and therefore this kind of racism appears less morally reprehensible than the traditional so-called scientific racism. Cultural differences are foregrounded without any explicit assertion that some "cultures" are better than others. But since the differences are often depicted as irreconcilable, this way of arguing can provide a basis for the view that different groups should live separately, each where it "belongs." I argue here that specific ideas about descent can provide a link between the "old" and the "new" racisms. My aim is thus to make visible the value concepts implied in what is now popularly considered natural, self-evident, and self-explanatory. The main point of the analysis is to demonstrate how cultural tensions between relations of consent (based on voluntary choice) and relations of descent (based on biological kinship) are currently articulated in new ways with a more pronounced emphasis on descent.[3]

My analysis is divided in two parts. I begin with a contextualization of the life narratives in three directions First, I present a few theoretical ideas about individualized identification in the present globalizing era. These ideas are developed in relation to my ethnographic work in Norway,[4] but I assume that on a certain level of abstraction they might also apply more widely. Individualization is probably more pronounced in the West than in the so-called Third World, and more pronounced

2. See Balibar, "Is There" and "Racism"; Barker; Goldberg; Rex; Stolcke; Taguieff; and Wieviorka. Some of these researchers still use the concept of "racism" (Rex, Goldberg, Miles, Van Dijk, Wieviorka, and Frankenberg). Stolcke uses the concept of "cultural fundamentalism"; Barker, Balibar, and Hervik write about the "new racism" or "neo-racism"; while André Taguieff uses "cultural differentialism." Goldberg uses "racist expressions." For Stolcke, "xenophobia" is also a central notion.
3. This way of formulating the analytical problem is inspired by Sollors.
4. See Gullestad, Art, "Defending," Det norske, "Each Person," Everyday, "Home," "Invisible", "Imagined," Kitchen-Table, Livet, "Mohammed Atta", "From Obedience," and "Passion."

among the middle classes than among the working classes. Second, I present some information about the cultural climate the authors write against. Third, I trace a few theoretical links among political economy, identity politics, and life writing. I then shift both the analytical perspective and the level of analysis in order to present the autobiographical texts. They offer an experience-near picture of the different identity strategies employed by three young persons whose self-images are routinely under attack.

Modern Self-Fashioning

Autobiographical writing can be analyzed as a metaphor of the self,[5] and as a mediation between private and public realms. I define the modern *self* as a continuous and processual effort of a person—with no definitive end product—to bring together her various roles, identities, and experiences. *Roles*, by contrast, are the dynamic aspects of the individual's positions in social institutions and subsystems, while *identities* are those qualities with which people identify and for which they desire social confirmation. Some identities are directly tied to social roles, while others, such as social class, gender, and ethnicity, can be more or less pronounced aspects of several roles. This is not always a question of self-definition but rather one of identities being imposed by relevant others. I thus combine a dramaturgical perspective on the self, based on the shifting performance of the various roles in different contexts, with a perspective focusing on the reflexive efforts of the individual to bring together her various experiences and performances in a more or less unified conception of the self. In a circle that can be good or vicious, each person develops his sense of self by taking the perspective of important others.[6] Each person is thus involved in a never-ending attempt at creating what I call a *sustainable self-image*, a concept that implies the possession of self-respect and dignity over time, in spite of challenges and attacks.

In modern society, commodification, social differentiation, and bureaucratization have for a long time resulted in a nostalgic longing for an assumed former wholeness, as well as the development of distinct autobiographical genres of reflection about the continuity of a self *behind* the various social roles of the individual. Reflexivity rests on the experienced distance between a person's various social roles and what she considers her "true self."[7] It is, so to speak, the hallmark of

5. See Olney.
6. See Mead.
7. See Høibraaten.

modernity, and has been developed and extended widely over the centuries.[8]

Ideally, each person has to choose her values among those available. There is today an unprecedented freedom and a new focus on play, aesthetics, and creativity in social life, but there are also new kinds of vulnerability, discipline, and power. One could say that the present duty for each person to "be herself" by "creating herself" is becoming the new guise of power. This ethos fits well with the flexibility cherished by contemporary work life.[9] The state and the market have in a sense entered "inside" the individual as specific forms of self-discipline. These ideas about selfhood can be summarized by the concept of individualization.[10] Individualization implies that the discourse of individual rights and liberties has become hegemonic, and that there is a foregrounding of specific value concepts such as freedom, rights, choice, independence, individuality, uniqueness, and achievement at the expense of the concepts of dependence, obedience, duty, togetherness, and community.

On the one hand, individualization in my view correctly places ethical responsibility within each individual. On the other, the intense focus on individuality hides the socially structured nature of social life and the fact that freedom and autonomy are not equally available to everybody, as well as the value of sociality. The idea in the working-class movement that a community gives strength, that it is only by standing together that social improvements can be made, is no longer prominent. The same goes for the value of sisterhood in feminism. In some middle-class contexts it is almost as if saying "we" has become illegitimate.

I therefore see the strong focus on individuality, autonomy, and freedom as a strategy that conceals both institutional barriers to self-development and what one has received from others. These others are still very much needed, but in partly new ways. For example, the ideology of "finding oneself" by creating oneself presupposes cultural pluralism. In order to create his or her unique combination of roles and identities, each person needs many established traditions to associate with, move among, pick from, and combine in new ways.[11] Self-creation also necessitates careful training.[12] Now, parents and teachers ideally do not transmit specific values, but rather give the capacity to choose among the available alternatives and to elaborate on inherited

8. See Giddens.
9. See Sennett, Piore and Sabel, and Sabel.
10. See Beck; Gullestad, *Everyday*, "From Obedience"; and Høibraaten.
11. See Gullestad, *Everyday* 17–32.
12. See Gullestad, "From Obedience."

cultural resources. Since nobody can just lean anymore on established norms, the transmission of values often takes place in more subtle ways, and with more open and uncertain results than before. Parents teach children to "find themselves," hoping that they will not go "too far." This instruction ideally happens by means of negotiations, persuasion, and inspiration rather than by claims of obedience. Such claims are today easily seen as authoritarian. In spite of the focus on uniqueness, the lifestyles, tastes, values, and practices of young people are usually not very far from those of their parents. Individualization is thus not necessarily contrary to continuity and conformity, but is rather a style that underplays these connections.

Thus, to raise children in Europe today ideally involves teaching them to be attuned to indirect and subtle cues, to take part in teamwork in which the power relations can be more or less hidden, to deal with and find their own solutions in the midst of many conflicting messages, and to make use of a rich variety of cultural resources for creative self-fashioning. To an increasing degree, legitimate authority is based on the ability to provide the most convincing argument. Present-day authorities (such as the government, the churches, and the sciences) do not command full authority. There is no authoritative center common to everyone, but only different offers in what we might call flea markets of value. For those in power positions, it may seem as if subjects, citizens, "users," members, voters, customers, clients, and so on are "treacherous," since they do not stick loyally to one party, organization, church, and so on but move among them while picking and choosing. A different and alternative way of putting it is that people attempt to solve new ethical tasks that have so far not been fully conceptualized. Of these tasks the main one is to "find oneself" by creating oneself out of the available cultural resources.

Faced with the specific and contradictory combination of freedom and discipline, some people manage to become their own authorities. They create their own forms of wholeness as if they were experimenting artists, and life itself becomes like a work of art symbolizing their self-image. I see styles—in life writing, clothing, home decoration, and so on—as popular expressions of the value of wholeness. Others react to the new demands in what might be called fundamentalist ways. Instead of picking and choosing in order to create unique wholes, the person embraces a ready-made package of identities and interprets it in a literal way. I see all these various reactions, be they experimental, fundamentalist, or something in between, as modern responses to the freedom and the discipline implied in the current stress on independent self-creation.

But individualization implies above all that each person depends on other people who are able and willing to confirm the presented identities and self-image. Confirmation is uncertain, and dignity and recognition have become key concepts in the present stage of modernity.[13] Rejection and lack of recognition routinely happen to many people, among them people "with a different skin color."

The Political Economy of Individualized Identification

I do not want to argue for a simple reflectionism between wide-ranging changes in the political economy of the world system and cultural practices such as the production and consumption of life writing. Nevertheless, I think it is important to discuss theoretical links among these realms in order to be able to frame our studies in more adequate ways. The end of colonialism in the 1960s and the fall of the Berlin Wall in 1989 are two key moments in recent world history. One moment undermined Western cultural and economic hegemony, the other discredited Marxism and the collective working-class movement, with the result that the resistance to economic neoliberalism is weak. The first industrial society is fading out, and we do not yet have all the necessary concepts to grasp the new tendencies. "Globalization" is a popular cover term for economic, political, and cultural processes of various degrees of intensity and extension. One of these processes is what is often called the "information society," based on the time-space compression made possible by the information technologies.[14] Related to this development is the increasing and changing role of the mass media and the culture industries, as well as the deregulation of capital, and the widening gap between investment capital and productive capital. The transformations of capitalism have been called a new form of "owner's capitalism," in opposition to the "managerial capitalism" of western Europe in the second half of the twentieth century. The strong professional manager mediated between labor and capital in a way that made capitalism bearable.[15] Now the owners of investment capital have increased their power, and their decisions are made accordingly. The stable well-being of firms, employees, and local communities is no longer necessary to secure increasing profits.

13. See Berger, Berger, and Kellner; Taylor.
14. See Giddens and Beck.
15. See Sejersted and Sennett.

In *Globalisation and Its Human Consequences* (1998), Zygmunt Bauman argues that the increasing power of investment capital, entering and leaving local communities with no social responsibility, has led to *freedom of movement* as a central expression of global inequality. Some people move freely as tourists and experts; others are stuck in poor regions. This goes for the world at large as well as within each country. In addition, parallel to the swift movements of capital is the loss of local autonomy for those who are forced to remain where they "belong."

The development of transnational labor, commodity, and capital markets and of multinational corporations has reduced the power of traditional political and social institutions to control and protect social groups within the state. Many people all over the world are turning to religious, ethnic, and national identities as a means of understanding themselves and of mobilizing themselves in defense of their interests.[16] Issues of collective identity are therefore hotly debated more or less all over the world. Who am "I"? To which "we" do I belong? To whom should I be loyal? These are crucial questions with profound ethical implications. Many people's need for direction in life, to see a clear role for themselves in society as well as a place in history, is not fulfilled. Therefore nostalgic ideas about social belonging have become more important to the forging of an autonomous "I" than the individualizing rhetoric might lead one to suspect.

In *The Well-Tempered Self* (1993), Toby Miller argues that the modern person has to balance off the contradictory roles of consumer and citizen and their associated discourses. According to the discourses of work and consumption, each person needs to be utilitarian and strategic and to think of her own good, while according to the discourses of parliamentary democracy, she needs to be altruistic and to think of the common good. Together these discourses constitute what Miller calls the cultural capitalist state. As a worker and as a consumer in the market, each person needs to be flexible, creative, and homeless. As a citizen in a parliamentary democracy, she needs community, togetherness, and stability. The parliamentary-political discourse, says Miller, encourages the creation of morally responsible political citizens with "roots," community feelings, and civic spirit who engage in public life. Because these various roles and discourses are incompatible and contradictory, they produce what Miller calls an ethically incomplete subject in need of training into humanness, and who therefore has to improve herself continuously. His main point is that the creation of specific sorts of morally responsible individuals is crucial

16. See Turner 419.

to the integration of the market, everyday life, and public life. Social integration takes place more and more *within each individual*—in her personal moral responsibility, in her recognition of social institutions, and in her feelings of community. For each person the task is simultaneously to be aware of his or her ethical incompleteness and to *unify the tensions into a single ethical substance*. The role of cultural politics and the culture industries is to help people reconcile these contradictory discourses and practices.[17] In other words, market and democracy are kept together by meaning-making cultural production conceived metaphorically to be "within" each moral individual. To unify tensions into what appears as a single ethical substance is to create what I call a *sustainable self-image*, a coherent, continuous, and yet flexible image of the self that can provide the basis for self-respect and dignity.

In my view, the rising importance of this ethical task helps explain the popularity of life writing, both for those who write their own or other people's life stories and for those who consume the various genres. In life stories otherwise incommensurable experiences and values can be brought together within a whole provided by a narrative structure (or by other kinds of textual structuring). But this ethical task does not in itself explain why the organic metaphors of roots, ancestry, and descent take precedence in many people's understanding of themselves, the way they express it in their life writing. What I argue here is that the popularity of naturalized ideas about descent is in part due to their usefulness in bringing together the contradictory identities and practices of the self. The focus on descent allows each person to foreground her sense of belonging, at the same time that her more utilitarian identities are also accommodated in a conception of a rooted self that is both malleable and felt to be continuous over time. And as I will show, for those whose self-concept is attacked by racial prejudice, the focus on descent also allows them both to find ways of reversing the stigma and to find a common ground on which to discuss their experiences of racialization.

What the Authors Write Against

The life writing of the authors of *Black on White* has to be read in relation to what they oppose. In Norway, as in most of the small, affluent European countries except Sweden, a right-wing populist party is today well represented in parliament. And not only that: according to the

17. See Miller.

opinion polls, the Progressive Party (Fremskrittspartiet) was, as of April 2003, one of the largest parties in Norway, with about 22 percent of the vote. Populist ideas about "immigrants" are also increasingly taken over by other parties, including the socialist party to the left of labor (Sosialistisk Venstreparti).[18]

Part of the populist appeal is expressed in a revitalized majority focus on descent, representing an ideological change that is generally not recognized as such. It occurs in the context of an increasing biologization of commonsense thinking about social relationships. While new technologies constantly challenge the conceptual boundaries between nature and culture, there is also a reinforcement of the conceptualizations of biological processes as the really real. One's "roots" are largely defined in terms of descent, and ideas about descent are closely connected to the specific understandings of "culture," history, and social space outlined earlier, and are currently central to the social production of belonging and exclusion. In fact, the idea of descent is now as much a spatial as a temporal concept. The ideological change can be interpreted as a "return to basics" in Europe that consolidates majority hegemony in relation to the new immigrants. It implies an imperceptible change of the ethical substance of people's lives, of the unwritten and self-explanatory rules of both everyday life and politics. Family and kinship are metaphors for belonging, as well as an experiential grounding for imagining social and moral communities.[19] The current cultural understanding of these social realms constitutes a key to understanding why and how new justifications of racism and ethnic nationalism in relation to "immigrants" have become naturalized as self-evident.

Most of the information about "immigrants" in the Norwegian mass media today concerns various sorts of problems, such as crime, the misuse of social security benefits, and the oppression of women. According to a study by Merete Lindstad and Øivind Fjeldstad, when "immigrants" are mentioned in the Norwegian mass media, it is most frequently in association with crime, with "immigrant men" as the perpetrators (44–45). The word immigrant (innvandrer) is today racially coded, and the dominant perspective is that the "immigrants" are a burden on and a disruption to Norwegian society. The focus on crime indicates that even police reports and statistics can be considered a form of life writing—not in the sense of being a person's existential reflections about his life, but in the sense of *writing affecting people's lives.*

18. Labor (Arbeiderpartiet) had 23 percent of the vote. See Gullestad, "Imagined," for an analysis of recent ideological developments in Norway.
19. See Gullestad, "Home."

Another theme in the mass media in connection to immigration is the racism and xenophobia of the self-defined racists of the extreme right—comprising only about two hundred individuals in Norway. Their attitudes and practices were discussed as much as nine times more often than antiracist attitudes and practices. While negative acts committed by political extremists were extensively covered, the everyday, nonsensational discrimination many immigrants experience in the labor market and the housing market was barely mentioned in the period studied by Lindstad and Fjeldstad (44–45).[20]

Over the last few years the media have also focused more consistently than before on the oppression of "immigrant women"—and Muslim women in particular—within their own families. The main themes have been forced marriage, female circumcision, and the murder of female relatives in order to save male honor. Some women have bravely gone public with their plight, exposing their families, and a few of them have afterward had to live in hiding. Among the majority they have become public icons and celebrated new voices in the fight against patriarchal traditions.[21] Unfortunately, the discussion of

20. Nevertheless, after they finished their study, the murder of a black boy in Oslo (Benjamin Hermansen) made majority discrimination the focus of moral panic in the media for a few weeks.

21. The most famous is Shabana Rehman, stand-up comedian and regular columnist in *Dagbladet*, a boulevard newspaper with a historical tradition of social criticism. In her own newspaper she has been characterized as one of the most powerful women in Norway. Her main focus as a columnist is the critique of Muslims in general. The daughter of parents who immigrated from Pakistan, she has presented a refreshing critique of the parent generation among Muslim immigrants to Norway, and is a defender of the right of the younger generations to chose their own lives, including their own spouses. Nevertheless, her column not only defends women's control over their own sexuality, but also follows tabloid genre conventions by focusing on the sensational and the sexually titillating. The first extensive and richly illustrated interview with her as a new celebrity was a six-page article in the Saturday supplement to *Dagbladet*, January 15, 2000. Rehman was photographed in three different modes: as an ordinary person with friends and family (small pictures in black and white and color), as an orientalized and exotic "Pakistani woman" (front page and full-page color pictures of just the face and of her in full figure), and nude with a Norwegian flag painted across her body while she is dramatically throwing away her Pakistani clothes (full page, full figure). She could probably not have signaled her conversion from "Pakistani" to "Norwegian" in a more striking way than with the flag image. Symbolically she takes off her Pakistani identity in a double sense: first, because she is physically naked, and second, because the value of female chastity in the form of being covered is central to her parents' social circles. At the same time, she puts on "Norwegianness" by accepting physical nakedness as natural and not sinful, and by putting on the Norwegian flag, the national symbol par excellence in Norway. Another media star is Kadra Noor (known in the media as just Kadra), a young girl born in Somalia who first participated in a TV documentary about female circumcision, revealing the lack of firm resistance to female circumcision of the Muslim leaders. Since then she has been interviewed in many media.

these very real problems has become part of the media panic, with "culture" and religion the main explanatory concepts. The way these painful issues have so far been debated in the mass media has had the unhappy side effect of stigmatizing large categories of innocent people. When a native Norwegian kills his wife, it is taken as a sad fact, due to specific psychosocial circumstances. When an immigrant man kills his daughter, it is taken as an act typical of his culture or religion. Thus, when one Kurd kills his daughter, all Kurds are labeled in the mass media as potential murderers. The information provided by the media thus need not be intimate in order to affect people's conceptions of self in negative ways. For the authors of *Black on White*, there is a marked difference between how the social categories they are assigned to are represented in the mass media and how they want to be represented.

Add to this the fact that since World War II, racism has become a very negatively loaded concept all over Europe, especially in the German-speaking and the Nordic countries. People in Norway generally associate the term "racism" with Nazism, the segregationist policies in the southern states of the United States, and the apartheid regime in South Africa. Nobody, except the very few political extremists, today identifies with ideologies that are explicitly racist. The word "racist" is associated with profound shame. As in other European countries, in Norway the word is therefore often mentioned as part of a denial, such as in the commonplace expression "I am not a racist, but . . ."[22] Fear of being called a racist is often used as an explanation of people's blameworthy acts as well as of their failure to take adequate action. In addition, many people see a contradiction between working against minority oppression of women and working against majority racism. For them, to support working against racism means not to support working against the oppression of women. Taken together, all of this paradoxically implies that the word "racism" is relatively common in public debates (as in denials of racism), while experiences of racism are seldom publicly recognized and debated. To put it briefly and bluntly, what the young authors write against is a society in which racialization and racism are both strongly present and intensely denied. The denial is based on feelings of innocence in relation to colonialism, Nazism, and fascism. People in Norway generally see themselves as victims of Danish colonialism and Nazi German occupation, but not as being influenced by an unacknowledged racist culture.

22. See Van Dijk.

Black on White: Introduction and Cover

The book *Black on White* (*Svart på hvitt*) includes many different experiences, but I interpret the main focus to be how the authors struggle to create a sustainable self-image in the face of stigmatization in parliament, the media, and everyday life. It is an edited volume containing fourteen differently constructed autobiographical texts written by nine young women and five young men, all born between 1967 and 1983, most of them in the 1970s. These texts are part of their individual projects of self-creation, written in the stage of life when identification is particularly important. At the same time, the book is a human document that makes it possible to feel out the Norwegian plural society right now. In a few years, much may be different, in the lives of the authors as well as in Norway at large.

Three of the authors were adopted and brought to Norway as small children, six were born in Norway to a parent or parents who had arrived as migrants or refugees, and five were born outside Norway and arrived in the country as children together with their parents. Through their biological parents, who for most of them are also their social parents, they are connected to different continents—Africa, Latin America, and various parts of Asia. In her introduction to the book the editor, Hadia Tajik, whose parents immigrated to Norway from Pakistan, stresses the uniqueness of each contribution. "The theme of this anthology is individuality," Tajik writes.[23] She continues:

> There is no fun in being held responsible for others' misdeeds just because one apparently has one's own roots in the same country, shares the same religion, or has the same skin color. . . . The first generation of multicultural and dark skinned Norwegians is growing up today without clearly defined roles in society. . . . Theoretically, members of the emerging generation are at liberty to define themselves.
>
> But there are individuals and groups who would restrict this freedom. The family desires respect, friends want a life of adventure and excitement, the religious community one of piety and virtue— and Norwegian society a charming little black mascot! There are far too many people telling the new generation of Norwegians who they are and how they are to conduct themselves for them to be able to find out for themselves. (7–8)

The focus is on voluntary relations of consent, in contrast to "roots," "skin color," and inherited religion. Tajik's use of the notion of

23. All quotations from the book are my own translations from the Norwegian.

generation also reintroduces an organic conception of commonalities across differences of origin. As a group the young authors actively resist the discrimination and lack of recognition they often encounter. I argue in what follows that the authors seem to take for granted both the contemporary individualized way of forming self-images, and the hegemonic resources for doing so by means of specific understandings linking history, kinship, and place. They demonstrate that they are fully assimilated—caught in the dominant frame of interpretation—while at the same time, given their specific positionings, they actively resist that framework.

Before I develop this interpretation, I should say a few words about the jacket of the book in order to bring out aspects of the presentation of self that are not emphasized in the text but are still very much present in implicit ways. Since discrimination based on appearance is the focus of the book, no wonder the editor and the publisher have chosen to picture all fourteen authors on the inside jacket. This is not common in books with so many contributors, but here the decision gives the reader the opportunity to compare the authors' expressed rage over racial discrimination with a photographic representation of their looks, and gives me, as an analyst, the opportunity to reflect on the often very important role of photographs in published life writing.

The photographs in *Black on White* demonstrate that in terms of appearance, the only feature that all the authors have in common is that to a majority eye they "do not look Norwegian." In Norway, what is perceived as "dark skin" need not be very dark. "Skin color" is a metonym for many different features of a person's looks, and can in some situations be regarded as a substitute for the word "race." But the portraits also carry other dimensions of meaning. Some are just pictures of a face; others also portray part of the upper body. Some of the authors look angry, some a little depressed, while others smile waggishly. Some look right into the camera with an angry, a laughing, or a questioning expression; others look away from the camera with a dreamy expression. The collection of portraits thus underlines the editor's focus on individuality: the authors are unique human beings who do not care to subordinate themselves to collective ethnic or religious identification.

Implicitly the photographs and the written information about each author also reflect their ambitions in the labor market—the utilitarian aspects of the self, in Miller's terms. As individuals and as a group they aspire to be part of the professional, intellectual, and creative sector of the middle classes—as a designer, stand-up comedian, actor, musician, journalist, politician, rap artist, youth worker, leader of a firm making and selling creative events, or as students of dentistry and law.[24] In terms of age and social class, they thus belong to a particular segment of Norwegian society, and most of them are women. All of this is both telling and typical. Thus, even if gender and social class are not thematically foregrounded, these identities are present in self-evident ways. The authors do not aspire to sell their time in a factory or a home for old people; they wish to sell their art, their knowledge, and their creative abilities in a market comprising both private companies and the public sector. The tendency in the organization of work life today is a change to creative and flexible processes.[25] Work processes are organized in networks focusing on thrust and the ability to solve problems. The reputation of each person is therefore an important good that has to be managed carefully. To picture everyone in his or her preferred mode can thus be regarded as a form of marketing, as can the rich verbal presentation of each of the authors. The portraits thus carry an implicit message with potential future implications for utilitarian relations of consent.

The cover of the book is also worth mentioning. It presents a striking photograph with high symbolic value. We see mountains with snow and glaciers at the top, and below them a fjord and green flowery meadows with cows grazing peacefully and cottages with turf roofs. The picture is a Norwegian national romantic cliché. For more than one hundred years this representation has been common both in works of art and on tourist posters. This is the kind of image the Norwegian Council for Tourism (Norges turistråd) uses to sell Norway abroad. But the cover is radically different on one point.[26] In the middle of the picture, in the forefront, is seated a giraffe. One need not be an expert on Claude Lévi-Strauss's famous concept of totemism in order to draw the conclusion that the picture carries an underlying message about physical and cultural difference based on the geographic distance between Norway and the African continent. The domestic cows here symbolize majority Norwegians, while the authors of the book are symbolized by a wild giraffe.[27] In Norwegian animal mythology,

24. There are also differences in family background regarding social class that are not made explicit, either in the texts or in the information about the authors.

25. See Piore and Sabel, and Sabel.

26. There is a similarity to the romantic symbolism of painters such as the German Caspar Friedrich and the Norwegian I. C. Dahl, who often place in the foreground of their paintings a symbolically strong object such as a cross, a church ruin, or a monument which largely determines the meaning of the painting.

27. A completely different interpretation of the picture is to see the landscape itself (naturen selv) as symbolizing the Norwegian majority. Then it is the high mountains and the still water (de høye fjell og det dype vann) that symbolize majority Norwegians instead of the grazing cows.

inspired by picturebooks for children, the cows refer to a whole series of animals—not bears, elk, and wolves but horses, pigs, chickens and cats—while the giraffe refers implicitly to a series consisting of lions, tigers, zebras, crocodiles, and so on.

The African is in many ways the prototypical "other" in Norway. Therefore it is only "natural" to choose an African animal to symbolize the authors. But why the giraffe? Why not one of the other animals on the African savanna? If the designers had chosen the lion, the cover might have called to mind the African lion in the Norwegian coat of arms. In addition, the lion is a dangerous predator who might frighten Norwegian readers instead of inspiring confidence in the authors as "individuals who are to be involved in forming the modern Norway," as Tajik writes in the introduction (7). The crocodile, for its part, is regarded as ugly and mean in Norwegian animal mythology.

In contrast, the giraffe is both friendly and a bit ridiculous. Because of its size, it stands out in almost any landscape.[28] At the same time, it has a long-necked elegance that sits well with the cultural capital and intellectual ambitions of the authors, and with the fact that most of them are women. The giraffe is therefore no doubt a sympathetic animal that is intended to reduce the xenophobia of the ruminating majority Norwegians. In addition, it is pictured lying down, in a relaxed and nonthreatening posture, in harmony with the grazing cows. The giraffe has no doubt come to stay, and like other good Norwegians it enjoys the view over the fjord. This is thus a well-chosen cover image in terms of catching the attention of prospective readers. Nevertheless, the question remains if its amusing symbolism does not contradict the very painful realities that are expressed in some of the contributions.

Imposed Identities: When Others Decide Who You Are

After Hadia Tajik's short introduction comes a text by Amani Olubanjo Buntu:

> The struggle, the analyses, the strategies and all the effort exerted to annihilate racism—this is what I really understand and can. This is my involuntary expertise. . . .

28. Literally speaking, the giraffe also has a particularly big heart.

I know many black youths who are just about to explode. They have the bit between their teeth and have put up with much. They have been chased by racists, suspected of shoplifting, beaten up by the police, misunderstood by the child welfare authorities, refused admission to bars. They have been the subject of threats and abuse, applications for fifty jobs in succession rejected, and not least, been accused of being oversensitive when they express themselves on these matters. They have been silent up to now. They can remain quiet a bit longer. But what happens after that?

Many African youths do not consider that they have a future in Norway. Irrespective of the fact that they have been born here, speak better Norwegian than Trine and Ståle, and eat porridge and brown cheese. What is an acceptable relation when time after time one is regarded with suspicion, excluded, ignored, made a mockery of, and degraded?

Many of us have voiced our opinion. Over a long period. Some have pointed to a systematic differential treatment, discrimination, and all the small details which have been accumulated into a "big thing." But we have been ignored because we asked difficult questions. Made too large demands. Spoke in a provocative manner. Said what we meant.

Soon, the situation will blow up in Norway. And nobody should be surprised. The warning light has been on for a long time. And switched off time and time again: "We don't want any trouble here." But trouble there may well be. . . . (9–10)

The worst are not always those who actively practice and are supporters of racism. But rather the silent majority. All those who do not bother to say anything. Who don't see the point of becoming involved. Their silence is so deafening. . . . (11)

It is extremely naïve to be black in Norway and believe that nothing will happen, that you may go about your business peacefully, never to be confronted with your skin color. The fact of the matter is that you do have the right to be angry. You should not put up with everything and anything. You must grant yourself that right because most around you will call you sensitive and unstable. It is neither healthy not acceptable not to react. You *have* to. Put your frustration into words. . . . (14)

The solutions are simple, yet simultaneously unlikely. Simple, because they are very largely a matter of platitudes such as showing respect, paying consideration, listening, evening out the imbalance. Unlikely, because so many choose not to take a stand and thus give negative attitudes free rein. (15)

In contrast to the emphasis on individuality in the introduction and in the collection of photographs on the inside jacket, there is a strong collective dimension to this text. Amani Olubanjo Buntu speaks on behalf of black youths in Norway.[29] The implicit reader in the quoted passages seems to glide from a "you" comprising both black youths and majority Norwegians to a "you" comprising black youths only. Buntu writes to young blacks who struggle with their definitions of self in a discriminating society.

The text is simultaneously well written and relatively unarticulated. For instance, what does Buntu refer to when he writes that "the situation will blow up" and "trouble there may well be"? The language is both dramatic and unspecified, the specificities being left to the imagination of the reader. The acting human beings are hidden behind sentences without a human subject. Amani Olubanjo Buntu seems to imply that the forces are so strong that they are going to overpower the individual. According to established gender stereotypes, he articulates a rough and also rather threatening masculinity. The text also demonstrates that the identity that is most attacked tends to become the most salient for the person.[30]

For Amani Olubanjo Buntu, black youths in Norway are "African" youths,[31] not just "Norwegians," "black Norwegians," or "African Norwegians."[32] He does not reveal much information about his family in his text. The information about the authors in the book tells us that he was born and bred in Oslo, and that his background is Caribbean. According to him, young black people in Norway want to be recognized and accepted in Norway. Most of them do not necessarily want to identify as Norwegians, and feel more comfortable with an identification as Africans: "They *actually* have an African background, an African ethos, an African aesthetics, an African body ideal, African cultural ties, special African features, etc. that they are *proud* of and *want* to identify with." According to Buntu, Africans in Norway have distanced themselves from majority ideas in which blackness is often associated with the primitive and the uncivilized. While these major-

29. In a conversation I had with Amani Olubanjo Buntu in Oslo (he now lives in South Africa) and in E-mail correspondence, he has emphasized that he wanted his essay in the collection to be based not on his private life but rather on his many years of professional experience as a social worker, cultural-political activist, and theoretician of the black experience in Norway. Buntu has worked practically and theoretically on the themes of black identification and black culture. Among other things, he founded the organization Afrikan Youth in Norway, the only organization in Norway working with and for black youths. He does not see himself as a young person anymore.

30. See Maalouf.

31. This is another contrast to the introduction by Hadia Tajik. She emphasizes that the authors regard themselves as "multicultural and colored Norwegians," while Amani Olubanjo Buntu writes about "African youths" and also sees himself as African.

32. This may be partly explained by the fact that most blacks in Norway have arrived as refugees over the past fifteen years.

ity ideas lead to feelings of shame, black youths, he says, find "a natural pride" in identifying with their "origin."[33] Buntu's focus on African descent thus gives a point of anchorage that helps to counteract discrimination, and to develop a collective identity on that basis. To be "African" in Norway is in this sense both ascribed and achieved, a matter of active choice and an identity that is constantly modeled and remodeled. In other words, there is a strong—but unstated— element of consent in his and others' emphasis on descent.

While Buntu's text simultaneously sounds both angry and matter-of-fact, Hannah Wozene Kvam tells in a more personal mode how she has developed a sustainable self-image in response to labeling and discrimination. She was adopted and brought to Norway from Ethiopia as a small child. In her fight for self-respect, she partly resists majority categories and partly takes them for granted:

> Many believe that it is sufficient to be culturally and linguistically integrated into a society in order to be accepted. This is wrong. In nineteen years of my life I have been so Norwegian that I have forgotten my own in order to satisfy others. For nineteen years I have gone round in a white and homogenous society as the gentle Hoa Hottentot.[34] That is more than enough for me. In the remaining nine years I have discovered who I really am—a proud Ethiopian-Norwegian woman with the right to define myself. "Negro" Hannah[35] is dead and buried forever. What a relief! (45)

She continues by relating some experiences from her past as "Negro" Hannah:

> I appointed myself as "Negro" of the class. I took the main role of Hoa Hottentot at the end of the first school year. . . . I dressed as a hula-hula girl at the carnival with an extra grass skirt round my waist and a rose in my hair. I called myself the black sheep of the family, the Negro-bun and the chocolate. I have several times presented myself to an audience and proclaimed, "I am Hannah and I am a Negro!" I have waited in company where the joke was to say how good it was to have a real slave girl in the house. With a smile on my lips. And a lump in the throat. . . . I have emphatically drawn atten-

33. All the information in this paragraph is from an E-mail correspondence with Amani Olubanjo Buntu. I thank him for his permission to use it here.

34. A figure in a well-known book for children.

35. The Norwegian word that is more or less equivalent to the English word "Negro" is *neger*. This is the word used in the Norwegian text. I have analyzed the intense media debate about this word in Norway in 2000–2001 (see Gullestad, "Defending" and *Det norske*). Many Norwegians see it as a neutral word, and insist on continuing to use it, in spite of the resistance of many (but not all) blacks.

tion to myself through playing the stereotype, and won the applause of the whites. Externally, I was a healthy girl who had nothing to complain about—with a secure upbringing, good friends, love and care. Inwardly, I erected a wall of sensitivity and bad feelings because I did not know how I was to come out of that evil circle. I crossed the street when I saw other blacks. I averted my gaze when I was confronted with other adopted persons. I did not like the person I was. (47–48)

Later on in her life, Hannah Wozene Kvam received new inspiration as a student and actor at the Nordic Black Theater in Oslo: "I met people with a similar background to myself, and could discuss my experiences out loud without being accused of being too thin-skinned" (48). She then traveled to Ethiopia, and found a country rich in cultural traditions and historical monuments. In a church she saw black angels: "I wept. They were so unbelievably beautiful. How banal it might sound, it was good to see that the angels were black" (50). The final sentence in her text reads, "That one should never disown one's background" (51). Like many others, she interprets her background in terms of a particular interpretation of her descent.

Like the "African youths" in Buntu's text, Hannah Wozene Kvam finds that her problem is to give her black appearance a positive value. Because the people around her are not neutral in relation to her looks, they force her, too, to focus on "skin color" and to examine, so to speak, where it comes from. Descent is closely associated with a particular vision of social space: the naturalized meanings of blackness (and implicitly of whiteness) seem in Norway to imply that white and black people have a different origin, come from different forebears, and that white people therefore are more closely related to one another than to black people within a global historical and geographical space. Black appearance is a marker of origin in a place that is both far away and culturally different.[36] In her journey to Ethiopia, Kvam discovered ways to appreciate her looks which circumvent majority racism. She "found herself," who she "really" is, by means of biological kinship and descent, and has created a hyphenated identity by elaborating upon her Ethiopian origin.[37] By identifying with Ethiopian arts and historic

36. This is underlined by the experience of people in Norway with one white and one black parent. In spite of having Norwegian ancestors, they are often regarded as outsiders to the Norwegian nation (see Gullestad, "Imagined"). "Race," as it is implicitly constructed in Norway (in terms of "skin color"), overrides both biological ancestry and social kinship in these particular situations.

37. Many adoptees choose differently. According to Botvar, 17 percent regard themselves as "immigrants." Johansen regards herself as Norwegian. Follevåg also sees himself as a Norwegian, but referring to existentialism, he holds that existence comes before essence (nationality). For him concepts such as nationality, ancestry, origin, culture, and so on are secondary labels, coming after the fact that he exists just as a human being.

monuments, and by developing new social ties to her biological kin in Ethiopia, she is in the process of providing the Ethiopian part of her Ethiopian-Norwegian self-image with social and cultural substance. In a way she has created a cultural difference corresponding to the symbolism of her looks within a Norwegian majority context. Also, in her focus on descent there is a strong element of voluntary consent.

Not only were the racial stereotypes difficult to tackle for Hannah Wozene Kvam, but so was the lack of understanding when she attempted to put her feelings into words and to communicate them to others. These experiences sound like an echo of Amani Olubanjo Buntu's statement that many black youths have voiced their opinions, only to be ignored. "Colored" children have painful experiences in relation to "skin color," while at the same time they meet well-meaning parents and teachers who stress that the children "should not be obsessed with skin color." By denying the discrimination actually taking place, the adults contribute to the powerlessness that arises from the lack of a language in which to express these things.

Both these authors were brought up in Norway. Both focus on their reactions to racism. Hannah Wozene Kvam gives a personal account of her success in coming to terms with it, while Amani Olubanjo Buntu exposes the unresolved problems of a broad category of people. Because of its emphasis on reconciliation, her emplotment can be characterized as a comedy, while the focus on unresolved problems in Buntu's text justifies characterizing the emplotment as a tragedy. In both texts the attacked black identity is the most salient, and in both a focus on descent is used to defend the attacked identities. Hannah Wozene Kvam's solution is a hyphenated self-image: she keeps her Norwegian identity, adding on an Ethiopian one. Amani Olubanjo Buntu has chosen to play down his Norwegian connection, focusing on the Caribbean link to Africa. Hannah Wozene Kvam writes in a personal mode without exposing her family, while Amani Olubanjo Buntu writes in a radical political mode that is angry and defiant. He conveys a general feeling of desperation, while she maps some of the thoughtless and tactless (but not necessarily ill-meaning) micro-acts of racialization. He demonstrates the urgency of political antiracism, while she indicates where to start changing the little everyday life practices of racialization and discrimination.

Both foreground particular interpretations of descent, and both also indirectly demonstrate other identities. For example, their texts reveal part of the reason why it is mostly women with a "dark skin color" who are active in the Norwegian media and public life. The silence— the resistance to any talk of what might be called everyday racism— probably hits men in a different and harder way than women. Owing to established and hard-wired gender roles, women often have a more direct access to spoken and written genres in everyday life which can be used to express complicated feelings and experiences.[38] I am thinking here of women getting together and discussing ethical problems by means of concrete personal experiences, as well as stories in the "my life" genre in women's magazines. In social life, men are often doers (they repair, fish, hunt), while women are talkers (sitting together chatting and exchanging confidences). There is a gender gap between these texts, even when the authors focus on similar ethical and political problems.

Nevertheless, *Black on White* does not contain only negative experiences. Some of the contributions tell of happy memories. The sons and daughters of immigrants, in particular, have early on found various strategies for dealing with discrimination. Some disarm their adversaries by being more proud of Norway than anybody else, while others react to discrimination and harassment by answering back in even harsher and more insulting language. Young people who have grown up in the large cooperative housing developments on the outskirts of Oslo seem in this way to possess a lot of hard-earned street smarts.

Adopting New Relatives

The editor Hadia Tajik's autobiographical contribution to the volume exemplifies the charming and light-hearted narratives. She regards herself as primarily Norwegian, and demonstrates much pride in her home country and the local community of her childhood in Norway. In particular she fondly remembers the day she was chosen to give the featured speech in her home village on the Norwegian national day, May 17, the day when the constitution of 1814 is celebrated:

> I was almost drowning in pride. For a while I had the desire to run hither and thither just to overcome the feelings inside of me: "I am going to give the May 17 speech. I am going to give the May 17 speech. Tra-la-la-la-la." The very thought that I was to be the focus of attention on that very day inflated my ego. Since that day my feelings about Constitutional Day have been particularly strong. The men at Eidsvoll [who drafted the constitution in 1814] somehow became my uncles as I stood on the podium for the four minutes' duration of my speech, painting a picture of how immigrants and Norwegians live in perfect union [*i skjønn forening*] in the country of Utopia. . . .
>
> For me the most significant experience was when I, as a rehearsed part of my speech, could raise my glance toward the Norwegian flag

38. See Gullestad, *Kitchen-Table* and *Everyday.*

at the top of the pole just twenty meters away and say, "When I hear the national hymn 'Yes, We Love Our Country,' and see the Norwegian flag waving in the breeze, then there is no doubt that I am a Norwegian. In spite of my dark skin, the fatherland pride is as strong within me as within anyone else. This *is* my country, my home, and I *am* proud of that fact." Even the wrinkled old lady in the first row who until then had stared rudely [*stygt*] at me, goggled in surprise [*fikk hakeslepp av forbauselse*]. I have warm feelings for my local community. Perhaps I am patriotic by nature. Perhaps I am just looking for a place to belong and call home. (41)

In this mini-narrative, racial prejudice and discrimination because of "skin color" are present in the implication that it was because of Tajik's "dark skin" that "the wrinkled old lady" stared rudely at her. Hadia Tajik takes the edge off the woman's racism by showing more pride in Norway than most others (and, one might add, by demonstrating a certain ageism in relation to the lady's wrinkles). Through participation in an important ritual event, she establishes a relationship of consent by means of metaphorical kinship. Thus in her case, too, descent is emphasized. By, so to speak, adopting new relatives, she creates a historical connection, and thus a new form of belonging in the present. It is significant that she adopts the founders of the constitution as her "uncles." With this choice of term she makes two simultaneous moves. First, she collapses almost two hundred years of history into the intimacy of the present. For a young woman like her, uncles are usually alive and kicking, not long-dead ancestors. Second, by talking about uncles instead of, for instance, fathers or grandfathers, she manages both to keep her ancestors and to add new ones. She thus does not replace her relatives but supplements her kin network with new members. This is probably the most acceptable choice both to her family and to the Norwegian majority.

Indirectly Tajik also illustrates the unstated expectation of many majority people that "immigrants" have to have a more positive attitude than most others in order to be accepted.[39] Still, there is no guarantee of success. The wrinkled old lady "goggled" in surprise, but the story does not tell if she (and others like her) was persuaded by the performance.

The Role of Descent for a Sustainable Self-Image

According to Frantz Fanon, whiteness is a category normally disregarded by whites themselves, and most clearly seen by those who are

39. See Gullestad, "Invisible."

excluded from that category. In the words of Ruth Frankenberg, it is not a natural biological essence but a structural advantage, a privilege, and a mental perspective associated with unmarked and nameless cultural practices. As this category is seldom discussed, it provides no basis for self-reflection. For the authors of *Black on White*, the situation is different. They have ample reasons to reflect on racialization and racism, but little encouragement to do so. At the same time, the combination of the current cultural climate and their (more or less) privileged class position—or at least class ambitions—does not inspire the same degree of self-reflection concerning social class. In this they are part of the general cultural climate of the times.

The contributions to *Black on White* show some of the ways that descent is implicated in present constructions of the self. Social class is usually in the background, while the relations between consent and descent are articulated in new ways. This is so both for majority and for minority people. The narrative examples demonstrate how the established majority frame of interpretation marks certain categories of inhabitants as visibly different, with the accompanying ideas of cultural and geographic distance. In many situations it is assumed that people "with a different skin color" belong somewhere else. As a reaction to discrimination, several authors embrace the territorially based identity that their looks point to within a Norwegian or European context. Many choose to become—and further develop—some part of what they already are in terms of descent, the way it is codified within the present hegemonic frame of interpretation. Others, such as Hadia Tajik, stress their current territorial identity as Norwegian citizens brought up in Norway. But as we have seen, their relations of consent are also often framed in terms of fictive descent. In many different ways descent thus seems to provide a "natural" anchoring point both for the bringing together of disparate and contradicting identities and roles in one sustainable self-image, and for the healing of attacked identities.[40] Majority and minority ideas of belonging seem both to be parallel to and to reinforce each other within a structured relationship of majority power.

Tajik emphasizes the Norwegian part of her "multiculturalism." Her solution is no doubt the most agreeable to majority Norwegians, and therefore socially the most effective. Her pride supports central majority ideas and self-images.[41] For Amani Olubanjo Buntu and Hannah Wozene Kvam, the experience of racial prejudice contributes instead to a search for alternative sources of belonging, resulting

40. There are oppositional voices, such as Follevåg.
41. See Gullestad, "Defending."

in what I interpret as a reversal of the stigma by investing it with positive value. All these strategies can be regarded as ethical choices that do not present themselves as such. As anchoring points for identification, family, ethnicity, and nationality have taken on new significance in the present neocolonial world. These identities appear to be natural and self-evident, and therefore part of "what is really me" in a different and more profound sense than achieved identities. Nonetheless, in the elaboration of these identities there is also an element of choice and achievement, both concerning which aspects are picked out for elaboration and cultivation, and concerning the intensity with which they are embraced. Discourses of descent have a potential not only for accommodating multiple, contradictory, and changing roles and identities but also for neutralizing racial discrimination, and thus for dignity and self-respect. The emphasis on descent by Kvam and Buntu may be interpreted as a precarious solution in the fight for dignity and self-respect within a prejudiced majority environment. While resisting dominant ideas about themselves, they inscribe themselves into those very same ideas. Thus, paradoxically, this solution simultaneously implies a more sustainable self-image for the individual, a basis for collective action across differences of background and experiences, and a social reinforcement of the racialized category.

The Reception of the Book: Both Success and Silencing

In this essay I have tried to tease out the ethical implications of what is often considered ideology or politics. A published life story can be seen as a way to take part in civil society, to exercise citizenship and democratic participation. The reception of Black on White tells a story of success, but also of a continuous silencing of the most painful experiences and the most radical views. As noted earlier, some young women with an immigrant background have been able to establish themselves as media celebrities fighting oppressive practices. The anthropologist and historian of religion Berit Thorbjørnsrud has characterized these media figures as "Muslim Cinderellas" inspiring majority tears. Like the Cinderellas, Amani Olubanjo Buntu, Hannah Wozene Kvam, and Hadia Tajik can be characterized as outspoken and courageous. But their message is not greeted with the same enthusiasm. They have not exposed their families, and they do not write about sensational topics such as forced marriage and female circumcision. The book has been a success, but few reviewers have discussed the overall focus on racism.[42] The most painful experiences in the book, ethically and politically, have not been taken seriously.[43] Why not?

I think that one part of the answer is that the book delivers many messages at once. It is proud, harmonizing, angry, amusing, and serious. The amusing aspects are particularly visible on the cover and the inside jacket, and may have made it possible for the reviewers and interviewing journalists not to focus on the more painful experiences and their implications for public life in Norway: the authors have encountered a white public space[44] with invisible fences guarding against a serious presentation and discussion of their experiences. Another part of the answer therefore has to do with the widespread denial of racism in Norway, and the profound unacknowledged shame associated with the slightest hint of being accused of racism. This shame acts as a barrier to self-reflection and empathy. Many readers may have read the texts of Amani Olubanjo Buntu and Hannah Wozene Kvam as unreasonable accusations.

The young women who have been most embraced by the media in Norway are those who have criticized aspects of their minority background. This has made them into honorary Norwegians. Several of the contributors to *Black on White* have instead focused their critical attention on majority racism. It is no doubt easier to gain sympathy among majority readers as a critic of "immigrants" than as a critic of majority practices. The reception of the book thus indicates some of the mechanisms working to maintain what Buntu calls the "deafening silence" surrounding these issues, in spite of the well-formulated attempts to break that silence. People "with a different skin color" are expected to be grateful for what they have and not to criticize Norwegian society. They are certainly not expected to speak out against racism. These expectations constitute a barrier to a well-functioning democracy.

---

42. This is also the opinion of the editor, Hadia Tajik (personal E-mail communication).

43. For example, in her review of the book in *Dagbladet*, Shabana Rehman praised the book and thanked the authors for having written it. But she did not engage in a consideration of its focus on majority racialization and racism.

44. See Page and Thomas.

WORKS CITED

Balibar, Étienne. "Is There a 'Neo-racism'?" In *Race, Nation, Class: Ambiguous Identities*. 1988. Ed. Étienne Balibar and Immanuel Wallerstein. London: Verso, 1991. 17–28.

——. "Racism and Nationalism." In *Race, Nation, Class: Ambiguous Identities*. 1988. Ed. Étienne Balibar and Immanuel Wallerstein. London: Verso, 1991. 37–68.

Barker, Martin. *The New Racism*. London: Junction Books, 1981.

Bauman, Zygmunt. *Globalisation and Its Human Consequences*. London: Polity Press, 1998.

Beck, Ulrich. *Risiko og frihet*. Bergen: Fagbokforlaget, 1997.

Berger, Peter L., Brigitte Berger, and Hans Kellner. *The Homeless Mind: Modernization and Consciousness*. New York: Random House, 1973.

Botvar, P. K. *Ny sjanse i Norge: Utenlandsadoptertes oppvekst og levekår*. Oslo: Diakonhjemmets høgskolesenter og verdens barn, 1994.

Buntu, Amani Olubanjo. "Når du er så svart at alt bare blir sint." In *Svart på hvitt*. Ed. Hadia Tajik. Oslo: Tiden Norsk Forlag, 2001. 9–16.

Fanon, Frantz. *Black Skin, White Masks*. 1952. London: Pluto Press, 1986.

Follevåg, Geir. *Adoptert identitet*. Oslo: Spartacus, 2002.

Frankenberg, Ruth. *The Social Construction of Whiteness: White Women, Race Matters*. Minneapolis: University of Minnesota Press, 1993.

Friedman, Jonathan. *Cultural Identity and Global Process*. London: Sage, 1994.

Giddens, Anthony. *Modernity and Self-Identity: Self and Society in the Late Modern Age*. Oxford: Polity Press, 1991.

Goldberg, David Theo. *Racist Culture: Philosophy and the Politics of Meaning*. Oxford: Blackwell Publishers, 1993.

Gullestad, Marianne. *The Art of Social Relations: Essays on Culture, Social Action, and Everyday Life in Modern Norway*. Oslo: Scandinavian University Press, 1992.

——. "Defending a National Self-Image." Paper presented at the presidential symposium "Initiating Cross-Atlantic Dialogues on Race and Culture in Anthropology" at the American Anthropological Association annual meetings, Washington, D.C., November 28–December 2, 2001.

——. *Det norske sett med nye øyne: Kritisk analyse av norsk innvandringsdebatt*. Oslo: Universitetsforlaget, 2002.

——. "Each Person His Family." In *Être soi parmi les autres: famille et individualisation*. Ed. François de Singly. Vol. 1. Paris: L'Harmattan, Collection Logiques Sociales, 2001. 23–36.

——. *Everyday Life Philosophers: Modernity, Morality, and Autobiography in Norway*. Oslo: Scandinavian University Press, 1996.

——. "Home, Local Community, and Nation." *Focaal*, no. 30–31 (1997): 39–60.

——. "Imagined Kinship." Paper presented at the workshop "Neonationalism in the EU" organized by the Wennergren Foundation and the Vienna Wittgenstein Prize, Brussels, February 1–5, 2002. In *Neo-nationalism inside the EU: Anthropological Perspectives*. Ed. Marcus Banks and Andre Gingrich. Oxford: Berghan Books, forthcoming.

——. "Invisible Fences: Egalitarianism, Nationalism, and Racism." *Journal of the Royal Anthropological Institute* 8 (March 2002): 45–63.

——. *Kitchen-Table Society*. 1984. Oslo: Scandinavian University Press, 2002.

——. *Livet i en gammel bydel*. Oslo: Aschehoug, 1979.

——. "'Mohammed Atta and I': Identification, Discrimination, and the Formation of Sleepers." *European Journal of Cultural Studies* (2003).

——. "From Obedience to Negotiation: Dilemmas in the Transmission of Values between the Generations in Norway." *Journal of the Royal Anthropological Institute* 12, no. 1 (March 1996): 25–42.

——. "A Passion for Boundaries: Reflections on Connections between the Everyday Lives of Children and Discourses on the Nation in Norway." *Childhood* 4, no. 1 (February 1997): 19–42.

Hervik, Peter, ed. *Den generende forskjellighet: Danske svar på den stigende multikulturalisme.* Copenhagen: Hans Reitzels Forlag, 1999.

Høibraaten, Helge. "Individualitet." Festskrift for Sverre Sløgedal i anledning hans 50-årsdag 06.04.1980. Ed. Ingemund Gullvåg. *Filosofisk institutts publikasjonsserie,* no. 1. Trondheim University, 1980. 76–85.

Johansen, G. M. "Farvede nordmenn—en selvmotsigelse eller en ny kategori?" In *Hovedfagsstudentenes årbok 1992.* Institutt og museum for sosialantropologi. UiO, Oslo, 1992.

Kvam, Hannah Wozene. "Svart pepper." In *Svart på hvitt.* Ed. Hadia Tajik. Oslo: Tiden Norsk Forlag, 2001. 45–51.

Lévi-Strauss, Claude. *Mythologies.* Vol. 1. *Le cru et le cuit.* Paris: Plon, 1964.

Lindstad, Merete, and Øivind Fjeldstad. *Pressen og de fremmede.* Kristiansand: Høyskoleforlaget, 1999.

Maalouf, Amin. *Les identités meurtrières.* Paris: Éditions Grasset & Fasquelle, 1998.

Mead, G. H. *Mind, Self, and Society.* Chicago: University of Chicago Press, 1934.

Miles, Robert. *Racism after "Race Relations".* London: Routledge, 1993.

Miller, Toby. *The Well-Tempered Self: Citizenship, Culture, and the Postmodern Subject.* Baltimore: Johns Hopkins University Press, 1993.

Olney, James. *Metaphors of Self: The Meaning of Autobiography.* Princeton: Princeton University Press, 1972.

Page, Helán E., and Brooke Thomas. "White Public Space and the Construction of White Privilege in U.S. Health Care: Fresh Concepts and a New Model of Analysis." *Medical Anthropology Quarterly* 8 (1994): 109–16.

Piore, Michael J., and Charles F. Sabel. *The Second Industrial Divide: Possibilities for Prosperity.* New York: Basic Books, 1984.

Rex, John. *Race and Ethnicity.* Stony Stratford: Open University Press, 1986.

Sabel, Charles. "Moebius-Strip Organizations and Open Labor Markets: Some Consequences of the Reintegration of Conception and Execution in a Volatile Economy." In *Social Theory for a Changing Society.* Ed. Pierre Bourdieu and J. S. Coleman. Boulder: Westview Press, 1991. 23–54.

Schneider, David M. "Kinship, Community, and Locality in American Culture." In *Kinship and Community.* Ed. A. J. Lichtman and J. R. Challinor. Washington, D.C.: Smithsonian Institution Press, 1979. 155–74.

Sejersted, Francis. "Struktur og legitimitet: refleksjoner over direktørkapitalismens kranke sjebne." *Søkelys på arbeidsmarkedet* 20 (2001): 53–57.

Sennett, Richard. *The Corrosion of Character: The Personal Consequences of Work in the New Capitalism.* New York: W. W. Norton & Company, 1998.

Sollors, Werner. *Beyond Ethnicity: Consent and Descent in American Culture.* Oxford: Oxford University Press, 1986.

Sørhaug, Tian. *Om ledelse: Makt og tillit i moderne organisering.* Oslo: Universitetsforlaget, 1996.

Stolcke, Verena. "Talking Culture: New Boundaries, New Rhetorics of Exclusion in Europe." *Current Anthropology* 36, no. 1 (1995): 1–24.

Taguieff, Pierre-André. *La Force du préjugé*. Paris: Gallimard, 1987.

Tajik, Hadia. "Forord." In *Svart på hvitt*. Oslo: Tiden Norsk Forlag, 2001. 7–8.

———. "Skyt meg hvis jeg blir en kamelon—eller bygdedyret ser deg." In *Svart på hvitt*. Oslo: Tiden Norsk Forlag, 2001. 38–44.

Taylor, Charles. *Sources of the Self: The Making of the Modern Identity*. Cambridge: Cambridge University Press, 1989.

Thorbjørnsrud, Berit. "Weeping for the Muslim Cinderellas." Degree lecture presented at University of Oslo, December 12, 1999.

Turner, Terence. "Anthropology and Multiculturalism: What Is Anthropology That Multiculturalists Should Be Mindful Of?" In *Multiculturalism: A Critical Reader*. Ed. David Theo Goldberg. Oxford: Basil Blackwell, 1994. 406–25.

Van Dijk, Teun A. *Elite Discourse and Racism*. Sage Series on Race and Ethnic Relations. Vol. 6. London: Sage Publications, 1993.

Wieviorka, Michel. *The Arena of Racism*. London: Sage Publications, 1995.

Afterword

Craig Howes

John Eakin's introduction to this collection assesses its many contributions to our understanding of life writing as a form of ethical inquiry, a field he has written about extensively himself. I take my task to be somewhat different: first, to give a sense of how the contributors responded to and influenced one another's work; second, to provide a more considered version of my response to the original colloquium papers and discussions; and third, to describe briefly how this collection has already enhanced my own understanding of how to approach ethical questions about life writing.

The colloquium's format and dynamics should be taken into account. October 2002 found us sitting along the sides of a very large table in the Memorial Union of Indiana University. Each participant had an hour to present the paper and to field questions. Discussion always ensued. The entire process took two and a half days, we were treated very well, and everyone participated fully—although one person did remark that our debates about betrayal, guilt, extenuation, and judgment made him feel at times like he was serving on a sequestered jury.

In one of his life writing courses, Timothy Dow Adams shows students that the order in which they read life writing texts will profoundly affect their response. It matters whether you read an autobiography before or after you read a biography—"A + B ≠ B + A," as Adams puts it—and the sequence in which we heard the conference papers strongly affected our discussions.[1] David Parker went first, for, as Eakin explains, Parker's and Richard Freadman's own 1998 collection on ethics in literature, philosophy, and theory contained an essay that eventually became part of Eakin's *How Our Lives Become Stories*, and provided the spur for the colloquium and the current volume. The focus that first morning on moral philosophy, epitomized in Parker's discussion of Charles Taylor, and reinforced an hour later by John Barbour's remarks on judging parents, led us into our shared topic and set the character of our deliberations, which neither began nor ended in consensus, as the resulting essays should suggest. (And thank goodness.)

A sampling of comments, removed from context and commentator, might give some idea of the degrees of difference at the table:

Can you forgive institutions?
I don't think you can assume there's an ethical unconscious.
Autobiographers cause harm! What do people have to say to that?
You're trying too hard to be good.
What about psychoanalysis?
I'm against forgiveness.
I am too.
Is posthumous harm possible?
As an autobiographer, are you a sadist or a masochist?
What about historical specificity?
The dead belong to the living.
What do your kids think?
Let's stick to writing.
Who would want to read about these people?

It soon became obvious that our assumptions about many key terms— harm, judgment, rights, ethics itself—were so various that some participants dismissed out of hand what others felt was fundamental. In fact, a major issue throughout the colloquium was whether ethics functioned at the level of ontology for life writing, or simply as a part of the repertoire of concerns that might arise for anyone while writing or reading lives. The entire project arose out of Eakin's own conviction that ethics is "the deep subject of autobiographical discourse." Paraphrasing Charles Taylor, he explains that if narrative is what allows us to understand "the direction and meaning of our lives," then

---

1. For the record, the order was Parker, Barbour, Mills, Wexler, and Deborah Nelson, who graciously stepped in for a participant who had to cancel, and who spoke very effectively on life writing and the law. Then Miller, Freadman, Middlebrook, Lauritzen, Frank, Gullestad, Couser, and my response.

"identity and morality are intimately and inextricably connected," and "ethics is not merely one possible perspective on life writing" but "constitutes it as a practice." For a number of the participants, life writing is instrumental in what they consider to be the defining ethical project: to answer the question *What is it good to be?* as David Parker, also citing Taylor, asserts, and which Arthur Frank calls "the core of what I mean by *moral*": "what ways of living are better than others, and how we become the sort of people we want to be." Viewed from this perspective, life writing can offer what John Barbour calls "a paradigm of what moral deliberation ought to be in ordinary life," with the goal of establishing ethical relationships to the past, present, and future, all conditioned by a clear-eyed examination of causes, extenuations, weaknesses, emotional crimes, and gifts.

Though delivered to none of the participants just mentioned, the remark "You're trying too hard to be good!" was clearly wielded as an axe to the ethical root, and as I think back on the colloquium, and read the essays now collected here, I believe that while such challenges did not cause any of us to snuff our own guiding ethical lights, they did make the essays less immutably foundational, or programmatic, and more dynamic. Sometimes with growing impatience, people listened, and the proof is in this volume.

When I made my concluding remarks, I did not therefore try to homogenize the very healthy cultures present. Dragging out once more Marx's stalking specter, though dislodged from any real political context, I instead identified the disciplinary and theoretical ghosts conjured up by, and still haunting, the colloquium. At that time I named them Psychoanalysis, Biography, Rhetoric, Law, and the Literary. Now, though, a less lurid "What about" rhetorical strategy, with some alterations in the cast, is more appropriate. My goal is to suggest how these essayists have drawn on their own training, previous work, and experience in Indiana to answer the questions that inevitably arise when we talk about what Arthur Frank calls "moral non-fiction."

What about Psychoanalysis?

The question of psychology came up in several forms, with the concern always over whether philosophical and ethical, or even political and cultural, explanations trump notions of psychology when we explore how life writing texts are created and received. Theorizing that seemed to appropriate psychoanalytic vocabulary was countered almost instantly. After David Parker laid out Taylor's argument that "conscious moral deliberation and choice are shaped from below by our

mostly 'prearticulate' but identity-orienting systems of value, commitment, and belief, which turn out themselves to be partly formed
by practical reasoning of another kind," one participant said, "I don't
think you can assume there is an ethical unconscious." Another person
placed all attempts to discuss "prearticulate" impulses on notice: "The
principle has to be that I'm ignorant of another's wishes; we can't know
the inner life." And someone else's opening caveat hit the same chord:
"I'm not looking at psychological dimensions, but social and cultural
dynamics."

These charges were gendered to a certain extent, and while it certainly wasn't planned, I admit it is interesting to note that every single
male participant chose to write about texts by fathers about sons, by
sons about fathers, by themselves about their own fathers, or, at least
in passing, by themselves about their attempts to become fathers.
Small wonder, then, that at times the topic of ethics and life writing
seemed patriarchal almost by definition, and by raising psychological
considerations, some participants reminded us that ethics can be seen
as a kind of censor, or superego, that stifles the impulse to write autobiography, or tries to channel it in appropriate ways. Claudia Mills's
reiterated "need to *tell* stories about my intimate relationships"
emerges not just from her strong belief that fulfilling this need produces "great benefit" for her, but also from a conviction that this
release makes it possible for her to function: "If I couldn't talk about
my relationships, I simply couldn't have them." Even more pointedly,
Nancy Miller notes that ethics can also act as a threatening social sanction and internal censor, working against free expression by women,
or any unwelcome thoughts: "Sometimes I have the uncomfortable
feeling that the truest ethical position is closely related to silence, to
self-silencing."

When the need to speak grows into the desire to publish, ethics gets
recast into guidelines that condition how talk can become a public
text. For Claudia Mills, the "great value" of "the widespread sharing
of *real* stories" must be balanced against the "painful costs," which
can include the public embarrassment or even betrayal of others. But
the psychological need to publish is still taken for granted, with ethics
entering the equation explicitly when she hopes that the life writer
will be "a responsible moral agent" who "will seek, if possible, to minimize" potential harm. Similarly, Richard Freadman presents a philosophically informed defense of his own ethical status, even though his
desire to come to terms with his father extends to making his conclusions public. "The 'need' alone doesn't seem sufficient to justify
publication," Freadman explains. "There has to be the additional
feeling that the book that was published as a consequence of this need

was acceptable, that its inevitable traces of indecency aren't gratuitous with respect to my father's and my own moral entitlements in the situation." For some of the contributors, then, while ethics may not initiate writing, it most definitely functions as a cluster of socially informed, often internalized considerations—possibly empowering, but just as possibly denying, or even silencing—that comes into play when the psychological need to speak is gratified.

And a primary ethical concern about such speech is what it says about others.

What about Biography?

Autobiographies "have become increasingly *biographical*," John Eakin notes, "featuring those others in our lives—parents, siblings, lovers, friends, and mentors—who have shaped us decisively." I would go further. Since autobiographers become biographers whenever they represent another person, which can sometimes amount to 80 percent to 90 percent of a memoir, many of the ethical quandaries discussed in this volume are biographical: what subjects, vulnerable or otherwise, are owed or entitled to because of their relation to the author, or because of the prevailing ethics in the containing society.

Recent life writing theory tends to draw a firm line between autobiography and biography. In *Reading Autobiography: A Guide for Interpreting Life Narratives*, Sidonie Smith and Julia Watson declare that "no matter how often" people "think of autobiography as the biography someone writes about him- or herself," life narrative and biography "are not interchangeable" (4–5).[2] In biographies, they write, "scholars of other people's lives document and interpret those lives from a point of view external to the subject," suggesting that the task is generally clear-cut, seldom self-conscious, possibly venal, and ultimately less interesting. At least some colloquium participants nodded toward this judgment. "The biographer is essentially a journalist, and therefore the ethics aren't nearly as complicated," remarked one person, and G. Thomas Couser observes that euthanography comes "as close, perhaps, as any life writing can to realizing the trope of biography as a kind of 'taking' of another's life," which he links to Henry Adams's famous remark that since biography is essentially a homicide, autobiography is a suicide designed to frustrate scribbling criminals.

2. In keeping with the comprehensive sweep of their *Guide*, Smith and Watson use the term "life narrative" to refer to "many kinds of self-referential life writing, including autobiography," which have as components "memory, experience, identity, embodiment, and agency" (3).

In life narrative, however, Smith and Watson note that "people write about their own lives . . . and do so simultaneously from externalized and internal points of view" (4–5). The internalization is crucial. A biographer may exhaustively document what a life looked like from the outside. Only a life narrator, though, while conscious of how her life appears to the world, can describe what living that life felt like, or record what certain experiences meant to the person who had them. Only the life narrator "writes her subjectivity."

Yet Smith and Watson, like Eakin, note that recently, "life narrators have blurred the boundary separating autobiographical and biographical modes by embedding their versions of the life of a family member in their own personal narratives" (7). (Given John Barbour's essay, it is significant that Kim Chernin and John Edgar Wideman are offered as examples.) Without going into a pointless "defense" of biography, I note that semi-buried assumptions about the relationship between the two life writing genres do affect how several essays treat ethical matters. Since autobiographers know the people whose narratives they are writing, the ethical implications are doubly personal—not just whether the subject was good or bad to the writer, but whether the writing is being bad by showing the person in a certain light. At least rhetorically, the journalist's or the life-snatcher biographer's moral nature is secondary to the act of writing. If ethics comes up, it's because there's something outrageous or fundamentally wrong about the biography—or because it's assumed that thanks to the nature of the work itself, the biographer, like the dyer, will unavoidably stain his hands.[3] Most autobiographers, however, seem to hope that readers will consider them to be, if not good people, at least understandable.[4] While we all know that biographies can be deliberate hatchet jobs, character assassinations, and so forth, we may therefore still hold on to a notion that ethics can remain "the deep subject of autobiographical discourse."

For some essays in this collection, the autobiography/biography bifurcation also stands in for the more important distinction between aesthetic impulse and legal responsibility. The need to write, and the right to exercise artistic license with all available materials, is the author's prerogative—what Nancy Miller calls "the excuse of Art."

3. The most famous treatment of this subject is of course Janet Malcolm's *Silent Woman*. A 1996 BBC documentary (*Bookmark* series), aptly titled *Lifers: The Rise and Rise of the Literary Biographer*, is a jaunty hour-long indictment of literary biography as a reprehensible and seedy act. And for an account of how a profile writer for major magazines sees this problem, see Kraus.

4. For a chilling account of how even notorious ethical monsters seek to accomplish this goal rhetorically, see Rosen.

The benefits are substantial, since the resulting text can be more valuable, even in ethical terms, than anything chained to the contingent, the factual. Or as Peter Ackroyd puts it, in an oft-repeated wisecrack: "If you want to tell the truth, write a novel. If you want to lie, write a biography"[5] Here Ackroyd suggests that the biographer's own agenda makes massaging the facts almost irresistible. While Desmond Mac-Carthy may think that the biographer is "an artist under oath,"[6] Ackroyd implies that most biographers are at best sophists, and at worst perjurers. Only writers exercising full control over their materials can be trusted, because as anyone familiar with biographies—or criminal trials—knows, reordering facts can make them serve a variety of ends that often have nothing to do with establishing the truth.

But what happens when we live in the age of memoir, and autobiography becomes "creative nonfiction"? This paradoxical—or perhaps even oxymoronic—term captures what became a crucial topic for the colloquium, and the resulting essays: the tension between literary aspiration and the danger of being held personally, or even legally, accountable for betrayal or libel by people who don't recognize art as a sufficient defense. John Eakin's brief opening remarks about the law are a useful guide to the public debates over privacy and their implications for life writing. During the colloquium, however, our comments tended to fluctuate between "There oughta be a law" and "The law is an ass." Legal language, if not actual proceedings, surfaced in some papers. "If it is sometimes possible to justify violating the privacy of others by telling, whom can we trust to adjudicate these acts of exposure?" Nancy Miller asks, and she goes on to describe *The Woman Warrior* as a text whose very existence results from Maxine Hong Kingston's "refusal to obey" an "injunction" from her mother not to tell. In a few essays, legal rights can be as important as ethical questions. G. Thomas Couser, for instance, presents Richard Galli's *Rescuing Jeffrey* as a kind of limit case for how law and ethics can clash. In it, a lawyer father describes how he successfully claimed his legal right to end his son's life, even though Galli ultimately chose not to exercise it. As Couser notes, the ethical implications here are staggering. One of the colloquium's most striking moments, however, occurred when Deborah Nelson explained that although neither the facts nor the represented person's sense of injury was disputed in the case she was exploring, whether or not the results met the *legal* criteria for harm was very much at issue. Following up on one of the many

5. I heard Ackroyd say it at a 1995 London conference, "Writing the Lives of Writers."
6. Leon Edel cites MacCarthy in *Writing Lives* (16).

implications of this question, another participant turned to the rest of us, and declared: "Autobiographers cause harm! What do people have to say to that?"[7]

The lack of any firm legal guidelines for measuring such harm did not, however, prevent participants from continuing to explore the ethics of life writing—and in several cases this investigation left the legal and the biographical behind, instead couching the inquiry in the familiar terms of the literary.

What about the Literary?

The literary work was the paradigmatic form for life writing at the colloquium. An early excursion into on-line diaries and blogs instantly provoked a firm request that the focus stay on "writing"—and, for the most part, we kept it there. Our proceedings therefore affirmed once more the defining influence of Philippe Lejeune's autobiographical pact. For protagonist and narrator to have the same name as the author, there has to be a title page, if only an imagined one, and in conception the text must be a book.[8] Nancy Miller succinctly describes how writing such an imagined book forces her to negotiate the strong pulls exerted by truth and the reader, memory and language. "I could write down what I remembered; or I could craft a memoir," she remarks. "One *might* be the truth; the other, a good story." In the same entry from September 2, 2002, she notes that "when I sit down to reconstruct my past, I call on memory, but when memory fails, I let language lead. The words take me where I need to go." Although Miller describes autobiographical writing as a literary act that "comes with responsibilities," she also insists that for herself "as a writer, the answer to the question of what 'really' happened is literary—or at least textual. I will know only when I write it. When I write it, the truth will lie in the writing. But the writing may not be the truth; it may only look like it. To me."

Two essayists pose this "conundrum" between literary and "real" truth through meditations on the nature of fiction. Rather than do explicit harm through publication, Claudia Mills opts for "fictionalization." And yet, while an "emotional core" may remain when she shares stories "through fiction rather than through nonfiction," she

7. For elaboration on a related issue, see note 9 from Eakin's introduction.
8. Lejeune's own activities with the APA (Association pour l'autobiographie et le patrimoine autobiographique) show how the idea of the manuscript, or the book, does not require publication to exert its influence. For Lejeune's own early response to Internet diaries, see *Cher écran*.

regrets losing the chance to write ethically about "real" actions. "I once read a quote that thrilled me, that the task of the historian was to hold up evil deeds 'for the reprobation of posterity,'" Mills writes, and when faced with transgressors, she would like to ensure that "their evil deeds are no longer hidden—but instead documented, dissected, despised." We're back then to Ackroyd's claim—if you want to tell the truth, write a novel—but with the added wish that the imaginary garden could occasionally have real toads in it. This argument cannot, however, be pushed too far. "I don't think bad people deserve the protections that good people do," Mills says, and I agree—but uneasily, since the statement reminds me of certain ethical problems raised, but happily left hanging, by the dialogue between Jamie Lee Curtis and Arnold Schwarzenegger in the aptly titled film *True Lies*:

"Did you kill anyone?"

"Yeah, but they were all bad."

In her account of how Emma Tennant has variously represented the lives of Ted Hughes and Sylvia Plath, Diane Middlebrook shows how the life writing/fiction conundrum can actually turn texts into weapons that cause ethical harm. The problem here is the reverse of Mills's. Although Tennant calls *Ted and Sylvia* a novel, the protagonists' names, and many details given about them, map exactly onto that huge, ever-growing, heavily scrutinized, and vexed mass of public information about Hughes and Plath. I return briefly to other aspects of Tennant's actions near the end of this essay; what should be noted here is that for Middlebrook, transgressing literary convention can in fact be an ethically reprehensible act. In *Ted and Sylvia*, "ethical problems are bound up with issues related to literary genres, and to the privileged position Tennant occupies as Hughes's intimate contemporary and memoirist." The problem lies not in using "real people in fiction," but in Tennant's own relationship to "the sensational and disturbing historical materials" that often appear in "nonfiction novels." Instead of making "imaginative interventions in order to fill gaps in documented events, and to create plausible inner lives for the protagonists in significant historical situations," Tennant "positions at the novel's front door an author who invites readers to assume that the most shocking, disturbing, and discreditable actions she represents in the novel may be 'based on facts . . . previously concealed or unknown.'" In short, as someone who had "personal access to witnesses and participants in the ugly story she tells," Tennant adopts "the stance of the gossip," and by doing so she "jams the signals by which a reader navigates the reality-effect of the nonfiction novel." This in Middlebrook's opinion is "a personal ethical failure," committed by an author whose known intimacy with her main "character" allows her to claim artistic license at the same moment that she assures us that we are getting "not a fiction but the real thing: dirt." Imaginary gardens with real people in them—and with toads as the gardeners.

It is the sociologist Arthur Frank, however, who arguably makes the largest ethical claims for life writing as literature. Drawing on John Gardner's *On Moral Fiction*, Frank makes a case for "moral non-fiction" that almost echoes Matthew Arnold in its belief that literary self-narratives offer the surest ground for "personal reflection on questions of value" at a time when "canonical, institutionalized standards of public and private morality have broken down." Frank extends all of Gardner's moral claims for fictional narrative to encompass life writing: "Moral writing is a medium in which people can express their intuitions about the ideal and their practices for attempting to reach it." He celebrates those disabled, ill, or traumatized individuals who tell counterstories as a way to preserve themselves in the face of "socially constructed and legitimated master narratives of identity." Since such master narratives are literally "demoralizing," writing autobiography is therefore an act of remoralization for those often denied social agency. Quoting Gardner, Frank sees art as a "careful, thoroughly honest search for and analysis of values," and claims that moral non-fiction contributes to freedom because it creates a space "in which people can consider who they are, what others require, and what consequences follow from one action rather than another." Moral non-fiction gives us the chance to test "whether one's own little voice expresses what's better and worse," and then to offer "one's own voice to others, for their affirmation and criticism."

Through literary-inflected readings of his narratives, and strongly stated convictions about the ethical importance of telling and responding to true stories, Frank goes as far as any of the contributors in suggesting that literary considerations are crucial to all attempts at writing, or understanding, a life narrative. And one final note: I find it interesting, if only biographically, that the strongest advocates for bridging ethics and life writing through the literary, the fictional, were the philosopher and the sociologist, while the participants most vexed and cautious about the interplay between the literary, the ethical, and the true were the literary theorists, the memoirists, and the biographers.

What about Theology?

With a degree of seriousness comparable to Frank's advocacy of moral non-fiction, several colloquium participants adopt the rationale, methods, and values of Western theological traditions for their own studies of life writing. For people trained in humanistic studies, such a course may seem almost inescapable. If ethics is the deep subject of autobiographical discourse, then the deep structure of that subject is frequently the judgment and forgiveness dynamic at work in texts like the ones Eakin lists—the Gospels and saints' lives, and works by Saint Augustine, Saint Teresa, Wordsworth, and T. S. Eliot. Whether a writer struggles to escape theological master narratives, like Rousseau in his *Confessions*, which Nancy Miller mentions, or like Gosse in *Father and Son*, which David Parker presented as the entryway into our sessions, or whether an essayist's emphasis is philosophical, moral, or emotional, this deeply embedded cultural narrative exerts its force. As his title suggests, John D. Barbour conducts the most sustained exploration of this tradition, and after completing his meticulous readings of his three-generation parent-author-child texts, in the last third of "Judging and Not Judging Parents," he tackles the question of what life writing can actually contribute to its readers' own ethical practices.

It is hard to imagine an essay that could argue more emphatically for life writing as a testing ground for learning how to balance notions of ethical judgment with the call of love or family attachment. Kim Chernin's rhetorical questions about her mother—"Should you judge a life by the ideology that inspires? Or by what that ideology, true or false, inspires the life to do?"—and Chernin's own affirmation of a transcendent "single motion of forgiveness" lead Barbour to ask "whether the desire to forgive a parent can negate or distort accurate moral judgment." On the basis of his readings, he concludes that "the final affirmation in these works, and their movement toward forgiveness, do not negate the work of moral assessment, or somehow move 'beyond judgment,' but rather display an integration of moral discernment and psychological understanding." Barbour seeks this synthesis for himself, and for all readers, claiming that it is "one reason for the ethical value of autobiography" as a genre. Since life writing can help us learn how to judge personal responsibility through a process of "causal understanding and moral evaluation," an autobiographer's task is therefore to be a "writer with good judgment," providing "a practical instance of fairness to others, imaginatively extending to another person the same considerations we bring to bear in self-assessment."

Barbour explicitly locates this example within the Judeo-Christian traditions of Scripture and literature. He quotes from Matthew and Luke on the need to judge, the perils of harsh judgment, and the link between judgment and forgiveness, pointing to these same concerns in "much of Greek tragedy," Shakespeare, Hawthorne, Dostoyevsky, Morrison, and Roth. The Christian theologian Marjorie Suchocki helps him clarify "how judgment may be related to, rather than the antithesis of, forgiveness," and he concludes that in his three texts, "the plot and the ethical signficance" must "be understood in terms of an unsentimental conception of forgiveness that does not undercut the importance of moral judgment." Barbour goes further. Although he acknowledges "the danger of imposing Christian assumptions on the genre of family memoir," his texts lead him to ask, "Do the dynamics of forgiveness shape and structure all family memoirs?" His own writers all turn "to religious tradition in the course of assessing a parent," whether that means Jonah, Pascal, Hölderlin, and Dickinson (Auster), African American spirituality (Wideman), or Jewish identity (Chernin). In fact, the patterns of ethical assessment Barbour traces in his three autobiographers replicate the Judeo-Christian tradition, which seeks "to balance the need for moral judgment with the equally great importance of mercy, forgiveness, and readiness to love persons on grounds other than their moral goodness." It should not be surprising, then, that when Barbour concludes that the "best," as in "most ethically instructive," autobiographies share with readers "a perspective that makes us judge ourselves, helps us to reevaluate our moral practice or ideals." Life writing is therefore "the best vehicle in our culture for sustained, probing, and public examination of the process of moral judgment." If Arthur Frank suggests that moral nonfiction is theology's successor as a guide for ethical judgment, John Barbour argues that the surest instructor is still the theological tradition itself.

I've rehearsed Barbour at length because he states explicitly many of the ideas and arguments underpinning—or contested in—this collection's essays. When such assumptions appeared on the long table, they provoked some of the most sweeping and energetic responses—"I'm against forgiveness" and "I am too" being only the most pointed and memorable. (Nor were such comments all directed at Barbour. "Are you trying to be a sadist or a masochist?" and "You're trying too hard to be good!" came up at other moments.) I am not resurrecting these remarks to suggest that they were flip, because what informs them was most certainly not. Rather, I would suggest that any claim to a shaping theological tradition got a strong reaction because all of the contributors to this volume were highly sensitive to what was at stake in any discussion of ethics, given our particular historical and institutional location. For this reason, perhaps the most pointed question posed to theological models of judgment had nothing to do with the writer and everything to do with the agent being judged. "Can you forgive an institution?" someone asked. "And should you?" This issue pervades not only *Father and Son*, where young Gosse determines that because his father can never be separated from his harsh faith, both must be rejected, but also many of the participants' essays when they turn to matters of institutional ethics—what I call politics.

What about Politics?

For many theorists, of course, ethics does not lie at the root of human nature, but exists as a product of social practice. When Marianne Gullestad says she is trying "to tease out the ethical implications of what is often considered ideology or politics," she is referring to the primacy of "civil society" in many conceptions of ethics. Although Charles Taylor is concerned with *What is it good to be?* perhaps the even more commonly asked question, as David Parker observes, is *What is it right to do?* Several participants just assume that doing the right thing will be resisted by others—whether as individuals or as parts of collective entities operating in the world. John Eakin identifies the autoethnography, the countermeasure, or any ethics of disclosure as markers of "the politics of life writing," and in this collection the essays foregrounding these markers appear together under the heading "Acts of Resistance: Telling Counterstories."

To state the obvious, the concerns about individual judgment and expression pervading psychological, literary, biographical, and theological approaches to life writing require the existence of larger communities which impede ethical self-determination, seduce individuals away from the difficulties of the task, or even determine, in different ways at different times, how it will be carried out. Within resisting texts, however, ethical attitudes tend to be less forgiving and more attuned to personal and communal survival. Alice Wexler, for instance, juxtaposes her personal sense of obligation, judgment, and forgiveness in relation to her father and "the woman in question" with her own "responsibility to this community of vulnerable subjects," composed of families with Huntington's disease. This responsibility is also ethical, and even fundamental. In the face of personal and institutional opposition, Wexler writes a memoir that asserts her community's right to exist. Profound suspicion must be part of this ethical stance, since the very act of identifying anyone as part of this community has consequences that are unimaginable for people outside of it. "What if a genetic truth about the dead can do harm to the living?" Wexler asks, noting that such a concern has "emerged with increased urgency in the context of both the new genetics and the tremendous explosion in information that makes tracing individuals on the Internet so much easier." In his essay, G. Thomas Couser bluntly seconds this point by citing Herbert Hendin: "If assisted suicide and euthanasia are given legal sanction, disabled persons are, in disproportionate numbers, likely to be seen as appropriate candidates."

The nightmarish circumstances that can make counterstories matters of life and death arise from widespread assumptions about "quality of life"—what kinds of life should be supported, or even allowed to happen. As Couser notes, the fact that "most people who live with severe disability (especially those disabled from birth) rate the quality of their lives higher than do those in the general population" means nothing if the larger community, through a massive failure of the imagination, willed or otherwise, decides that no one should have to live such a life. Wexler links such assumptions to the predictable return of eugenics at various points throughout the nineteenth, twentieth, and now twenty-first centuries as a supposedly benign, or "scientific," solution to what often proves to be a political problem. Couser identifies this as "the 'cure or kill' response to disability, according to which the disabled are tolerated only if, and as long as, their condition is deemed rectifiable; when cure or improvement proves impossible, sympathy often turns to hostility or aggression." Citing Wesley J. Smith, he labels this hostility as economic, political, and institutional—"in an age of managed health care and far from universal health insurance," terms like "futile care" tip the balance away "from the duty to live toward the duty to die, so that the burden may now be on those who wish to be treated."

That the political and the ethical often function as two sides of the same coin parallels the inseparability of other familiar life writing terms. Couser's euthanographic texts, for example, are necessarily "political *and* ideological," since feminism has shown us that the personal is political, and postmodernists have shown us that "the denial of ideology is itself an ideological position." Arthur Frank also stresses the need for politically engaged autobiographies that argue for the right not just to self-determination but to life itself. After quoting Hilde Lindemann Nelson's description of counterstories as "tools designed to repair the damage inflicted on identities by abusive power systems," which produce "stories that identify certain groups of people as targets for ill treatment," Frank draws the political and ethical implications together: "What is moral is also political: because demoralization is a political project to delegitimate the values, perspectives, and identities of some persons, remoralization affects the distribution of social resources conventionally known as power. Put more bluntly, life writing about illness and disability upsets the conventional identities assigned to these groups." In his account of "moral nervousness," Frank again allies himself with Gardner by emphasizing the need to confront "what is at stake in life writing about illness and disability." I would further suggest that the nervousness Frank recognizes in "academic audiences and illness groups" when he uses the word "moral" also points to a reluctance to act in the face of unethical political behavior. Audiences may agree with his "values," and even incline toward valuing the lives he talks about—including his own. But if ill and disabled people are treated immorally, then the community presumably should do something about it, and any individual, ill or well, who recognizes the problem is obligated to agitate for change—lobbying that will not necessarily be welcome, or even recognized. Hence the nervousness.

Marianne Gullestad also shines a light on similar kinds of moral nervousness, and for explicitly political reasons. Her clear-sighted, depressing account of the ways in which state and market have "entered 'inside' the individual as specific forms of self-discipline" reveals that while "the discourse of individual rights and liberties has become hegemonic," any sense of solidarity with anything but the state and market has become self-denying or self-erasing. The result? Gullestad suggests that the public focus on "uniqueness" is in fact "authoritarian": "Individualization is thus not necessarily contrary to continuity and conformity, but is rather a style that underplays these connections." Drawing on Toby Miller's work, she argues that a sense of ethical incompleteness in the modern subject stimulates efforts at social integration *within each individual*—in her personal moral responsibility, in her recognition of social institutions, and in her feelings of community." To be ethically complete requires an individual to be an active social being—a political person, in short—and Gullestad links "the rising importance of this ethical task" to "the popularity of life writing," because in such stories "otherwise incommensurable experiences and values can be brought together within a whole provided by a narrative structure (or by other kinds of textual structuring)."

The depressing aspects of her study appear when she explains how, in their various life narratives, young Norwegians of color "demonstrate that they are fully assimilated—caught in the dominant frame of interpretation—while at the same time given their specific positionings, they actively resist that framework." What she assumes this resistance points toward, however, is what I consider to be her most astute contribution to this collection. Her anthology writers' individual success in creating *"a sustainable self-image*, a coherent, continuous, and yet flexible image of the self that can provide the basis for self-respect and dignity," is really not what is at issue. I suspect Gullestad feels that despite the forces of assimilation and self-erasure, her writers are actually a fair distance along in that process. The real question is whether *white* Norwegians will ultimately fashion such an identity, such a life story for themselves. Although the great value of life stories is their power to bring "incommensurable experiences and values" together in narrative, white Norway is resisting any such union, and refusing to admit that its own current social self-image is unsustainable. "To put it briefly and bluntly," she writes, "what the young authors write against is a society in which racialization and racism are both strongly present and intensely denied." As a result, the success of the anthology *Black on White* was only partial. The individual writer found it "easier to gain sympathy among majority readers as a critic of 'immigrants' than as a critic of majority practices," and the overall response to the life stories amounted to "a continuous silencing of the most painful experiences and the most radical views." In an individual, this might amount to an ethical fault—in Gullestad's terms, a willful refusal to create a sustainable self-image because this social self will not act on the new awareness of racial discrimination that these life stories cause. What Gullestad does, however, is take the argument one stage further, insisting that as a political and social entity, majority Norway cannot sustain its self-image in the face of such countermeasure narratives. It must respond in an encompassing way or it will eventually collapse. This is what I understand Gullestad to mean when she says that Norway's widespread conviction that people "with a different skin color" should not "criticize Norwegian society," not "speak up against racism," but should be "grateful for what they have" represents "a barrier to a well-functioning democracy." In this way, she draws life writing, ethics, and politics more intimately, inextricably, and significantly together.

Life Writing and Ethics in Practice: What about Rigoberta Menchú?

While it does point out what doors these essays open, simply cataloguing the various debates that occurred at Indiana University, and now continue in this collection, does not exactly suggest what together these essays do. I conclude by suggesting how familiarity with this volume can enhance the ways a reader might engage with one or more of the essays, or with some of the larger ethical issues that life writing raises in general. I'm not proposing a "new" reading, or any sustained contribution to what are already fully developed arguments. Rather, I hope to suggest what cumulative effects this collection has had on my own understanding of ethics and life writing.

When looking through these essays once more, I noticed that on the first page of Diane Middlebrook's manuscript I had written the following: "I'm truly disturbed by the 'fictionalizing' act described here—but what is the transgression?" Middlebrook of course explains eloquently why I *should* be disturbed, but when I read John Eakin's introduction again, I had an even stronger sense of being bothered. "The very idea that these personal narratives by Menchú, Wilkomirski, and Tennant could cloud access to the historical record testifies to the potential power of life writing," he says. True enough—but after attending the colloquium, I found myself becoming almost involuntarily indignant that Menchú and Tennant could appear in the same sentence. (A few paragraphs later, Eakin himself replaces Tennant with Kathryn Harrison.)

What was annoying me? I now think it was a concern that drove so many of our discussions: the issue of "vulnerable" subjects. The final "conundrum" in Nancy Miller's essay states the problem this way:

> After listening to me read a much earlier draft of this essay, a seminar participant asked (with a slight edge of disdain, or was it incredulity) why he should care about "these people"? I can't say I know better now how to answer that question. If not "these people," then which people do (or should) readers of life writing care about? For some in the seminar, the people readers (like writers) should care about are, in G. Thomas Couser's phrase, "vulnerable subjects," people who suffer from grave and multiple medical disabilities. True. But ethical as well as aesthetic dilemmas arise in the telling of any narrative, no matter how unsavory a story—not to say life—they emerge from.
>
> When we expose the narratives of our lives to others through the forms of life writing, do we not all become vulnerable subjects?

Leaving aside whether most of the seminar participants could be described—or would want to be described—as "vulnerable subjects," I would certainly argue that, on the basis of evidence provided in the other essays, vulnerability cannot be confined to disability. Marianne Gullestad makes a case for thinking of Norwegians of color as vulnerable subjects; Claudia Mills sees her children as vulnerable; David Parker argues that Gosse's progress in *Father and Son* is a movement out of vulnerability; the main figures in John Barbour's three texts are acutely vulnerable at various points; and Richard Freadman is so con-

cerned about his dead father's vulnerability that he imaginatively res-
urrects him to present the case for publication. I would therefore
suggest that readers responded so strongly to Binjamin Wilkomirski's
Fragments and *I, Rigoberta Menchú* at least partially because they perceived the authors to be profoundly vulnerable subjects—a little boy
in Auschwitz, a young woman caught in the maelstrom of another
kind of genocide.

This observation takes us only so far, though, because presenting a
writer, narrator, or character as "vulnerable" can, and often does,
accompany some of the most manipulative appeals to sentimentality
and bathos imaginable. (Without going too far into it, I suspect that
some of the outrage at Wilkomirski's "deception" results from the fact
that while an autobiographical narrative of this kind can be a powerful statement, a novel with the same story, written at second or third
remove from the historical events, runs a very serious risk of being
exploitive schlock.) Here I find John Barbour's comments on moral
luck extremely useful. If judging another's actions requires us to take
into account factors lying outside that person's control, then Rigoberta
Menchú seems to have suffered some truly horrible circumstantial
luck, which Thomas Nagel defines as "the kind of problems and situations one faces." Binjamin Wilkomirski's exposure greatly reduced
the perceived badness of his circumstantial luck. The questions raised
about Menchú's veracity, however, never "improved" her luck or less-
ened her vulnerability. Her parents and siblings may not have died in
precisely the way she describes, but they are still all dead. When
Barbour remarks that "sometimes causal understanding and moral
evaluation both seem necessary, yet we are perplexed about what an
agent can be held responsible for," he could therefore be summing up
the entire Rigoberta Menchú controversy, and in a way that provides
a map for negotiating some parts of the treacherous mix of politics,
history, ethics, and testimony that Paul Lauritzen describes as the
scene for exploring that controversy.

And conversely, moral luck can also shape our assessment of Emma
Tennant, for Diane Middlebrook certainly draws the picture of
someone who acts voluntarily, freely—even willfully. It is not just that
Tennant exploits "the value of information" about Hughes; plenty of
people have done that. It is what Middlebrook calls Tennant's "privileged position" that makes her account so inexcusable. The aristo-
cratic background, the public school education, the family castle, and
the access to the court suggest that her circumstantial luck was quite
good. As for what Nagel calls the "luck in the way one's actions and
projects turn out," even with her pen and notebook hidden somewhere,
Tennant seems to have made her way through her London circle of

upper-class young marrieds successfully. Her entry into literature comes through a roman à clef, though an introduction to the ethics of life writing at the hands of lawyers immediately followed. Given her many advantages, Tennant's willingness to tie herself to the British poet most famous at the time for a horrific domestic life is almost perverse, and her deliberate and confessed harming of other women seems sadistic. Had she only written a memoir, then, she would probably be the kind of autobiographer that the question "Why should I care about this person?" was made to be asked about. But Middlebrook goes on to point out that our own biographical knowledge of Tennant, when coupled with her self-proclaimed familiarity with the "facts" of Ted Hughes's life, allows her to contaminate sheer speculation or invention with the truth. Like Rigoberta Menchú, Tennant writes as a "contemporary insider," but in her case absolutely nothing indicates that her questionable actions are involuntary. Quite the opposite, in fact. With all the good moral luck to spare, Tennant nevertheless sees fit to suggest that "the most shocking, disturbing, and discreditable actions she represents in the novel" involving Hughes "may be 'based on facts . . . previously concealed or unknown.'"

If we extend these considerations to Paul Lauritzen's own framing narrative, another possible explanation emerges for the reactions he describes. As someone struggling with issues of infertility in his earlier essay, he is not just a person with experience in the process but a vulnerable subject whose "constitutive luck ('the kind of person you are')" includes being someone who can't conceive a child with his partner. His friends, colleagues, and readers had this understanding of him as a narrator, and valued his essay accordingly. Unlike in the Menchú case, then, the problem here is not that he lied, but that he is no longer the subject his readers and friends took him to be. A change in his moral luck changes how others judge him.

And I would go so far as to claim that an author's perceived vulnerability, her moral luck, powerfully conditions our ethical judgments of her life writing text. Deborah Nelson remarked at the colloquium that in legal circles, the facts of the narrative are often not at issue; what's important is the nature of the harm. That so many of Emma Tennant's facts are not in dispute, or even familiar, is what makes her integrating totally unverifiable material into her insider narrative so ethically dubious. In the case of Rigoberta Menchú, however, it should at least give us pause that while some of the facts may be in question, the harm to her people and to herself is not—or not, at least, for anyone who does not wield moral judgment purely as a weapon in ideological warfare and international power politics.

These brief comments on Rigoberta Menchú are only meant to suggest how a reading of the entire collection has deepened my understanding of the individual essays. Disagreement, dismissal, difference remain—but as spurs to active, inquiring reading and ethical assessment that will change habits and opinions.

■

"Omphalos" was an elaborate nineteenth-century theory that reconciled creationism and evolution by arguing that God created the world in six days, but placed within it the evidence that seems to disprove his act. According to Stephen Jay Gould, this theory is the "classical example of an utterly untestable notion, for the world will look exactly the same in all its intricate detail whether fossils and strata are prochronic or products of an extended history." The theory is therefore fundamentally unscientific, because "science is doing, not clever cogitation; we reject Omphalos as useless, not wrong" (110–11). Since the creator of Omphalos was Philip Gosse, the father in *Father and Son*, perhaps we might ask whether what is scientifically useless might be ethically useless as well—for so the son found his father. The strength of this collection lies in its capacity to tease us repeatedly into ethical thought, without presenting us at the same moment with a recipe for what this thought should be. I have learned a great deal about the ways other people are thinking and writing about ethics and life writing. More important, I also have a sense that my understanding of life writing has changed—at least, as far as I can judge.

WORKS CITED

Adamson, Jane, Richard Freadman, and David Parker, eds. *Renegotiating Ethics in Literature, Philosophy, and Theory*. Cambridge: Cambridge University Press, 1998.
Eakin, Paul John. *How Our Lives Become Stories: Making Selves*. Ithaca: Cornell University Press, 1999.
Edel, Leon. *Writing Lives: Principia Biographica*. New York: Norton, 1984.
Gould, Stephen Jay. *The Flamingo's Smile: Reflections in Natural History*. New York: Norton, 1987.
Kraus, Carolyn Wells. "On Hurting People's Feelings: Journalism, Guilt, and Autobiography." *Biography: An Interdisciplinary Quarterly* 26, no. 2 (spring 2003): 283–97.
Lejeune, Phillipe. *"Cher écran . . .": journal personnel, ordinateur, Internet*. Paris: Éditions du Seuil, 2000.

Malcolm, Janet. *The Silent Woman: Sylvia Plath and Ted Hughes.* New York: Knopf, 1994.

Rosen, Alan. "Autobiography from the Other Side: The Reading of Nazi Memoirs and Confessional Ambiguity." *Biography: An Interdisciplinary Quarterly* 24, no. 3 (2001): 553–69.

Smith, Sidonie, and Julia Watson. *Reading Autobiography: A Guide for Interpreting Life Narratives.* Minneapolis: University of Minnesota Press, 2001.

Contributors

JOHN D. BARBOUR is Professor of Religion at St. Olaf College. His work on ethics and autobiography includes *The Conscience of the Autobiographer: Ethical and Religious Dimensions of Autobiography* (1992), *Versions of Deconversion: Autobiography and the Loss of Faith* (1994), and "The *Bios* of Bioethics and the *Bios* of Autobiography," in *Caring Well: Religion, Narrative, and Health*, ed. David H. Smith (2000). Barbour has recently completed a book titled "Solitude and Autobiography: The Ethics and Spirituality of Aloneness."

G. THOMAS COUSER is Professor of English at Hofstra University. He has written four books: *American Autobiography: The Prophetic Mode* (1979), *Altered Egos: Authority in American Autobiography* (1989), *Recovering Bodies: Illness, Disability, and Life Writing* (1997), and *Vulnerable Subjects: Ethics and Life Writing* (Cornell University Press, 2004). With Joseph Fichtelberg he edited *True Relations: Essays on Autobiography and the Postmodern* (1998).

PAUL JOHN EAKIN has published three books on autobiography: *Fictions in Autobiography: Studies in the Art of Self-Invention* (1985), *Touching the World: Reference in Autobiography* (1992), and *How Our Lives Become Stories: Making Selves* (1999). He has also edited two volumes, *American Autobiography: Retrospect and Prospect* (1991) and a book of essays by Philippe Lejeune, *On Autobiography* (1989). Eakin is Ruth N. Halls Professor Emeritus of English at Indiana University.

ARTHUR W. FRANK is Professor of Sociology at the University of Calgary. He is the author of *At the Will of the Body* (1991) and *The Wounded Storyteller: Body, Illness, and Ethics* (1995). One of his current research projects analyzes interviews with people who use their own experiences of serious illness as the basis for works of service to others; another considers the ethics of surgical interventions that normalize children with congenital anomalies. His most recent book is *The Renewal of Generosity* (2004).

RICHARD FREADMAN is Professor of English and Director of the Unit for Studies in Biography and Autobiography at La Trobe University, Melbourne. His recent books include the co-edited *Renegotiating Ethics in Literature, Criticism and Philosophy* (1998), and *Threads of Life: Autobiography and the Will* (2001), and his auto/biographical book about his father, *Shadow of Doubt: My Father and Myself* (2003). He is currently writing a study of Australian Jewish autobiography.

MARIANNE GULLESTAD is a social anthropologist currently working as a senior researcher at the Institute for Social Research in Oslo. Among her many publications in English are *Kitchen-Table Society: A Case Study of the Family Life and Friendships of Young Working-Class Mothers in Urban Norway* (1984, with a new edition in 2002 with a foreword by Daniel Miller), *The Art of Social Relations: Essays on Culture, Social Action, and Everyday Life in Modern Norway* (1992), *Everyday Life Philosophers: Modernity, Morality, and Autobiography in Norway* (1996), and an edited volume, *Imagined Childhoods: Self and Society in Autobiographical Accounts* (1996).

CRAIG HOWES is the Director of the Center for Biographical Research, the editor of *Biography: An Interdisciplinary Quarterly*, and Professor of English at the University of Hawai'i at Mānoa. The author of *Voices of the Vietnam POWs* (1993), he is currently co-producing *Biography Hawai'i*, a television series that airs on PBS Hawai'i.

PAUL LAURITZEN is Professor of Religious Studies and Director of the Program in Applied Ethics, John Carroll University, and author of *Religious Belief and Emotional Transformation: A Light in the Heart* (1992) and *Pursuing Parenthood: Ethical Issues in Assisted Reproduction* (1993). He has also edited *Cloning and the Future of Human Embryo Research* (2001) and, with Diana Cates, *Medicine and the Ethics of Care* (2001).

DIANE MIDDLEBROOK is a professional writer and Professor of English Emerita at Stanford University. Her book *Anne Sexton, a Biography* (1991) was a finalist for the National Book Award; she selected Plath's poems and wrote a new introduction to *The Bell Jar* for publication in the Knopf/Everyman Series. Her biography *Her Husband: Hughes and Plath, a Marriage* was published in 2003.

NANCY K. MILLER is Distinguished Professor of English and Comparative Literature at the Graduate Center, CUNY. Her most recent books are *Bequest and Betrayal: Memoirs of a Parent's Death* (1996), *But Enough about Me: Why We Read Other People's Lives* (2002), and *Extremities: Trauma, Testimony, and Community* (2002), an anthology.

CLAUDIA MILLS is Associate Professor of Philosophy at the University of Colorado at Boulder, where she writes and teaches on ethical theory and applied ethics. She is also the author of over thirty children's books, including *7 × 9 = Trouble!* (2002) and *Alex Ryan, Stop That!* (2003).

DAVID PARKER is the author of a novel, *Building on Sand* (1988), and a collection of short stories, *The Mighty World of Eye* (1990). His academic publications include *Ethics, Theory, and the Novel* (1994); *Shame and the Modern Self*, co-edited with Rosamund Dalziell and Iain Wright (1996); *Renegotiating Ethics: Literature, Theory, Philosophy*, co-edited with Jane Adamson and Richard Freadman (1998); and *Anglophone Cultures in South East Asia*, co-edited with Rudiger Ahrens, Klaus Stierstorfer, and K. K. Tam (2003). Professor of English and Department Chair at the Chinese University of Hong Kong, Parker is currently working on identity and the good in autobiography.

ALICE WEXLER is the author of *Emma Goldman in America* (1984), *Emma Goldman in Exile* (1989), and *Mapping Fate: A Memoir of Family, Risk, and Genetic Research* (1995). She has also published articles in journals such as *Raritan, Caribbean Studies, Feminist Studies*, and the *Bulletin of the History of Medicine*, and has received fellowships from the American Council of Learned Societies, the John Simon Guggenheim Foundation, the National Endowment for the Humanities, and the National Library of Medicine. A Research Scholar at the UCLA Center for the Study of Women, she is currently working on a book-length manuscript on the social and cultural history of Huntington's disease.

Index